Gynicide

Gynicide

Women in the Novels
of William Styron

David Hadaller

Madison • Teaneck
Fairleigh Dickinson University Press
London: Associated University Presses

Associated University Presses
440 Forsgate Drive
Cranbury, NJ 08512

Associated University Presses
16 Barter Street
London WC1A 2AH, England

Associated University Presses
P.O. Box 338, Port Credit
Mississauga, Ontario
Canada L5G 4L8

The paper used in this publication meets the requirements
of the American National Standard for Permanence of Paper
for Printed Library Materials Z39.48-1984.

Library of Congress Cataloging-in-Publication Data

Hadaller, David, 1954–
    Gynicide : women in the novels of William Styron / David Hadaller.
        p.   cm.
    Includes bibliographical references (p.   ) and index.
    ISBN 0-8386-3633-0 (alk. paper)
    1. Styron, William, 1925– —Characters—Women.   2. Women in
literature.   I. Title.
PS3569.T9Z73   1996
813'.54—dc20
                                                95-10401
                                                CIP

PRINTED IN THE UNITED STATES OF AMERICA

for my wife and son

Contents

1

The Depiction of Women in the Novels of William Styron: Feminist Dialogics, Bakhtin, and the American Heroine as Casualty

Elizabeth Ermarth has written with insight on the phenomenon of female casualties in realistic fiction by men. She explains that in representational fiction there is a preoccupation with the conflict between an individual and society, or between individuals and what Ermarth calls the "prevailing consensus" (Ermarth 1983, 10). By "fictional representation" Ermarth means "verisimilitude [and] realism" which make up "an aesthetic form of consensus" (2). She notes further that the relatively "high proportion of important female casualties" results primarily from situations in which women's psychic needs are not understood and therefore not met by this prevailing, inevitably patriarchal, consensus. Indeed, in her discussion of the deep intimacy between psychic and physical existence, Ermarth demonstrates that the continuance of one is endangered if the other is damaged. The end result is that the heroine is "cut off" from the chief resource in her community: the medium of growth and development Ermarth associates with the prevailing consensus (2). These breakdowns are fatal to a surprising number of heroines who become suicides or, indeed, even *gynicides,* a term of mine which is more specific than *homicides* for such fatalities. Women also endure a psychic death-in-life existence, as "automata" (15), and suffer a kind of ongoing *psychogynicide,* a denial of self and the proscription of the formation of any self beyond the formulaic ideals of womanhood based on patriarchal definitions.

Because of their extreme victimization, fictive heroines, Ermarth claims, "do not participate in the objectifying consensus but instead are objectified by it" and are therefore represented in the margins of social existence, becoming irreversibly isolated from the mainstream and thus cut off from the lifeworld of the community (15). In this move toward potentially deadly solitude, heroines find that their "attempts to recover from this solitude with a friend or lover are fragile [and] isolate them only further" (13). They will not survive because the "gaze" of the patriarchal consensus can be met only at great peril, and the heroine's progress in a fictive plot is in actuality a slow war of attrition against societal norms that eventually destroys or leads to the gynicide of such a heroine. Ermarth explains that a heroine in realistic fiction experiences "not time for growth, but time running out" (2). Ermarth further argues that consensus in its best sense should include "rule" by mutual understanding and agreement, in contradistinction with the rule of force. But the nature of the prevailing consensus comes down to an irresistible force that maintains itself by expelling or repressing certain female members of the community. If, therefore, a woman, in spite of a narrator's sympathy, challenges the system, she may be driven to a psychic suicide, a denial of her will, of which physical death is at times "only a final corroboration" (16).

Significantly, this phenomenon of psychic/physical death of important female characters is portrayed in each of William Styron's novels. Consistent with Ermarth's thesis, a patriarchal/societal consensus drives Styron's women characters to the "margins of social existence," to an isolation from which there is often no return. Ermarth's own examples of such women include Tess Durbeyfield and Emma Bovary, characters who have come to symbolize female alienation and victimization. From American literature Dale Marie Bauer, in *Feminist Dialogics: A Theory of Failed Community* (1988), adds such examples as Edna Pontellier, Maggie Verver, Lily Bart, and Zenobia (*The Blithedale Romance*). To these examples must be added the four major novels of William Styron: *Lie Down in Darkness, Set This House on Fire, The Confessions of Nat Turner,* and *Sophie's Choice.*

M. M. Bakhtin's theory of dialogism, or heteroglossia, offers a useful mode of analysis of such female characters and their situations. Granted that, as Wayne C. Booth has pointed out, Bakhtin himself made "no shadow of a suggestion . . . of the influence of sexual differences, no hint that women now talk or have ever talked in ways different from men's" (Booth 1982, 54), the method is nonetheless productive. In her feminist reconsideration of Bakhtin, Bauer explains that "the authoritative community works by disarming and mastering the desire for resistance or aggression; however, the precondition for [such] resistance and contradiction is unsettling the *disciplinary gaze*" (Bauer 1988, xiii; italics mine). When female characters struggle to meet this gaze by refusing to succumb to social stereotypes, they find themselves unsettled by the scrutiny to the degree that they quite literally lose their own voices—or find that they *never had* their own voices—in the face of this hostile and intimidating *coup d'oeill.* Bauer's observations about the "failed community" of a social system that is primarily "exclusionary and androcentric" support Ermarth's similar discussions concerning the heroine's isolation from community supports (xi). Further, "[c]ommunities (and these include communities of postmodern critics) exercise their power by the threat of exclusion or by the misuse of power" (xi).

Bauer contends that few critics have closely examined how the "disciplinary gaze" has silenced female voices and denied them entry into communities that control social systems. In her study, inspired by the idea of "linguistic community" (xii) advanced in the work of Bakhtin, Bauer attends to this critical oversight and employs what Peter Hitchcock refers to as a "materialist feminist reading of dialogism" which examines several nineteenth-century American novels "against the grain in order to track the conflicting voices" making up each work's synchronic view of its social realities, the actual "material" of the times in which women's voices are "situated or silenced" (Hitchcock 1993, 19–20). Bauer argues that what is absent from Bakhtinian scholarship is a clear discussion of the importance of gender theory or sexual difference in a "materialistic-feminist practice," that is, with a concentration upon the material and social conditions dictated primarily by *male* privileged authority structures (xiii). What most post modern critics do not see, Bauer insists, is that the "feminist voice (rather than the male gaze)" (2) deconstructs and challenges the debilitating aspects of patriarchal discourse in a novelistic discourse by voicing dissenting interpretations of societal hierarchies. In this way, "women readers in the text assert their otherness not by surrendering," but by engaging a dominant language with their own voices (10).

The notion of "materialistic" dialogism is important to pursue at this juncture, insofar as it is a cornerstone of the method of analysis employed by Bauer. Peter Hitchcock explains that "a material understanding of [an] utterance depends on a realization of the extraverbal or nonsaid conditions in which the utterance takes place" (Hitchcock 1993, 18). Alan Singer adds that Bakhtinian assumptions about the novel reinterpret subjectivity "under the valid materialist constraint which refuses to allow interpretation to rest outside the tumult of historical changes" (Singer 1988, 175). In short, the importance of a Bakhtinian/dialogic approach as modified by my interpretation of Bauer lies in its emphasis on "the specific situations of dialogic exchange" or cultural contexts that reflect or re-present societal power structures (Hitchcock 1993, xv). Wayne C. Booth, in his important early study of feminism and Bakhtin, relates that this method of inquiry is dedicated to the close scrutiny of specific passages and even "examination of the *actual language* of almost any passage" (Booth 1982, 63; italics mine). Further, Booth admits, "I am forced now to look closely at fragmentary evidence showing who is included and who is excluded" (63). Indeed, the process of exclusion is of major importance with regard to female characters and their psyches precisely because writing, as Walter Ong argues, "is a particularly preemptive and *imperialistic* activity" even though the written word is but the "residue" of language's basic orality, its basic economy of articulated sound brought forth from the unconscious (Bakhtin's "utterance") which is paramount (Ong 1982, 7, 11; italics mine).

The method used by Bauer emphasizes the careful reconsideration of selected passages to determine what the actual "material" of the text re-presents to the reader in terms of a central assumption of feminist scholarship: the thesis put forth in Simone de Beauvoir's *The Second Sex* that "one is not born, but rather becomes a woman . . . it is civilization as a whole that produces this creature" (Beauvoir 1953, 301). Based on this assumption, Gayle Greene and Coppelia Kahn argue that feminist scholarship "undertakes to 'deconstruct' the social construction of gender and the cultural paradigms that support it" (Greene and Kahn 1985, 2). A materialist feminist dialogics examines the multiplicity of voices re-presented in fiction which "constitutes a form of cultural agency at specific moments in history" (Hitchcock 1993, xvi). Toril Moi writes:

> The fact that the oppressors tend to equate the oppressed group with ontological Otherness [exotopy], perceived as a threatening, disruptive, alien force, is precisely an ideological maneuver designed to mask the *concrete material grounds* for oppression and exploitation. (Moi 1988, 12; italics mine)

Moi concludes that materialist analysis alone "can provide a credible explanation of why the burden of Otherness has been placed on this or that particular group in a given society at a given time" (12). Ultimately, such an analysis depends upon the exegesis of passages of text that reveal the interplay of characters' voices with the "will-to-monologism" of the patriarchy as re-presented in the novelistic discourse which itself also serves as a record of contemporaneous material and social conditions.

Ermarth's investigations of Hardy and Flaubert (an idol of Styron's) and Bauer's study both reveal that the tragic stories of women's deaths and/or marginalization often reflect discernible patterns of male authorial exploitation of women that reinforce patriarchal norms. Ermarth in fact contends that, although the realistic novel can dramatize the story of an individual's challenge to the social consensus in the name of freedom or humanity, it often does not itself challenge that consensus (Ermarth 1983, 2). In this view, the narrator, as the chief administrator of a particular rendering of patriarchal consensus, is merely reinforcing the shortcomings of society. On the other hand, by employing aspects of M. M. Bakhtin's theory of the dialogic novel, Bauer maintains that novelists who represent marginalized women and other groups in their fictions in fact undermine the disciplinary gaze of societal norms whether they seek to do so consciously or not. "Through Bakhtin's principle of the dialogization of the novel," she writes, "we can interpret the silenced or suicidal voice of female characters compelling a dialogue with those others who would prefer to think they do not exist" (Bauer 1988, 14). Hitchcock puts it this way: "The dialogic can never be erased completely even within the most authoritarian speech contexts" (Hitchcock 1993, 18). In this sense even the silenced women characters represented by male writers speak; as the powerful feminist voice of Adrienne Rich reminds us: "All silence has meaning" (Rich 1979, 308).

William Styron's work, this study will argue, is non-exploitive inasmuch as he portrays the complex variables surrounding the lives of his female characters as they are experiencing them; his is a critique of conventional mores and societal codes rather than a defense of them. In his portrayal of women's suicides and gynicides at the hands of males, Styron employs narrative strategies that invite a reader to realize Judith Fetterley's challenge and "become a resisting reader rather than an assenting reader and, by this refusal to assent, to begin the process of exorcising the male mind that has been implanted in us" (Fetterley 1979, xxii). With this changing of consciousness, the reader may then approach the women in Styron's novels, especially in relation to their suicides and gynicides, as important speaking voices and not merely as exploited textual artifacts. As Margaret Higonnet explains, a woman's death by suicide, whether psychic or physical, does not finalize, eliminate, or trivialize that woman's discourse. Suicide is, rather, a narrative strategy used to ensure that death is addressed by other characters. "To take one's life is to force others to read one's death," writes Higonnet (103). In fact, the fatal suffering of women has been used as subject matter for some of the greatest works of literature, "from Antigone to Anna Karenina," in an effort to "juxtapose silent resistance with the *dominant discourse,* and to demonstrate the costs of the social order to the individual" (116; italics mine).

One such example is readily seen in *Lie Down in Darkness* and in Styron's attention to the inner machinations of Helen Loftis's mind as she grapples with a troubled marriage and with her own psychological difficulties concerning her complicity in her daughter's suicide. Patterned on interior monologues from Faulkner and Joyce, the collection of thoughts, impressions, and memories that populate Helen's sections propels the reader into nightmarish visions of domestic relations gone awry in upper-class Tidewater Virginia society. In particular, Helen's horrific dreamscape of the female dead presents a woman who fails to see her own daughter as another women, as another victim in her own right. As a result of their conflict, both mother and daughter vent their displaced anger on each other "rather than on the cultural system by which they have been defined" (Bauer 1988, x).

"The Land of the Female Dead,"—a scene in which Styron has Helen Loftis reveal a dreamscape filled with the corpses of her female "enemies" (SC 120)—is important for this study because it dramatically presents the influence of oppressive social and psychological forces endured by women characters in Styron's fiction, forces that define mid-twentieth century American cultural mores. In Helen's case, her nightmare land of the female dead shows how even the central, albeit culturally constructed, mythic role of Mother can torment a woman and produce in her grotesque visions of younger women, including her daughters. Eventually, male characters in the novel, Helen's husband and her Episcopalian spiritual advisor especially, see her as a "monster" and as "quite mad." Helen's dark interior imaginings are the result, ironically, of her obsession to appear before her community as the devoted wife and mother who sacrifices all for her family only to be spurned, she believes, in spite of all her "Christian" efforts. Other women in Styron's works also suffer egregiously and either commit suicide or succumb to violent physical death at men's hands; still others are doomed to the death-in-life experience of psychological submission and/or dependence on men. This study contends that these female casualties, while reflecting Elizabeth Ermarth's formulations about the gynicide in realistic fiction by men, are more precisely seen as Styron's critique of societal influences and not as examples of the author's overt or covert misogyny, as some critics contend.

Such criticism of Styron's *oeuvre* is a subsidiary question in this study. Georgiana Colville, for example, writes that Styron in *Sophie's Choice* has written "one of the most male chauvinist novels 'ever penned by man or beast'" (Colville 1986, 113). Colville maintains that Styron's novels are attempts to "kill" his own dead mother by sacrificing again and again his female protagonists to a rabidly chauvinist patriarchy. Joan Smith takes the argument a step further when she pronounces that Styron's "model of female sexuality" as presented in the character of Sophie "has nothing to do with real women but exists to legitimize masculine sexual fantasies which are violent, vicious, and ultimately lethal" (Smith 1992, 137). The popular success of Styron's novel suggests to Smith that a large portion of the reading public, socialized by the same patriarchal consensus that dooms Sophie, are entirely receptive to such "fevered imaginings" (137). And, although she does not write about Styron directly, Shoshana Felman problematizes a collateral issue in her discussion of Balzac's story "Adieu" in which a man is willing to kill his former lover in order to cure her "insanity" (Felman 1975, 10). Felman expands her argument to show how male critics repeat the male protagonist's dominance of the female by exercising the same mastery over the female character: "the critic also, in his own way, kills the woman, while killing, at the same time, the question of the text and the text as question" (10). Bauer attends to this problem by arguing that feminist dialogics is in fact concerned primarily with just such a "killing" or marginalization as the one Felman articulates. In order to "silence its threat," the interpretive community "anxiously" incorporates and domesticates the "alienated female voice," the voice that feminist dialogics seeks to reveal.

Yet another group of critics chastise Styron for reasons arguably more conservative in nature than those of Georgiana Colville. Some see Styron's novels as loose, baggy, structurally inept, and even morally reprehensible. Critics berate Styron for wasting narrative on supposedly prurient sexual details, as in Stingo's adventures in losing his virginity in *Sophie's Choice* (Alter 1979, 43). Similar concerns have been voiced, especially by African-American intelligentsia, about the structural and thematic irrelevance of the character Margaret Whitehead in the Pulitzer prize-winning novel *The Confessions of Nat Turner* (Clark et al. 1968). These critics see Styron's suppression of Nat's real-life wife as proof of the exploitive and sensationalistic purposes behind the novel's publication. In short, these readers see Styron's studies of oppression as forms of oppression in themselves.

This study seeks to show, however, that a more balanced critical approach may be found in work such as Carolyn A. Durham's overview of the structural and thematic criticism attached to sexism and racism in Styron's works. Durham sees Styron carefully exploring sexism and other prejudices through networks of complementary parallels and repetitions. We can see Stingo, for instance, reflecting, however naively, that he too is a survivor like Sophie. The older musing Stingo/narrator relates that his younger incarnation "survived" the sexual "malaise" of the midtwentieth century in America, which the elder Stingo/Styron looks back on as a "sexually bedeviled era" (SC 120). The idea that Stingo, although he is basically a virgin, is a "survivor" from a time of duplicitous sexual mores which privileged male sexual expression while condemning women who acted out their sexuality openly serves to intensify the reader's awareness of Sophie's contradictory position in her world; we see and hear her world through the eyes and ears of one of her unwitting oppressors—unwitting because of his devotion to her as well as to his own priapic libido.

As Durham notes, every chapter of *Sophie's Choice* contains a certain structural pattern in which systems of organized oppression are first described, followed by particular examples of oppression articulated into a commentary on the impact of these systems on language or literature—"thus creating a structural paradigm in which sexism illuminates both the systems that oppress society and the literature that can lead toward an understanding of how they function" (Durham 1984, 451). Built into this structure is the mature Stingo's anticipation of reader objections to detailed renderings of his masturbatory visions, his breathy preoccupation with his virgin "status," and his subsequent attempts with Leslie Lapidus and Mary Alice Grimball to relieve his sexual tensions. Styron/Stingo concedes that the narrative drive of Sophie's tragedy may appear compromised by such apparently trivial goings-on:

> In itself this saga, or episode, or fantasia has little direct bearing on Sophie and Nathan and so I have hesitated to set it down, thinking it perhaps extraneous stuff best suited to another tale and time. But it is so bound up in the fabric and the mood of summer that to deprive this story of its reality would be like divesting the body of some member. . . . (SC 120)

Stingo's trysts, imaginary or otherwise, are in Durham's view an integral part of Styron's ongoing critique of the sexism of the period. Indeed it seems clear that both Stingo and Sophie struggle against the *same* constraints, although in different ways and with different results, as shall be seen.

In William Styron's four major novels, then, I will analyze the depiction of women and the various gynicidal acts that determine and define them, in order to explore the largely unexamined view that Styron's works "are not oppressive but about oppression, not racist but about racism, not anti-Semitic but about anti-Semitism, and . . . not sexist although . . . persistently about sexism" (Durham 1984, 449). Styron's art, as Durham relates, shows convincingly that "the experiences of women can be particularly effective means to understanding an experience of oppression, otherwise foreign" (463). Styron re-creates the oppressive conditions of women's lives "as a central metaphor for the general degradation of the self and others" (451). This central thematic concern reveals itself time and again as the various narrators in Styron's novels address the problem of how systems like Stingo's "beehive" at MacGraw-Hill Publishing house or the twentieth century's ultimate bureaucratic nightmare-system, Auschwitz, reduce and degrade the self, especially the female self, with cruel and yet banal effectiveness.

Thus building on the arguments of Ermarth and Durham, my study adapts certain aspects of Dale Marie Bauer's materialistic feminist dialogics as a means of exploring synchronically character descriptions and examining important narrative scenes in detail. I am in this heeding Michael Holquist's definition of heteroglossia as the basic condition of meaning in any utterance: "It is that which insures the primacy of context over text" (Bakhtin 1981, 428). Bakhtin employs the term *chronotopes* to describe such scenes and their use of "time-space" to reflect social and material conditions in the novel. The analysis of chronotopes is especially useful as "an optic for reading texts as x-rays of the forces at work in the culture system from which they spring" (426). I then place these discrete scenes together in a diachronic schema that follows the textual development of the character under consideration in the same way that Bonnie Kime Scott investigates James Joyce's works in her discussion of gender, discourse, and culture (Scott 1987, 47). That is, I follow the development of selected characters from their earliest portrayals to their final scenes (chronotopes) in the progress of the narrative discourse. This method makes it possible for me "to analyze descriptively dialogical structures in actual texts," as Paul De Man would have it (De Man 1983, 102). The method, De Man explains, "is by no means unusual to 'formalist' practitioners of an American style of close reading" and is a boon for study that seeks an "itinerary beyond form by ways of formal analysis" (103). The tools of such analysis allow for an examination of certain cultural/patriarchal questions relevant to a study of the silencing of female voices/casualties by that very patriarchy. As Bauer argues, "The explicit and implicit interplay of these [social] voices reveals the way a specific historical and cultural context fashions the self" (Bauer 1988, 1).

In Bakhtinian terms, I describe the heteroglossical world of Styron's novelistic fictions: the way in which many languages, female as well as male, are present in his novels. The polyphonic structures of Styron's narratives are strategies of inclusion in that they represent the voices of "the beaten and butchered and betrayed and martyred children of the earth" (SC 515), that is, the casualties, in the same text with the voices, and "reasoned" arguments in some cases, of their antagonists and oppressors. The value of Bakhtin's analysis, Dale Marie Bauer argues, is that it provides a theoretical framework from which to study the oppression of women and minorities, a central concern of Styron's. Bauer's use of feminist dialogics demonstrates that Bakhtin's understanding of the inclusive nature of the novel can itself be informed by feminism's attempts to examine and detail both the voices of domination and the voices of the marginalized. In what Bauer calls the dialogic American novel—of which Styron is clearly a practitioner—the struggles and the voices of the disenfranchised are represented along with those of the powerful; and this inclusiveness particularly illuminates the resistance, however marginalized, of the female heroine to the monologism of patriarchal norms and conventions. The novels that Bauer examines in her own study present situations where women misinterpret their social "texts" and are sacrificed because they cannot realize their own "social power" (Bauer, 1988, 3). The American "heroine" in this sense is doomed by the roles foisted upon her by a patriarchy resistant to her inclusion in the power structures of the society. In a linguistic sense, the American heroine finds herself, as she attains the crucial self-awareness, without a language of power, without the words even to express her exclusion or powerlessness. Sophie reflects on just such a dilemma when she tells Stingo that she had no way to object to her father's anti-Semitic tracts or even to challenge him about other day-to-day abuse:

And I was a grown woman and I wanted to play Bach, and at that moment I just thought I must die—I mean, to die not so much for what he was making me do but because I had *no way of saying no.* (SC 246; italics mine)

In terms of form, the evolving pattern of Styron's narrative structures suggests a movement from a multi-voiced *Lie Down in Darkness* to *Set This House on Fire,* a narrative that employs a strategy of including multiple voices by embedding a confessional first-person novel within another first-person novel (Cass's novel inside Peter's). The development of polyphony and multivocality is heightened in *Nat Turner* as the first person narrative includes not only the discourse of Tidewater folks of all socioeconomic levels, but also that of the King James version of the Old and New Testament whose Elizabethan cadences Nat hears in his revelations from spirit-voices. In *Sophie's Choice,* we again find a first-person-within-a-first-person narrative along with a series of powerful polyphonic meditations that inculcate several informed voices on the sociohistorical importance of domination and slavery in America; in Nazi camps; and in the triangle of Nathan, Sophie, and Stingo. In *The Dialogic Imagination,* Bakhtin describes the kind of linguistic consciousness we see in Styron's narratives:

> The actively literary linguistic consciousness at all times and everywhere (that is, in all epochs of literature historically available to us) comes upon "languages" and not language [per se]. Consciousness finds itself inevitably facing the necessity of having to choose a language. With each literary-verbal performance, consciousness must actively orient itself amidst heteroglossia. . . . (Bakhtin 1981, 295)

Stingo acts as this "linguistic consciousness" as he reports Sophie's various renditions of her past; the elder Stingo has listened to additional voices and has read texts that try to interpret the Holocaust experience, and he adds his own mature resonance to the heteroglossia of *Sophie's Choice.* What results from the process is not any one single, closed language, but a dialogue among voices that asks the reader to enter into the ongoing process of understanding which Styron has designed.

This active engagement of the reader's voice emerges when he or she is drawn into a constantly adjusting dialogue with the novel's voices. Richard Law refers to this salient aspect of Styron's work as an ability to encourage in the reader "a sense of involved discovery" very much like the actual emotional experience of consciousness itself by "drawing the reader into constructing the text" and thereby creating the novel anew, in some sense, each time (Law 1990, 53). In Styron the text invariably concerns the evils of human domination and repression, especially in relation to women. Like Stingo, the reader encounters the "unspeakable"—although it is spoken—in texts and in Sophie's own various changing voice. These texts polemically invade, as Bakhtin explains, "the reader's belief and evaluation system, striving to stun and destroy the appreciative background of the reader's understanding" (Bakhtin 1981, 293). Bakhtin refers to Tolstoy here, but a comparison between Styron and the Russian master is apt: each defamiliarizes experience by surrounding the reader/listeners with texts/voices from a varied panoply of human discourses meant at once to appear realistic and within the boundaries of normal experience and to function as multivalent points of view that frustrate a single monologic "understanding" of text that would "kill" it in the Felmanian sense (Felman 1975, 10).

Styron's work has evolved, notes Gavin Cologne-Brooks, such that the pattern of voices in his discourse has become increasingly "decentered" and concerned more with sociohistoric rather than personal and literary issues (Cologne-Brooks 1989, 1611). In this, Styron reflects the concerns and evolution of literary criticism itself as it becomes more self-aware of particular biases and more sensitive to the inclusion or exclusion of alternate voices in its own discourse. Feminism has been no small contributor to this evolution. However, as Bonnie Kime Scott has asserted in reference to Joyce, some might question why we need yet another study of yet another canonical male author. Part of my answer to this query resides in a determination to test feminist claims about the cultural hegemony of a well-developed patriarchy. In researching this problem, feminists (male and female) seek to question a perceived male dominance of the literary and critical canons by exposing the limitations of patriarchal norms. Jonathan Culler has explained that, as a term, *feminist criticism* in this sense may be applied to "all criticism alert to the critical ramifications of sexual repression" (Culler 1982, 56). Further, "[by] confronting male readings with the *elements of the text* they neglect," as indeed I do in my study, such readings "identify the specific defenses and *distortions of male readings* and provide correctives" (54; italics mine). As Scott writes, "Instead of seeing literature as pure and disinterested, feminist critics are apt to detect previously unassessed power structures (politics) in the text and its production" (Scott 1987, 2). As to the problem of my own gender limits in this study, Peter Hitchcock notes himself that he accepts Tania Modleski's arguments about the problematic existence of a "feminism without women" but that he is nonetheless optimistic, as am I, that such "strategic alliances can contribute to, rather than undermine, feminist projects" (Hitchcock 1993, xiii).

William Styron compels his readers to question the culture, mostly Western, mostly Judeo-Christian, that can give us African-American slavery and Auschwitz, as well as dehumanizing stereotypes of women. Scott writes that feminist questioning leads to a "basic deconstruction of male-organized western thought" by critiquing its mainstay, binary logic (Scott 1987, 13). In Styron we find narratives of women related by and framed by men and their "logic," narratives that demand we question both "male" discourse as well as the "process of interpreting experience as text"; thus, as Richard Law explains further, Styron "illustrates the arbitrary nature of the discourse in which knowledge is ordinarily framed" (Law 1990, 53). In this sense my study argues that Styron's art is also concerned with understanding male dominance and the discursive processes by which it promulgates its patriarchal, monologic visions.

Peter Hitchcock explains that dialogism does not "homogenize" the voices of oppressed peoples; instead, "dialogism throws into sharp relief their heterogeneity" (Hitchcock 1993, 1). In this way, a feminist dialogics serves my purposes of creating a studied collection—in some cases, as in important scenes between Peyton Loftis and her father, Milton, a point-by-point data bank as it were—of synchronic and diachronic discourses that describe female characters in the works of William Styron. I address the material aspects of how the specific details of Styron's language reflect or capture a society's underlying ideological bases as they are described in the social and material conditions of a particular time. As such, I endeavor to assert a basic chronology of development in which scenes may be properly *contextualized* through careful observation of their particularities. In this, I am concentrating on deconstructing the actual depictions of women in these novels rather than defining methodological terms I may be employing at any given time. Hitchcock relates that such defining "is a form of monological contraction, a limitation, that is, of the 'terms of the debate'—but only in the voice of the speaker" (2). I wish to problematize in an exploratory way the limits of dialogism and observe with my reader the pushing of dialogism's limits not only beyond the formulations of Bakhtin, but also beyond those of Bauer. Rather than seeking closure (or the "harmony" of monologue) for the ongoing "conversation" here presented, I wish to add my own voice and suggest *possibilities*. In Wayne C. Booth's words:

Propositions about women can tell us nothing . . . until we ask who utters them? In what circumstances? In what time? With what qualifications by other utterances? And most important of all, what is the quality of our emotional response, point by point? (Booth 1982, 59)

Booth further explains that the usefulness of M. M. Bakhtin's discovery of a "dialogic imagination" as an integral part of human existence is that it "demolishes the notion of the atomic self, authentic in its privacy only, clearly separable from other selves and identified as free to the degree that it has purged itself of 'external influences'" (51). Such a definition of the "atomic self" is challenged by Bakhtin's idea that each of us is made up of "a collective of the many selves we have taken in from birth" and that any attempt to exorcise all voices except "my own" is impossible. "We are," says Booth, "constituted in polyphony" (51). For Bakhtin, this "polyphonic self" is best explored literarily in novelistic discourse because the novel inculcates the "supreme value" of resisting monologue. Booth concludes that in art and life "our essence and our value are found in whatever counters the temptation to treat human beings as 'objects' reducible to their usefulness to us" (52).

In terms of a descriptive, materialist analysis, a rereading of the representation of women in the novels of William Styron invites a dialogic activity that requires, as Hitchcock notes, "taking others into account without dominating them" (Hitchcock 1993, 24).

2

Bring Home the Bride Again:
The Women of *Lie Down in Darkness*

Bring home the bride again, bring home the triumph of our
victory.

—*Lie Down in Darkness* (247)

WILLIAM Styron wrote *Lie Down in Darkness,* his first novel, with
an achronological structure in the Southern modernist tradition of
Faulkner, Wolfe, and Penn Warren (Rubin 1981, 71). John Kenny
Crane divides the novel into five levels of narrative time, levels that
include major and embedded flashbacks called up in associative
patterns designed to reveal contexts for the lifeworlds of the various characters (Crane 1984, 145). The reader is invited to create
these contexts, and thus recognize the text's multiple discourses
as they grow out of a series of overlapping episodes. In this way,
Styron avoids monologism in the novel, and, like Faulkner in *The
Sound and the Fury,* he presents subjective versions of crucial
scenes as witnessed by the main characters and described in their
respective flashbacks (Rubin 1981, 73). In Bakhtinian terms, Styron
presents voices in competition with one another in a dialogic structure: "one point of view opposed to another, one evaluation opposed to another, one accent opposed to another" (Bakhtin 1981,
314).

I will examine first the women who are important but who receive much less textual space than Helen Loftis or her daughter,
Peyton. The chapter continues by examining in careful, chrono-
logic detail key scenes (chronotopes) from both Helen and Peyton's
narrative discourses. My method is to observe closely the specific
language and structural devices, especially the fragmenting of narrative chronology, used in the portrayal of these women. By considering point of view in addition to the aforementioned details,
I adapt Bauer's materialistic feminist dialogism to document the

23

presentation of what Thelma J. Shinn refers to in her study of American novels, *Radiant Daughters,* as Styron's "gallery of women" in the novel (Shinn 1986, 78). In this "gallery," Styron's organization of the novel allows the reader to examine the problems of "telling the tale from the inside" and the "social languages and codes of reading" which Styron employs to dramatize the novel (Bauer 1988, 18). In this process of producing a communal experience, Styron creates what Bauer refers to as "a heteroglossic polylogue of ideological discourses" that critiques the social, and therefore necessarily patriarchal, structures involved (18).

A close analysis here will "unveil the workings of the patriarchal system of values and display structures which control the social and cultural order," as Nelly Furman puts it (Furman 1985, 59–60). Furman's own method, which she employs as she scrutinizes specific marriage vows and the politics of other language related to marriage as an exchange of women that "assures the continuity of the social structure," is itself informed by Helen Cixous's point that "no political reflection can dispense with reflection on language" (Furman 1985, 60). Furman sees the literary text as a space where an ongoing dialogue between writer and reader takes place in the context of a "literary system" which is itself representative of the social reality surrounding the literary enterprise (Furman 65). The literary text, in this sense, is "the result of an interaction" which exists only in discourse: "Because it is the result of a dialogical process of exchange between reader and writer concerning the signification provided by the materiality of the linguistic medium, each and every reading is unique, and this in turn explains the inherently plural character of textual criticism, understood as a post-structuralist activity" (68–69). Furman's basic message here supports the notion that no monologic interpretation of a text is credible in light of the reality of the novelistic discourse; moreover, examination of the specific use of language further sensitizes a reader to the "values woven through the fabric of our society" (59). This study seeks also to unveil the strictures that result in the ritualistic literary gynicide and psychogynicide that punctuate Styron's critique of Port Warwick, and therefore midtwentieth-century American, society.

Perhaps correctly viewed as "minor," but a particularly important female character in spite of her "supporting" role in the discourse of the novel, Milton's mistress, Dolly, reveals much about the social structures that define her. After flirting with Milton on and off since 1933, she enters into a liaison with him in 1939 which continues, except for an eleven-month hiatus beginning after

Maudie's death, until the close of the novel. A physical description of Dolly comes early in the novel from an omniscient point of view.

> She was a dark and pretty woman and would perhaps have been beautiful except for a slightly receding chin which lent to her features an expression not so much of weakness as fretfulness, as if at any moment her jaw and lips might tremble in sorrow, like a little girl's. (LDD 37)

Dolly's flashbacks reveal a character far more interesting and complex than Milton's first impression of her as "common" and having "a certain naive, little-girl wit which wouldn't be too hard to take provided one weren't around her for too long" (LDD 54), suggesting Styron's own avoidance of female stereotypes in the novel. She is unhappily married to Pookie, a potbellied, glad-handing man who nevertheless reappears in the novel later and proves through Milton's view to be a dedicated spouse, in spite of his lack of sophistication which Dolly had so loathed. Indeed, Dolly's own social climb apparently began with Pookie who took her away from a "little peanut town" and a hardscrabble existence. Dolly has a son by Pookie who seems more a bother than a source of pride for her, since the hapless boy appears to be a carbon copy of his father. Pookie and Dolly eventually divorce, and her son goes off to college, leaving her, by 1945 "free" to share Milton's room at the country club and hotel rooms where they have "hot, sweet" nights (70). So for Dolly, the journey from Pookie to a "sophisticated" lawyer has been worth the trials.

> Together we can never die. A farm girl from Emporia: what would Papa say now? I sophisticated and fancypants . . . member in good standing of the Tidewater Garden Club, too. (71)

Milton began his affair with Dolly the night of Peyton's "sweet sixteen" birthday party; they made love on a couch in the golf museum of the country club. "Sweet and ruinous" is what Dolly tells us Milton says of her, and she relishes his sexual attraction to her. "Knowing he wants me, that's what's so good" (LDD 71); she makes him "warm with desire each time, with a silken whisper, she crossed her legs" (53). It takes Milton six years to consummate his flirtation with Dolly, a period she wishes had been shorter, but she is not simply a gold digger or a nymphet. She stands up to Helen during their confrontation at the Bide-a-Wee Club lunch after Peyton's party; Helen's desire to humiliate and regally defeat her rival in a public place crashes about her as Dolly's secret weapon, her "easy indifference" to Helen's fury and outrage, out-flanks her threats. Dolly taunts Helen further with her declaration of love for Milton, a love that's more than Helen can give, says Dolly (130). Not quite a strumpet or "the other woman" or tempt-ress or even the classic divorcée, Dolly defies the easy labels by exhibiting a healthy sexuality that Milton appreciates in contrast to his perception of Helen. Dolly shows her emotions, again unlike Helen, whose life with Milton after 1939 consists of a series of retreats to her bedroom and Nembutals. Styron forces the reader to discover the complex, palpable nature of Dolly by allowing her a page of italicized internal monologue in which she muses on her "tender rapture" and on her own role "upcaught in the tragedy of middle class morality" (70–71). It is Dolly who lectures Helen, whom Dolly refers to in her section as a "succubus," much to Helen's surprise and indignation, when they meet one-on-one: "Just remember that whatever Milton does it's because he's just been lonesome" (131).

Dolly is an essentialist who focuses on what she sees are the basics of her relationship with Milton, but she too has conventional hopes in her own agenda, and her fanciest hopes (or worst delu-sions) include her daydream of a future with Milton. This dream is periodically threatened by his preoccupation with Peyton; Dolly feels "the girl cast forbidding shadows across her tenderly hopeful destiny" (LDD 68). Dolly also sees the sober Milton as a "gentle spirit" who promises "to envelop her like a tender flame, radiating decent contentment" (68) and who promises to take care of her. But, again, wrenching feelings pull at her dreams when Milton speaks of Peyton's troubles, ironically on the very night he re-ceives news of her suicide: "when he spoke of [Peyton] she felt an emotion that . . . was nothing but wretched jealousy" (68). So Dolly's feelings parallel and, in a sense, confirm Helen's jealous reactions toward Peyton. Dolly's dreams of a conventionally happy and respectable future also come to naught as Milton leaves her sobbing in a limousine after Peyton's burial. Her other, more gran-diose visions of achieving perhaps some National Democratic Committeewoman position when Milton finally succeeds in politics are likewise destroyed. All she receives from Milton at the close of the narrative is a "brief glance" as he runs from the cemetery through a blinding thunderstorm.

In his portrayal of this "other woman" Styron peels away layers to unveil a woman who is indeed hopeful of improving her social standing by entering into an extramarital relationship with what appears to her an influential man of substance, but she is engaged in more than social-climbing. She has a desire for less difficult circumstances and a wider, fuller gratification of quite normal needs; she seeks a more significant role in a marriage as well as in the larger community. She is also desperate not to fall back into the peanut town she escaped, where she will have to return to nurse her aging aunt and endure certain poverty if she cannot make a life with Milton. For her, the cost of her divorcing Pookie in order to devote herself to Milton is high: the gossip "runs" (LDD 71) about the two of them, and so she will not be able to remain "socially acceptable" if Milton returns to Helen or if he rejects her out of grief. Because it is only through him that she retains a veneer of "respectability" among the country club society, she is heavily invested in her pursuit of a conventional life with Milton. But to Milton, a male with wider options, she is "one among the assortment of props and crutches" (40) which have supported him through his awakening to the fact that "life was not rich and purposeful and full of rewards" (40). This underlying mercantilism of sex in which the "other woman" can sometimes be typed as a "social climber" has created the very role Dolly finds herself in: she views men as commodities because she herself has been a "dolly," a "kitten," a plaything and object, and, given the slenderness of her resources, it is clear that for women like her the stakes are high indeed. Society matrons confirmed in their positions may scoff at Dolly, but it is the system that supports *them* which also encourages the Dollies to crash the party.

It may not be too reductivist to say that the novel is primarily about the evil that results from the dehumanizing of people into conformist, even Procrustean roles, especially women. The primary roles explored here, mother, beautiful daughter, mistress, all appear to revolve around the uncertain moods and appetites of a profoundly troubled, alcoholic male, Milton, who, even as a mediocre lawyer, enjoys measures of prestige and power that his moneyed wife, privileged daughter, and "social" mistress cannot. Thus in this tidewater community of the mid-1940s, women's lives are defined in male-privileging terms which are then rigorously enforced—as we see in Helen's severity toward Peyton and Dolly—by the patriarchy's most dependable defenders: women who have their own power bases granted by the patriarchy. Dale Marie Bauer refers to such women characters as those who mimic their fathers' voices and repeat their fathers' monolithic, authoritative speech as a means of accessing cultural authority (Bauer 1988, 53).

Another important "minor" character in the novel, Maudie, the eldest Loftis child who is also mentally retarded and who lives in a perpetual suspended animation as the family's infant child, in constant contrast with Peyton, is significant beyond her apparent voicelessness. In this sense, Maudie, as a Loftis daughter and as a source of primal guilt feelings for the rest of the family, is perhaps more centrally involved in the discourse of the novel than other supporting female characters. In one of Helen's major flashbacks, Maudie has an interlude with a drifter named Bennie who imparts to her foreknowledge of her own end, at least as Helen views the encounter (LDD 211). Helen is convinced that this little juggler mystically provides Maudie with "a lover, father, magic—something" (212). And then Bennie departs as mysteriously as he had come, leaving Maudie "silent and peaceful" during the month before her death. She and Helen sit together in the yard, dozing; Maudie, says Helen, did not feel her own "strength flowing out of her like a dying flower" (213). Earlier references to Maudie in the novel are fairly repetitive: she is the baby who "hollered" in the night and causes Milton to ask testily: "What's wrong with the kid?" (28) Later Maudie ages but does not mature or improve; she manages to say "Pretty!" from time to time as well as "Papadaddy" to Milton who longs "for an affection that could never really blossom" with Maudie.

Although Maudie is not neglected physically by Milton and the others, two incidents—Maudie's being gagged and tied and later "dropped" by Peyton—obtrude in the lives and in the memories of each family member, subsequently distorting their lives with agonizing guilt feelings. Helen feels guilt for bearing Maudie and for condemning the child to such dangers and to the cruel emotional rejection of her father who expected only beautiful children. Milton's sense of guilt resides in his anguish over siring a defective child, although he selfishly postulates that Helen's body is somehow more to blame than his. Peyton's guilty feeling over her binding and torturing Maudie and then dropping her in another incident—accidentally or out of spite and anger at her mother—is compounded by a sense of abandoning her sister after she leaves home to escape Helen's taunts. An emblem of sorts of "the sins of the fathers," Maudie can also be seen as a focal point of this family's fate: they are handsome, moneyed, educated, poised in public, but in their midst, day in and day out, Maudie reminds them of some mysterious genetic error that does not quite fit their pleasant surroundings.

"The miracle of birth" is all Milton can muster as he muses on Maudie during those rare moments that he does think of her. Like

Benjy in *The Sound and the Fury,* Maudie's muted presence adds another dimension to the Loftis household which we must remember is in the South, a land where, as Milton's father says, "the ground is bloody and full of guilt" (LDD 69). Helen ostensibly devotes herself to Maudie, but at the expense of her marriage and in so doing she takes on a martyr complex, becoming self-righteously indignant that she is not recognized in her role as a devoted and caring mother. Indeed, in one dream sequence, she sees Maudie as part of her land of the female dead, and thus she suffers even more pangs of guilt: that she should hate her own beloved Maudie, the innocent. The family, in the end, loves but is deeply appalled by Maudie; as Milton reflects: "Poor dear gentle child. Now his heart went out to her yearningly. But . . . she caused him dreadful unhappiness" (46). Thus, even though Maudie in one sense is a "voiceless" character, she is nonetheless an important presence affecting the members of the Loftis family. Perhaps it is Maudie more than any other character who provides a solid base of evidence for Bakhtin's assertions that "the development of the novel is a function of the deepening of dialogic essence, its increased scope and greater precision" (Bakhtin 1981, 300). Her "space" in the novel is more one of an overheard voicedness, rather than a conversant interlocuter, except in the case of Bennie, who himself remains mute. Maudie represents, then, how "the novelistic word . . . registers with extreme subtlety the tiniest shifts and oscillations of the social atmosphere; it does so, moreover, while registering it as a whole, in all of its aspects" (300).

Like Maudie, the African-American female house servants Ella Swan and her daughter La Ruth create by their largely silent presence much of the ambience of the Loftis household and its encompassing social milieu. Although these characters are at times presented in uncomplimentary, stereotypical terms, the descriptions are reflective of the time, 1930s and 1940s Virginia, and the respective characters' points of view. Indeed, it is their stereotyped roles as black domestics that establishes the veracity of Styron's presentation of the Loftis household. Ella, who like Dilsey in Faulkner's tale of another crumbling Southern family, presides over the domestic services provided to a family plagued by disunity and domestic strife. She is first described in one of Milton's sections: "She had a wrinkled, wizened face, like that of an aged monkey" (LDD 11). We next see her through Helen's judgmental eyes as a "black wraith with yellowed, aqueous eyes. 'Lawd God, Miss Helen, cain't I help . . .'" (24); and Ella sets off, leaving to attend Daddy Faith's meeting to find redemption and some meaning in Peyton's suicide. Milton in another scene offers Ella a drink but she scoffs at his alcoholism; his view is: "old nigger cooks and nurses and laundry women from birth to death casting up eyes of blame and self-righteousness" (47). A little while later Milton encounters La Ruth and we see her for the first time: "a huge, slovenly Negro with steel-rimmed spectacles and an air of constant affliction. . . . She lumbered past with a sullen flat-footed sound, a great, aching hulk of a woman, moaning and groaning" (52). It may appear from these images that Styron is merely repeating stereotyped black mammies, but he layers in other details such as Ella's appearance in one scene "old and bent and stooped-over, dressed fantastically in one of the cast-off gowns Helen had worn in the twenties" (114). Still, it is a scene from Helen's perspective and she adds that Ella looks "like a wrinkled ape someone had costumed for a side show in silk and tassels and clinging beads" (114). Neither Milton nor Helen see their black maids as anything more than these passages relate. Ella and La Ruth are more beasts of burden and part of the background than people for the privileged whites; thus Styron's descriptions are appropriate and informative in their honest clarity of white peoples' views of "their" blacks.

La Ruth deserves special attention, however, because she has the audacity, as Helen might say, to compare her own misfortunes with those of Helen on the day of Peyton's burial. To Helen, La Ruth appears as a set of "enormous buttocks reared before her . . . the faded skirt hiked high, revealing fat mahogany limbs and the sandy crater of a vaccination scar" (LDD 139). As La Ruth searches for an umbrella, Helen's mind offers an observation of La Ruth's intellect. "And then down the endless tunnels of her mind, without tributary where no thought could diverge . . . only link with a sister-thought like an elephant trunk-to-tail" (139). What Styron suggests by staging such a scene, however, is something quite different from Helen's racism. La Ruth's grief for Peyton launches her at Helen, cold, white-haired Helen, and Helen finds herself in the grips of La Ruth's scaly callouses and sweaty arms, "a Negro touching her" thinks Helen (140), "but behind those greasy spectacles the eyes, always so full of muddled despair, had in them now . . . the shine of revelation" (140). La Ruth trippingly explains how when her own child died she was "soured," but she prayed to Jesus to send her man, a wayward man like Milton she says, back so that she could "get" her love, she says, "even if dat was de onliest thing I could get" (140).

But La Ruth's entreaties are ignored and then rejected with Helen's abrupt "Shut up, La Ruth. Be quiet!" (LDD 141) Yet for all the negative descriptions, La Ruth is the final character in the novel to mourn "po' Peyton." At the close of Daddy Faith's service during which Ella achieves a revelation and a sense of redemption, La Ruth continues to moan that she "don't know" and that she is "comin' around to thinkin' about all dat time and everything" (381). And in her grief she snuffles into the wet sleeves of her robe and cries in anguish and true angst, "God knows, I don't know." Ella, however, has an affirmation of "yes, Jesus," in a soft voice that announces her acceptance of Peyton's fate in light of Daddy Faith's assertion that "sho'ly the people is grass" and "grass withereth, de flower fadeth" (380).

In this way Styron compares the voices of women from different worlds and examines how rich, white, more empowered women may appear to lack the spiritual resources they need to face tragedy, and not only to endure it, but to rise above it with vision and understanding. For all that, a note of criticism enters even here as Styron portrays Daddy Faith as a charlatan in a Cadillac, offering poor Ella and La Ruth the same idols of money and power that white men offer white women; La Ruth still hasn't been properly baptized and "washed": she harbors dimly expressed doubts about the entire system, but she has scant resources with which to raise questions. And even in the black revivalist society there is a woman present to reinforce the message of the male authority figure, Daddy Faith. It is Sister Adelphia who chastises La Ruth for even voicing her muddled doubts. Ella may have felt a cleansing from sinfulness that Helen does not enjoy, but even Sister Adelphia's admonishment cannot quiet La Ruth's profound doubts. Ella ends by crying out that she has "seen Him," and so the novel closes with affirmations of faith in the final male authority figure: Jesus. Supplicants are encouraged to accept their lives as in His hands, under His control. For them, redemption comes in the form of self-annihilation; their meaning in life comes from abandoning doubts about the system over which they are instructed to see they have no control. As Daddy Faith instructs, the people, like the grass and the flowers, fade, but God, the overarching patriarchal force, "shall stand forever" (LDD 380).

Some critics charge that Styron's oeuvre is an attempt to explore and then excise his feelings about his own mother, so it is worthwhile to examine particular mothers and how they are portrayed in the novel. Milton's mother is remembered early in the narrative when he recalls her whispering to him about a parade outside: "It's music, Milton dear, music, music" (LDD 12). Her face, vacant and "hovering" above, remains for him "unseen and finally unknown"

(12) because she dies before he can memorize the lovely features his father speaks of. Herein lies a commonality Milton shares with another male character, Dick Cartwright, Peyton's college beau, who also lost his mother at an early age and was therefore reared by his grandmother. Dick's grandmother is portrayed not as a "vacant" face, but as a religious woman, with a "stern old eagle's face, the beak clapping endlessly over words of iniquity and damnation" (217). The old woman speaks of Heaven and hell and woman, "full of abominations and the filthiness of her fornications . . . the mother of harlots" (217); again, we see here a woman reinforcing patriarchal mythology about "woman as harlot." Another mother, Carey Carr's, on the other hand, is described as a widow with lovely skin and a "sweet thoughtful" disposition, a woman who "encouraged his sensitive nature" which he eventually purges, says Carr, when he marries a woman of whom his mother does not approve. The fine sweet woman with the "deep liquid eyes" dies in a delirium so great that she cries out that "somehow she had been all her life tricked and cheated" (99). Helen Loftis's mother by contrast is remembered hardly at all, and when she is, it is not by Helen but by Milton as he recounts how he and Helen had built their fine new home "thanks to Helen's mother who had auspiciously died two years [before]" (46).

Thus are some mothers remembered and described in the novel: from the supportive and sensitive but "cheated" to the vacant and even absent; whether Styron's body of work seeks to investigate his relationship with his own mother is problematic. But since much of his fiction is inspired by incidents from his own life, it may be useful to note here that in his latest book, *Darkness Visible,* Styron reveals that his fight with his own very serious depression and subsequent suicidal state in the mid-1980s took a decided turn for the better when in a fit of despair he heard a passage from Brahms's *Alto Rhapsody.* Immediately his mind was flooded with thoughts of his long-dead mother who had sung such a passage to him in their home. Styron writes, "my own avoidance of death may well have been belated homage to my mother" (DV 81). As for his stepmother, Elizabeth, Styron recalls chiefly that she tried to make his life a "hell" (Coale 1991, 7). To the young Styron, the woman "was as close to the wicked stepmother image as one can possibly imagine"; Styron has also admitted recently that "the basic torment between Peyton and her family [especially Helen Loftis] was really a projection of my own sense of alienation from my own tiny family—that is, my father whom I really loved and this strange woman. . . ." (7).

The first time that Peyton's mother, Helen Loftis, appears in the narrative discourse, she is contextualized by Milton, her husband, in one of his major flashbacks. Milton recalls their first meeting long ago at an officers' dance on Governor's Island, New York, during the First World War. Grieving terribly in the fictional present of August 1945 as he awaits the arrival of the train from New York carrying his daughter's casket, Milton describes his initial meeting with Helen as one in which she fled from him when he tried to give her a drunken kiss. His memory of the young Helen's flight from his drunken advances is, ironically, still couched in a romantic haze: "then she fled, the raindrops on her cape leaving a trail of trembling sparks" (LDD 13). Milton goes on to relate that, like himself, Helen was handsome, liked parties and dancing, but was also straitlaced and in many ways "rather severe" (13). She categorically forgoes any sexual encounters with him before they are married; she does not drink, either: "She loved a good time, but a sober good time" (13). Later, when Milton tries to force a drink on her at another social event during their courtship, she runs off again, "unaccountably," according to Milton, and "weeping a little." "Now, Little Miss Muffet," says Milton to his young bride-to-be, "don't be scared" (14). In reality, this snippet of memory from Milton's viewpoint reveals more about Milton's soon to be announced hopes for their reconciliation after their daughter's tragic suicide than it does about Helen, although it does dramatically underline Helen's own inability to face her husband's drinking as alcoholism. The most she can do during her engagement is weep and leave Milton to his stupor, but in this she is certainly a young woman of her time. The reader's first encounter with Helen hardly prepares the way for the image of this character at almost fifty on the day of her daughter's burial.

A few pages later in the narrative, Casper the undertaker has his own flashback concerning the manner with which Helen had informed him of the arrival of her daughter's casket. Casper recounts that Helen's voice is cultured, polite, if faintly superior, but that it is also a voice "oddly calm and devoid of feeling" (LDD 18). So odd, in fact, that he remarks to his fellow mortician afterwards: "That was funny, she sounded so . . . cold" (18). When Casper goes to the Loftis home the following morning, he encounters Helen's "ghostly face" and "lovely hair, stark white, although she couldn't yet be fifty" (18). Thus are we presented, quite literally "faced with," Helen Loftis, the materfamilias, at the two extremes of her life: as a "little Miss Muffet" and as the prematurely aged woman she has become. That Helen is observed so early in the novel by a mortician who has a professional eye for the details of her "fine tapestry of wrinkles" on her "ghostly face" is significant in that we can sense immediately the tragedy in that face; a mortician's objectivity is our necessary antidote to Milton's sentimental and boozy memory of his Miss Muffet. That he does not see his own wife's face as a tragic mask heightens the irony of the situation for the reader.

Casper's viewpoint presents Helen as she is in what Crane refers to as the "transcendent present" of August 1945 (Crane 1984, 149). Casper represents the very community before which both Milton and Helen strive to keep up an appearance of "decency" by playing down the family's dysfunctional behavior. As Casper waits for specific instructions concerning Peyton's burial, he overhears Milton's pleas that Helen accompany him to the train station; in fact, Milton, whose affair with Dolly Bonner has been public for two years, now pleads that "decency" demands that Helen attend. He begs her with a quintessential social concern: "What will people think?" (LDD 19). Helen ridicules Milton's tardy emphasis on public decency by parroting Milton and repeating tonelessly if sarcastically, "What will people think." She then retires to her room, her sanctuary, but as she goes she taunts him further by suggesting that instead he take his mistress and the black family servant, Ella; and Milton, dutiful in this if nothing else, does take the two women with him for company. Ella's presence and her right to attend are simply and succinctly explained by Helen: "She loved Peyton" (20). Casper's interior comment on this exchange, as a member of the Port Warwick community, is his brief but italicized and therefore doubly significant "*Lord Almighty.*" Here Styron effectively heightens the irony of the moment by underscoring how Helen, who has been supremely concerned with her own appearance before her community as a long-suffering mother, has abandoned even the pretense of family reconciliation. At the grave site later in the day, Helen repeats over and over "Nothing!"—which is what remains of her family after the ceremony is complete. Through Casper, who doubtless will bear witness of this dialogue to others, the community is represented even as Helen finally rejects its rules of "decency." She has journeyed far from her "strait-laced" youth and courtship when she obeyed social strictures unconsciously (13). The one attribute she has kept, a trait she cherished in her puritanical West Point father, Colonel "Blood and Jesus" Peyton, is her severity.

Once Helen has retreated to her room, she herself reflects on how she received the news of Peyton's suicide; in her reverie she recalls that she has let the beds go unmade and that she herself retrieved the morning paper from the front steps, "an act quite out of keeping with the serene and orderly character of her life" (LDD 20). In her "queer, abstracted way," reports the narrative, Helen reflects, "This is the first day that I have awakened knowing that I am a mother no longer and that I shall never be a mother again" (21). Instead of presenting Helen merely as an angry country-club housewife whose marriage is a disaster, Styron delves into the Helen's psyche and exposes her quite poignant thoughts. At this juncture in the narrative, the reader is presented with evidence that invites empathy with Helen's grief. Critics have complained that Helen's behavior and interior monologues do not make her psychological motivations apparent enough, and therefore she is "less effectively drawn" than other characters (Rubin 1981, 75). But such criticism appears to ignore Styron's efforts to reveal the depths of Helen's sense of betrayal and loss. Until the day of Peyton's burial, Helen has worn her tragic masks of the mother and wife scorned, but over the years the mask has become her own face, and the tragedy is not a public ruse any longer. As she examines her face in the dresser mirror, she finds "an old woman's face . . . haggard and spooky," the skin of which she pulls tightly over her cheeks to eliminate for a moment the lines of time. Squinting, she sees "smooth skin as glossy white" as gardenia petals and the lips of a sixteen-year-old "unblemished by any trouble." But the fantasy fades as soon as she releases the folds of skin and turns automatically to scan a newspaper.

The simple everyday humanity of Helen's reaching for a newspaper in such a moment of wrenching realizations is another example of Styron's ability to frame a character in her world, to draw the reader into that world more fully than if Helen had at this moment behaved in terms of some stereotyped notion of female grief. Helen Loftis has been seen by various critics as a woman filled with "insane jealousy" that leads to her acts of "great cruelty" toward her family (73, 74) and as a mother who wears a "hypocritical mask" of love and understanding when in reality she feels naught but jealousy and hostility (74). Her "madness" has been characterized as the end result of her perception that Milton had failed to "provide her with the protection of a dead Southern aristocracy" (Shinn 1986, 79). She has also been described as a recluse bent on revenge like some midtwentieth-century Medea-as-Calvinist who is nevertheless "another of that lost and dying breed haunting the pages of Southern writers, the ideal Southern lady" (79). The initial scenes here presented further problematize a monologic understanding of the character and suggest a much more variegated portrait. Helen began as a virginal, innocent daughter of a well-to-do Virginian, a pious military man whom she adored and thought was "just like God" (LDD 107). Even Milton's own sententious father pronounced on their wedding day that Milton was indeed a lucky young man: "Believe me, my boy, you have a good woman" (41). So here was the ideal young wife and mother of the time, class, and place: beautiful, genteel, chaste, conservative, and religious; for her time, Helen appears to have been quite a "catch" for Milton, a bride with respectability and money in addition to her personal qualities.

Styron's text examines a woman who cannot be dismissed with clichés such as "insanely jealous mother." In fact, it appears that such critical comments in the early book reviews reflected the era in which they were conceived: critics could not meaningfully reconcile Helen's behavior with what they saw as the role of the true mother. But Styron critiques such gender-bound assumptions in the novel itself: it is acceptable for Helen's father to be severe, cold, and distant; but for his daughter as a woman and mother to exhibit the same behavior is taboo. The stern Blood and Jesus Peyton is "loved by his men" as Helen tells it; he is the "strong, silent type" much admired in American popular myth. But Helen's own similar behavior is seen by the "objective" mortician as "cold and odd," because it runs counter to the warm and comforting mother role the stereotype demands. In a word, Helen is seen as "unnatural." However, Helen can and does more objectively examine her own background as she shares her story with Carey Carr, her erstwhile Episcopalian minister. She comments on her father's influence. "And severe and strict he was. But it was good for me. I learned what's right and what's wrong" (LDD 108). Later in Styron's *Sophie's Choice,* we will see a similar approach taken by Sophie herself as she *first* tries to explain her relationship with her stern father.

Helen and Carey Carr also discuss her marriage's decay. Shortly after Peyton's sixteenth birthday, Helen begins to visit Carr on a semiregular basis, and during these meetings, she unveils her awareness of Milton's first negative reactions toward her. Helen postulates that Milton began to drink heavily and subsequently spent more time away from her for perhaps two reasons: their daughter Maudie's infirmities became more pronounced and/or Milton's "need for her" sexually had died (LDD 108). The importance of alcohol as Milton's elixir for escaping his parental responsibilities and for maintaining his at times fatuous opinion of himself is paramount.

On one Sunday in the mid-1930s we see from Milton's point of view Helen's efforts to chastise her husband for beginning his drinking at nine o'clock. At first she confronts him about his drinking. "What's the big idea?" (LDD 49) But he simply jokes and asks her: "Have a drink?" Instead of getting "crazy" or "bitter" and "raising hell" as he projects she will, Helen's "face softened; a shy look, quizzical, playful, almost tender, came to her eyes" (49). Even the now-tipsy Milton admits that she has become "beautiful once more" as she tries to cajole him out of his drinking. His response is to think to himself: "Why did she put on the mother act?" For the rest of the brief passage, he ignores Helen's entreaties to go to church with his daughters and her; he belches in her face, and he sees Helen swim "towards him on a cloud of alcohol, filling him with sudden, intolerable discontent" (50). He refuses church, and later that day makes his initial flirtatious overtures to Dolly, who also uses the elixir to escape her fat but jovial husband. Later that same day Dolly and her husband visit, a visit Helen suspects has other purposes, and, of course, Helen's concerns are validated for the reader in Milton's interior monologue as he admits to ogling Dolly's legs, which she crosses often "with a silken whisper." Helen confronts him. "Isn't it you just want to be with her? Isn't it! Well, isn't it?" (55). Milton's mind is immediately filled with horror, and he thinks, "She's not supposed to know." "I'm not blind," Helen mutters and walks away, leaving him quite alone (55). Clearly in these moments when their marriage is on the brink of dissolution, Helen is the perceptive, sensitive one of the two partners who is attempting reconciliation and tolerance; after the incident over Dolly's visit, during which the surprised and flustered, not to say inebriate, Milton denies all, the reader is aware that Helen has indeed been shouldering the primary burden of parenting their two young girls in addition to parenting her husband. Helen has played by the rules only to have her dreams shattered by her indolent, alcoholic husband who now seems bent on publically humiliating her by flirting with another woman. And yet another thing is clear: Helen is no fool; she does know her husband and what he is thinking about Dolly. She is no longer Little Miss Muffet.

The evolutionary change of Helen's character from a young beauty to the emotionally paralyzed woman she sees reflected in her mirror in August 1945 has its beginnings in the crucible of Blood and Jesus Peyton's stern Army of the Lord. "I'll tolerate no misconduct in my outfit" (LDD 108). Although she began her life as a shy soldier of the Lord and of her father, young Helen elected to marry Milton who was then a handsome young officer and quite obviously a younger version of Blood and Jesus himself. But Milton turns out to be the antithesis of her strict, no-nonsense father, and thus it is she who becomes the disciplinarian in the family, a fact which poisons her relationship with Peyton. However, the power of the ideas of "right and wrong," of conventional, patriarchal morality that her God/father instilled in her prevents her from asserting herself as something more than a long-suffering wife. She has no other options, given her background; there is simply no socially acceptable role in her community for "the angriest woman in the world," as she will later call herself. In spite of Milton's abdication of his parental duties, in spite of his drinking, and in spite of his obvious indolence and dependence on her money, Helen refers to him as "poor Milton" when she describes him to others. She regards him as hapless, subject to temptations he cannot control, as if he were a child. After the mid-1930s, Helen increasingly considers Milton a man lost in the "stupid progress" of his life and subject to the temptations of booze, Dolly, and Peyton. She assumes more and more the role of a severe mother to his wayward boy; and most tragically, she begins to blame Dolly and even Peyton for his abandonment of her sexually.

The "bees" scene in the novel provides the first evidence of Helen's consuming obsession with the relationship between Milton and Peyton. The scene occurs early in the narrative, within the first flashbacks Styron has Helen's mind enter on the day of Peyton's burial. Brought on itself by a flashback of Milton's in drunken reminiscence of "better" times from their early married life, Helen's recollection of the "bees" incident begins as she recalls a summer visit to her brother Edward's Pennsylvania farm, probably in the late 1920s (LDD 27). It is a brief two-page scene that opens with Helen startled and amused as Peyton, about four years old, rushes with cries of delight and fear from some woods, yelling, "The bees, Daddy, the bees!" (26) Helen rises, "arms outstretched," and thinks, "my dearest baby." But Milton runs to Peyton first, scoops her up, tossing her playfully as both of them seem to "buzz like bees" themselves. Suddenly, Helen feels "helpless frustration" in the face of the "buzzing of the household," of the attention Peyton receives from the other adults present. Peyton is her uncle and aunt's "pretty girl," her father's delight, and thus is the veranda—in Helen's memory—filled that day with delight and approval for Peyton. Instead of feeling joy herself as the mother of this beautiful little girl who has ventured into the woods, Helen rebukes the child, lightly, for going off by herself and instructs Peyton that she needs a good combing.

Styron's description of the frieze of mother and daughter is telling, is darkly foreboding in its simplicity. "Peyton stood stiffly against her as Helen brushed and combed and groomed" (LDD 26). Milton chimes in that it is really safe for Peyton to explore on her own; Helen feels a sudden "hot embarrassed flush" as the other adults, she senses, are watching her closely. Peyton squirms; Helen holds her lightly and whispers, "Keep still," only to release the child and loudly, for the adults, proclaim that she would love to walk with such a "pretty girl." But of course Helen does not walk with Peyton to see the bees; when the others go off with Peyton, she feels chilled and "terribly empty." The Polish maid instructs her that Peyton is spoiled and that her own children are spanked "most every day" (27). And, using this Polish woman's comments, Styron intensifies this brief moment a fraction more. "She's a nice little girl, though. Pretty. You got a pretty daughter, Missus Helen. Me, I love children" (27). This last comment communicates an awareness between the two women who are far apart in terms of class and education. The Polish maid in her none-to-subtle way raises the issue of Helen's love for Peyton early in the novel. Helen turns this over in her mind and thinks to herself, "Why last night [Peyton] crawled over against me on the bed—'Mama,' she said, 'do you love me?'" (27)

Here Styron has the nearly fifty-year-old Helen reflecting back to the twenty-four-year-old's first inklings of a "silly, selfish" idea: that perhaps she does not love her daughter as other women seem to love their children. In a panic, the younger Helen leaps up, spilling cream, and rushes to her crippled, retarded first-born daughter Maudie and "crushes" the child into her arms, and contentment begins "to steal over her like a warm and loving flame" (LDD 27). She can, she reflects, "go on being a mother forever," as long, perhaps, as she has a child who is absolutely dependent upon her, who returns love absolutely, and who is not as prescient as Peyton.

Thus in this brief scene Styron has laid the groundwork for the ensuing relationship between mother and daughter. And in so doing, he explores the psyche of a young mother caught up in a defining moment. The mere fact that Styron has the older Helen reflect back on this scene so early in the narrative at first seems to intensify his presentation of Helen as obsessive about her daughter's being spoiled by her husband. Motherhood for Helen is, in this sense, all a matter of *control;* she mistakes a part of mothering for the whole. But Styron focuses the discourse more clearly on Helen's bitterness and goes beyond the simplistic notion of her blaming Milton. Helen herself locates the problem—again letting Milton off the hook—in Peyton: it is Peyton who asks: "Do you love me" so early. It is Peyton who is willful, unlike Maudie who is "my first, my dearest" for Helen.

Dale Marie Bauer's point about women blaming women echoes throughout this short, enigmatic, but crucial scene (Bauer x); just as Wharton's women in her short story "Roman Holiday" fail to develop a shared sense of being, of themselves as women in their society, Helen is unable to reflect meaningfully on her own sense of jealousy; all she can manage to do is intone how "silly" her feelings are. She is jealous of the attention her daughter receives from her husband, but she is only dimly aware of the depth of her feelings at twenty-four. Later, as she muses in 1945 on the day of her daughter's burial, instead of calling up delightfully sentimental and therefore escapist memories of Peyton as Milton does, she concentrates on the seeds of her alienation from her daughter; she attends to this memory-scene in its minute detail and investigates the unfinished emotional business it represents. Clearly the passage is meant to inform the reader that Helen is only too aware of the roots of her alienation from her daughter. Not attending to this "silly" idea of her love for her daughter has cost her dearly, and this brief scene enables the reader to discover yet another level of Helen's anguish and guilt. In so revealing Helen's mind, Styron effectively contextualizes later scenes between mother and daughter; this text of Helen's first flashback candidly presents the character outside the stereotype of mother-as-nurturer. Helen is, in this sense, freely exploring herself, and Styron's own textualizing of this mother can be seen as giving voice to a woman who has grave troubles with defining herself as a mother, except as a facade. Is Styron thereby reinforcing an idea of the self-effacing mother figure as an ideal? That is, is Styron here unconsciously reaffirming through this negative portrait the patriarchal imperative for a woman-as-mother?

In my view, Styron presents the scene to flesh out the discourse, to give voice to Helen's own grappling with Peyton's suicide and her possible complicity in the events leading to it. Styron depicts Helen as a product of a social consensus that demands she appear very proud of her "pretty little girl," but he adds the dimension of Helen's problematic feelings of jealousy which she cannot, and Styron does not, evade. If Styron is merely reinforcing cultural

norms by using Helen Loftis as an obsessed foil, he is also calling
into question the system that leads such an obstensibly religious
and morally "correct" woman as Helen to question her own love
for her child. Helen's repetitions of "how silly" and "how silly
and absurd" concerning her doubts about her love for Peyton are
evidence of her inability to minimalize her own feelings or rationalize them away. There is an emptiness that motherhood, even her
own control-directed idea of motherhood, cannot fulfill in her, but
she does not have the capability of expressing that feeling because
in her society pondering such things is literally "unthinkable." So
strong has her socialization been that she is left without the tools
to interact with the patriarchy and to find a way to create a more
positive space for herself. Because she was raised to be a good
soldier in the Army of Lord, she has not learned to question
women's roles; to question such things would be to question directly the primacy of that grand patriarch, Blood and Jesus Peyton,
by whose rules she has lived her entire life. But even the Colonel
did not prepare her for the abyss of Peyton's suicide.

Another important scene depicting Helen revolves around the
"sweet sixteen" birthday celebration for Peyton at the country
club. Once again, at the beginning of the passage Styron describes
Helen's face and emphasizes her fixation on facades, both public
and private. Helen looks much older than her "little past forty"
years because she has "surrendered up" her beauty to time (LDD
73), although there is a "whisper of loveliness" that lingers on her
face. The time is August 1939, apparently before the Nazis invade
Poland and begin World War II, but the atmosphere at the country
club is anything but somber. Milton and Helen dance together
briefly, surrounded by "young girls' perfume"; the mood is festive.
Helen sits out the rest of the dancing, claiming her by now chronic
"tiredness"; her face once so beautiful is "full of discontent" and
"sullenness." A cinematic effect is achieved as Helen sits watching
Milton dance with first Peyton and then Dolly and then Peyton
again: Helen is pictured before a mirror at an angle that gives off
"twin-reflected Helens" in a blue gown, contrasted against the yellow afternoon light. Thus is Helen shown and her inner self is
likewise bisected; she must go see how Maudie is, but she watches
Peyton, convinced that Peyton has been drinking. She also watches
Milton with Dolly, watches his fingers on Dolly's neck, caressing.
When she is complimented on Peyton's loveliness, Helen replies
that the dance is nice, but she merely ignores the sentiments directed at Peyton, pretending not to hear.

At this point Helen's mind appears to wander from the dance to her doctor's warnings that menopause causes "physical complications"; she then postulates that Milton and Dolly are having an affair. She projects in her mind a conversation with a passerby about the truth of her husband's infidelity, but to the dance crowd she presents only her wanly smiling facade. She continues to muse while the dance swirls around her, and she falls into a reverie in which she yearns for darkness to enfold her in her room, her "home" where no intrusions can reach her, where she longs for "those strong and constant arms" of her father. But the country club world intrudes as Peyton runs up to invite her to join the dance; Helen immediately rebukes her for drinking and for something more elusive: "She was beautiful, she was young, and those two things together caused Helen the bitterest anguish" (LDD 77). Styron's characterization of Helen here advances the complexity of the relationship yet again. Helen's hero-father fixation has crippled her emotionally, and now when she should be basking in her daughter's social success—if we are to believe the myth of the generous and therefore satisfied mother figure, Helen's mind is a torrent of loathing because of her perception of her own body's aging and a tumult of toxic jealousy aimed at both her daughter and the younger Dolly with whom Milton dances. And so, as she ran from Milton during their courtship, as she ran to Maudie and away from both Milton and Peyton in the "bees" scene, Helen runs from the country club, bringing Maudie (and therefore herself) home to the safety of a hushed bedroom/womb.

But before she leaves, she lectures Milton on his chief sin: "I love my God and you don't. . . . you don't have any God at all" (LDD 89). It is important to reflect on which Christian god Helen refers to here. She received her religious indoctrination from her severe "Blood and Jesus" father, but she says that she cannot forgive Milton for a "whole lot of things" even though later she will say simply that Milton is helpless before temptation. In terms of religion her father, although Jesus and blood are part of his sobriquet, did not teach her the message of forgiveness in the New Testament; so Helen's God, like her father's, is the Old Testament God of righteousness and vengeance who tolerates no misconduct and who metes out punishment to the unworthy, the sinful. In times of severe stress, Helen reverts to this vision and becomes again a soldier in the Army of the Lord because she is incapable of dealing in any meaningful way with her own feelings of jealousy and resentment towards Peyton and Milton. She has no language with which to express even to herself ideas of accommodation and acceptance; this is the legacy of the stern patriarchal teachings of her father.

Importantly, Helen calls nine-year-old Peyton a "little devil" (58) after Maudie is found gagged and trussed up during a prank. Later, Helen tries to forgive Peyton, but is only able to apologize for slapping her. Helen is also unable to accept Milton's many apologies for inviting Dolly to their home; in fact, Helen again uses Maudie as an emotional crutch and tells Milton that he is "going to destroy" them all, and that only Maudie keeps her in the marriage (61). With apocalyptic epithets of destruction on her lips, Helen does a curious thing: she turns to the Episcopalian minister Carey Carr as a "brother," not as a "father" confessor, and to Carr she speaks of God in more detail.

As Carr begins his ruminations on his initial interview with Helen, he mentions that his own wife had said "Helen Loftis is a nest of little hatreds" (LDD 105). Thus prefaced, Styron has Carr recall that Helen appeared at their first meeting, just after Peyton's tumultuous birthday party in 1939, "like some advertising man's idea of a woman professor" (106). But one who has come to tell Carey of her God: her own father who put the "fear of the Lord" into his men at Fort Meyer, and who tolerated no misconduct. Helen also relates in Carr's flashback that for six years she watched Milton turn towards Dolly, "following his stupid progress" objectively (109). Curiously, once again she does not blame Milton even though she cannot forgive him: she refers to him as "poor Milton" and then in a fit of pique adds: "So damn them both. . . . God please damn them" (109). It is righteous, continues Helen, to want to see Milton and Dolly "swallowed in their own filth" (109). Her wish is for retribution; she sees Milton's flirtations with Dolly as an injustice that has made her sicker and sicker, and each night she has prayed that "this wouldn't go without reproach" (109). It is as if she expects Blood and Jesus Peyton to smite Milton and Dolly.

However, Helen's most deeply felt resentment is reserved for another; she tells Carr of her hatred for Peyton, her "shameless" daughter who is already "not-so-innocently good" with men at sixteen (LDD 111). Feeling a devil at her side, as she puts it, Helen watches Milton and Peyton together the night before Peyton goes off to college, and she thinks of how Peyton is pressed against Milton; "and I kept on watching, hating, too" (111). Father and daughter are reading a catalog, but Helen sees them as betraying her: Milton through his infidelity with Dolly and Peyton through "the ingratitude of a shameless child" (111). When Helen hears the voice of the devil—the voice of her long-dead father?—time seems to stop as if a film projector had halted, she explains, on a particular frame. In this intensely cinematic moment, Helen feels all at once "unburdened," then suddenly time resumes for her, and she goes down to join the other two, presumably satisfied that her anger has passed for the moment. Carr interjects and tries to put a rationalistic gloss on the event: "So you had a moment of real hatred—or evil and temptation, as you put it?" And then in his own mind, Carr reflects that Helen's problem is rather more simple: "actually it was the tragedy of frustration, probably of sex. . . ." (112). Thus is Helen's complex of feelings and background reduced to her genitals.

"Really an odd woman," continues Carr as he reflects on Helen's religious fundamentalism; to him, she is like a "cowardly Puritan" (113) who uses the Devil as a scapegoat to rid himself of positive action: "'The devil forced me, [says the Puritan] instead of, 'I turned my eyes from Christ's example'" (LDD 113). Carr resolves to let Helen "have her symbol" of the Devil. At worst it is merely childish, he thinks, for her to believe such "bosh," but his resolve is tempered with a strong irritation. He sees Helen, finally, as a selfish woman, "too unwilling to make the *usual compromise* to be happy" (119; italics mine). Thus we see Carr as a spokesman for the patriarchy that demands from women "usual compromises" in which they must sacrifice their identities for the hearth, a sacrifice Elizabeth Ermarth refers to as "psychic starvation" (Ermarth 1983, 10). He ventures that Helen is "a complete prig" who needs to have some charity at certain times. Helen, meanwhile, reacts to his tossing off the adage "small kindness makes love grow" with scorn and says, "but I guess you're like all the rest," the "rest" here probably meaning "males in positions of authority," a group she will rail against in some detail when she speaks with Carr at Peyton's wedding.

Styron's implicit critique of the interview, then, is surely that the deep psychological problems evidenced by Helen's narrative to Carr are simply ignored or minimalized/marginalized by the quaint adages Carr prefers to quote in his comfortable den. In short, perhaps Helen has it right enough, and indeed the narrative confirms that her husband has had sex with Dolly, that Peyton is "shameless," and that Carey in his own internal musings is indeed "like the rest." At this point in her life Helen fears she is going crazy and contemplates suicide by Nembutal overdose when she feels that the seesawing of her "crazy words" will teeter her over an edge into oblivion. Nevertheless, she tries to come to grips with the devil she feels and the message the apparition brings. "Dear Lord, I can't hate my own husband; dear Lord, I can't hate Peyton, my own flesh and blood" (LDD 125).

Indeed, Helen's thought on this Devil is analytical too: "hadn't this devil or whoever he was, perhaps disguised himself in order to make her think such a vain mean thought?" (LDD 123) Is this simply "fundamentalism" as Carey Carr has it, or is Helen's inability to concentrate, her dreamy obsession with a devil figure, and even her preoccupation with her daughter's nubile hips, are all these symptomatic of Helen's deep and abiding fears of being alone? Even in the midst of her reflection on suicide—which she dismisses eventually as too "gross" a thing to contemplate for very long—she posits that it is only the season which makes her unhappy: "this tail end of summer" (124). In his presentation of multiple views of Helen through Milton, Carey, and her own mind, we see how Styron refuses to stereotype Helen; she is presented as a complex woman whose behavior arises from a welter of past influences, psychological stress, and even the physical trauma of the onset of menopause.

In any case, the presentation of Helen must impress the reader as one of an individual who, on the traumatic day of her daughter's burial, is desperately trying to piece together a sense of meaning, of identity, of context for herself. Styron's purpose in revealing the inherent complexity of an endeavor such as Helen's and drawing the reader into the very process itself exhibits the author's thematic concern with not only women's identities in American culture, but also with how problematic the process is even in the fertile reaches of modernist/post-modernist fiction. No matter how closely we follow Helen's mind/voice/text in the process of the narrative, we find ourselves like Carey, Milton, and Helen herself, groping for understanding in the midst of apparently cogent language. Milton's descriptions, for example, of Helen's "quirks," her "unfortunate neurosis" do not, finally, explain in a truly meaningful way Helen's tormented behavior; "unfortunate neurosis" as a phrase does not give Milton the insight or explanation he desires. It names, but it does not explain.

Another scene that sheds light on Helen's character involves the family's celebration of Christmas in 1941. After an eggnog gathering, Milton finds Helen upstairs in her room, lying on the bed "in an attitude of death"; she had left the party because Dolly has telephoned. Quite suddenly, Helen asks Milton: "Do you think we can forgive each other?" (LDD 149). Helen refers here to the misery they have lived with since 1939 when Milton began his affair with Dolly. Once again they discuss the main reason they remain together as boarders and not as husband and wife: Maudie, their special, helpless woman/child. But Helen confronts Milton in another way by placing his hand on one of her naked breasts: "'feel that,'" she said trembling; "' haven't I got love down there, too?'" (150). Just as swiftly she pushes his hand away and sinks back into her bed as if a spell has been broken. This simple, poignant action of Helen's, this reaching out in the context of her previous inability to use forgiveness as a means of bringing Milton back to her again, presents the complexity of Helen's motivations. She appears to want a reconciliation, but she pulls back just at the moment when she may be influencing him; further, she recalls for Milton the days and nights when they were a newly married couple and he would call her "love," but she digs her fingernails into his hand and pushes it away. Milton, in the meantime, sees her breasts fall "heavily, no longer youthful" (150). Helen's simultaneous desire for both love and retribution paralyzes her actions toward a reconciliation and results in a fever that is the physical manifestation of her internal conflict. Milton will later recall this as their last tender moment together, and it ends when Peyton enters the house and Helen whispers to Milton, "She hates me" (150).

The next morning, after Peyton has returned very late from partying with her friends, Helen and she confront one another in the kitchen as Helen tries to create the perfect Christmas dinner. Helen castigates Peyton for drinking and for being rude to Uncle Edward, himself a drunkard, but to this Peyton, now eighteen, reacts with sarcastic taunts at which Helen fumes in red-faced rage. Helen continues the meal preparations while the rest of the family sits meekly waiting. Milton sees her then as a shadow,"a brief pale reflection in its passage from the kitchen to the dining room . . . a reluctant acolyte, votive, long-suffering . . . footsteps so quick and determined and ceremonial" (LDD 158). When a glass of water is spilled during the meal, Milton is shocked to see Helen quickly on her knees mopping up water like "a charwoman immersed in a flood of atonement" and "like a nigger she wants to be, a black slave" (159). Thus does she appear to Milton, but he further laments her mind set as he thinks: "What crazy furied winds, bearing the debris of what wicked imaginings, sour suspicions, balked hopes, had swept her mind?" (160). Suddenly, a glass of water is again upset, and Helen erupts in sobs as the terrible tension between Peyton and her breaks wide open and Peyton rushes out. The attempt at reconciliation through the shared Christmas has failed miserably, and Helen runs to telephone Carey Carr while she drags Maudie behind her. Once again Helen approaches her family with an outward attempt at forgiveness and reunion, but, again, she is incapable of entering into a meaningful dialogue with them. Instead, she dedicates herself to the all but mute Maudie and engages Carey Carr in one-sided discussions about the suffering she endures because of Milton's drunken adultery and her daughter's selfish ingratitude. Peyton's opinion of her mother's behavior at Christmas is swift and adolescent. "She's crazy. Absolutely off her head" (162), while Milton yells up to Helen after he has had four whiskeys: "you're a real horror. . . . God damn your soul!" Later he will notice with optimism that Helen keeps a photo of Peyton on her dresser, in a silver frame alongside Maudie's. And in June of the next year Helen kisses him good-bye as he goes off to Washington—their first kiss in over a year. It is precisely this presentation of Helen as a complex woman who is caustic and unforgiving as well as suddenly tender and even sentimental that allows Styron to bring the reader to a deeper understanding and appreciation of the character's divided sensibility.

By November of 1942, Milton and Dolly have resigned themselves to a publically acknowledged yet nominally discreet form of adultery. Helen is "generally silent and preoccupied with Carey Carr," according to Milton. Abruptly, Milton is summoned from Dolly's arms to the hospital in Charlottesville where Maudie lies dying. A tragic scene unfolds at the hospital as Helen, exhausted, informs Milton that Maudie has but a slim chance to recover; confused in his alcoholic haze, his attention wanders as Helen stares in disbelief at his disheveled drunken face. "You aren't sane enough to know what's happening," she says (LDD 181). And so they wait together miserably as Maudie's condition worsens, Milton acutely aware now that he has "failed utterly in Helen's eyes" (182). Determined to make some amends for his behavior by supporting her, he tells her Maudie will recover, and to his surprise, Helen takes up his proffered hand by the fingertips, "looking up at him with eyes sorrowful, almost kindly" and withholding the "eternal crushing weight of her judgement" which he so fears. She pleads with him to stay with her, but again takes her hand away from him and intones that she knows what's happened with Maudie. And in a more agitated voice she continues, cryptically. "And I'm the only one that knows. Only if anything happens I'll tell you" (182). She may be referring to Peyton's accidental dropping of Maudie years earlier which Helen had seen as purposeful. Then, quickly, she seizes his hand again, calmly saying, "stay with me, Milton," a moment after Milton had reflected that she had gone "mad." Again we see Helen's anguished pattern of approach and disengagement in a crisis situation.

But of course Milton does not stay to comfort and support her; he leaves to find Peyton and winds up attending a football game and various festivities at the university. Eventually he and Peyton return to the hospital to find Helen still waiting and furious at them both. At this point, Helen is beyond mere grief and launches into a fierce commentary about her lifetime spent waiting for the two of them. "One word and I'd be saved, a word that I could have said as well as you, it didn't matter, so long as we both understood: 'love' or 'forgive' or even 'darling,' it made no difference" (LDD 206). Helen then recalls her last days with Maudie, especially the time Maudie met Bennie the magician, who enchanted her by making balls seem to disappear and who captivated her only to leave her desolate when his work at a nearby yard was completed. After the story, Helen begins a tirade against the other two which culminates in a venomous rage directed squarely at Peyton: "You're half the cause. Remember when you let her fall?" (214). In her grief and rage, Helen blames Peyton for contributing to Maudie's death and further holds Peyton responsible for her father's abandonment of his responsibility to keep a vigil for Maudie: "Guilty?" Helen rages at Peyton; "You with your whoring around and your drinking." Of course, the irony of the situation is that, although Helen is wrong about Peyton's direct influence on her father's drunken ramble over the university, in another sense Peyton *is* the reason Milton sets out for the campus in the first place. Milton never has been able to come to grips with his older daughter's infirmities and has showered more attention on his attractive second daughter. Helen's taunt likewise displaces her own terrible guilt feelings of giving birth to a deformed child by heaping abuse on her more "perfect" child, Peyton.

Perhaps the scene in the novel which presents Helen in her most intensely manic stage is Peyton's wedding in the Loftis home in October 1943. Between the debacle of Maudie's death and the wedding, however, Helen suffers a suicide attempt that sparks a reconciliation between Milton and her. They spend a three-week vacation together at a resort where they make love even though Milton reflects that he does not like the act itself as much as he appreciates his ability to elude the wiles of a divorcée he meets at the resort; and, of course, he thinks of Dolly. In his arms, Helen clings to him and asks him for forgiveness, confessing that she had been a fool and had wasted much time in the misery of their apartness. Their reunion is in April, and as they move toward the fall, Helen's mood improves and she makes plans to have Peyton return home; the wedding provides an ideal setting for a harmonizing of disparate familial voices, or so Milton hopes. But his hopes are soon shattered when Peyton tells him just before the wedding ceremony that she has returned only "to play the good sweet role, the prodigal daughter come back home at her parents' whim . . . but somehow today it all seems phony" (LDD 255). Distraught, Milton listens as his daughter continues. "Mother. She's such a faker. Look at this circus" (256). With that, the reunion begins to disintegrate.

As far as the structure of the wedding scene is concerned, the narrative first lights on Helen's susceptibility to Carey Carr's wedding service; Helen herself notes that she has been as enthralled "as much as any of the dimmest and most susceptible of the women present" (LDD 259). It is all part of the recent reconciliation with Milton, she reflects a little later: through Milton's groveling and pleading after Maudie's death she has been saved from death; but more than this: she has triumphed over Dolly. In the first weeks of their reunion Helen is so intoxicated with her success that when her thoughts turn to Dolly—as a vanquished corpse "face downward in a stream" (260)—she laughs aloud in spasms of hysterical laughter in her room. Helen muses that the wedding is another triumph because she successfully acts out the role of the long-suffering wife and mother who, in spite of all sacrifices, presents herself courageously and with "gentle good will" (260). The irony is that, although Helen thinks to herself that "no one would ever know the struggle," Peyton has identified clearly the "circus" of her mother's grand production of the wedding. Helen further considers that her success after Maudie's death depended on Milton's gullibility, on his belief in her honesty, on her sincerity."After so much suffering," she reflects, "did a woman really have to be honest to fulfill herself?" (261). She would do anything, she emphasizes, "Anything that people should know Helen Loftis was a good mother, a successful mother" (261). Helen feels she has a right to her feelings, her "profound and unalterable loathing of Peyton" (261).

True to the novel's relentless dissection of the Loftis family's relationships, this internal discourse of Helen's poses several challenges to the reader's sensibilities. Styron, however, has Helen build her own case for herself and what she sees as a triumph. But Helen is not "evil" here so much as she is reflecting—as she senses herself—a lifetime of frustration. It is true that her expectations that her life should have been "a nice, long, congenial tea party" (LDD 260) are unrealistic, but they are not any less human for all that. She feels that she had come to the tea party of life and "it had been ghastly: everyone misbehaved, and no one had a good time." Helen further admits in this interior section that she had cast aside religion as a toy or a trifle when Maudie died. Her winning Milton back has thus given her a new life, and this new life revolves around appearing the happy, fulfilled mother before her community; her new religion, then, is her dedication to what she calls her "most villainous intentions": to have the world see her as "that suffering woman, who had brought together the broken family" (261). With the moral underpinnings of her religion stripped way, all that is left for Helen to believe in is the artifice, the appearances of moral rectitude.

The wedding, predictably, collapses in upon itself by virtue of the sheer weight of the tensions shared by the major participants. The dissolution begins when Milton suddenly realizes, when he finally "reads" correctly the two women, Peyton and Helen, and sees: "God help him, hadn't he known all along that they hated and despised each other?" (LDD 270) Milton, now disabused of his naive belief in a true familial reconciliation, is chilled by each woman's smile: "women smiles—great God, so treacherous, so false . . . like the hateful wings of bats" (271). In this stupor of blinding terrible insight, Milton grabs at Peyton and kisses her desperately on the mouth "much more than a father," and this act of his moves Helen to abandon her heretofore pleasant, public party exterior which has artfully contained her loathing of Peyton. But again, curiously Helen does not see Milton at fault for his boozy kiss; she blames Peyton for pushing her father rudely away. Helen is furious that Milton loves Peyton so "when it's obvious she despises him" (279). Carey Carr is Helen's auditor as she thus rails against Peyton; and he, again, becomes a voice of authority and objectivity when he observes that "a girl comes home on her wedding day . . . where relations, to put it mildly have been strained," and "her father is jolly and tight, too, and maybe gets a little bit too affectionate, and so she snaps at him" (280). Styron's use of Carr as a sort of a neutral but not very astute internal narrator carefully underscores the power of the more subjective internal views of Milton and Helen. In fact, the narrative switches dramatically at this juncture to Helen's point of view wherein we see Carr carrying on in a male, authoritarian, prosaic, "reasoned" manner as Helen's mind reacts.

Carr's direct confrontation of Helen and his announcement that she is "a very sick woman" (LDD 281) elicits from her a curiously calm assurance that she's never felt better, but as she watches Carr's "prissy" mouth, she begins an internal diatribe on men: "a whole array of ministers, doctors, men (men! she thought) protest her stubbornness, her wrongness. What did they know of a woman's suffering?" (282). Men, Helen muses, would be shocked to feel how her blood angrily pounded through her; they would not believe that she had such a pulse, the pulse of "the angriest woman on earth!" (283) And if they did know, Helen would have another triumph because they would acknowledge her righteous "woman's fury" and the "defeat of men in general." But Milton she would forgive, since he had yielded, had said "I quit" and "had admitted she had been right all along" (283). Then Helen begins her recollection of her dreamscape of a "land of the female dead" where she visualizes female corpses strewn about through which she walks always in the company of a man, Carey, Milton, or even her father (284). And in other dreams, she reveals, she slays Dolly on a field of battle astride the white horse Champ, just like her father's, that buries its hooves deep into Dolly's skull. Triumphant in her dreams and in her apparent deception as the Good Mother, Helen in her reverie sees Carey as the enemy and chokes out that her God "is the devil" (286); and just as suddenly, Helen realizes that it is not Dolly she destroys in her dreams—it is Peyton. She rushes back to the wedding party to "fix" Peyton, as she puts it to Carey.

Styron leaves it to another male point of view to describe Helen's "fixing" of Peyton later at the party; the man is the apparently kindly family physician Doc Holcomb, a sixty-eight-year-old bachelor. His first description of Helen is notable for its comparison: "only her head moved, and her blue crazy eyes: it was like watching an adder . . . surely she was ready to strike" (LDD 291). Milton's view picks up the narrative at the moment of the collision between mother and daughter; filled with foreboding, he sees that "it was a final moment, signifying everything" (294). And in a "voice unemotional, polite, but direct," Helen "fixes" Peyton by chastising her for the ill-treatment of her father earlier when she had shoved away his drunken advances (296). The women attack each other, first Helen pushing Peyton and then Peyton gouging Helen's face; ironically, they both accuse the other of "fakery" and duplicity in the day's events. Peyton rushes out and Helen is left moaning in pain as blood trickles through her fingers, out of the "raw, deep slits" in her otherwise "dead and white" face (298). Seeing her, Milton pronounces through a whisky-thick tongue, "God help you, you monshter."

And that is our final picture of Helen before the day Peyton's body returns by train to Port Warwick in August of 1945. As was mentioned earlier, by 1945 Helen is described by Casper as a white-haired woman not yet fifty, but hardly a "monshter." The complexities of Helen's psyche, as laid out by Styron, suggest all too clearly how human she really is. The shocks of her daughter Maudie's death compounded by the unresolved feelings she holds for Peyton, Milton, and even her father all contribute to her collapse at Peyton's wedding. As in *Sophie's Choice* where Styron explores the limits of fiction's ability to provide an instrument by which readers might understand the evils of Auschwitz or the mind of the camp commander Rudolph Höss, Styron peels back the layers of Helen's experience to contextualize Peyton's tragedy. Above all else, Peyton's suicide is a human failure, and Helen's complicity, her desire to "fix" her own daughter, is not rooted in some mysterious evil force. It arises from Helen's deep-seated alienation from her family; it is her aloneness, her retreat into her own world, her own reality—a reality half given, half created—that dooms Helen to the "Nothing!" she feels at the very close of the novel.

Transcending the human failures of Helen's existence, however, are the aspects of her life over which she has no control, especially but not exclusively the societal demands of the roles she has been taught she must play. Unable to develop a meaningful dialogue with the representative authoritarian males in her life, including her father, Carey, and to some extent Milton, she reverts to affixing blame on those women she perceives as threatening her idea of domestic bliss, or, rather, the patriarchal ideal of domestic bliss drilled, undoubtedly, into her since childhood. Helen is precisely the kind of American heroine whom Dale Marie Bauer sees as forced into a psychic rather than a physical suicide, a psychogynicide victim. Unable to communicate with even the most "sensitive" of males in her culture—represented in Carey Carr—Helen retreats to her room/womb and takes her Nembutals. And so it is in her last appearance in the novel—after the scuffle with Milton, who tries to kill her to somehow assuage his own guilt and frustration—Helen can only press her head against the wall of the funeral chapel and say, "Oh, God, Peyton. My child. Nothing! Nothing! Nothing! Nothing!" Helen has no language, no words for the grief she is experiencing. But in a larger sense and as a voiced text in the novel, she has become part of the heteroglossia that is American literature; her voice in this sense speaks most eloquently and honestly about some American women's lives in the first fifty years of this century. Somewhere between the extremes of Little Miss Muffet and the "monshter," many Americans lived their lives and made their voices heard in spite of efforts to silence them.

In terms of Dale Bauer's feminist dialogics and her study of

American heroines, Helen can be seen as a woman who is a "sign" inscribed by the patriarchy, in particular by her father. Her internal dialogic remains paralyzed because she is unable to recognize the "other": the fact that *she* is "other" to the patriarchy and that the patriarchy is "other" to her. She has not developed self-consciousness sufficiently to discover class consciousness in a internally dialogic process. She is a woman who submits, albeit with great bitterness, "to the imposition of meaning" from the patriarchy as "woman-sign" rather than as woman who is a *maker* of meaning (Bauer 1988, x). In this sense, Helen is a "sign," a Southern Lady, who loathes the male patriarchy (*"Men!"*) but nevertheless enforces its strictures upon her daughter Peyton. Helen, like Maggie Verver, has been trained by her father "to desire what he desires, to speak as he speaks" (82). In the final analysis, however, Helen is not a villain; like other female characters who remain "signs" in American literature, "she merely reproduces the exclusions which the social hierarchy upholds" (119).

In turning now to Styron's depiction of Peyton Loftis, I am asserting my contention about the preeminence of her position in the narrative as not only the obvious textual focus upon which the other characters are led to their own dialogic moments—during which they reveal their inner voices and pain, but also her representation of a generational shift that Styron announces with his first novel. By entering the mind of Peyton as he does in her "monologue," Styron personifies the angst of his own "lost" generation. Lost in her mind and in the monumental urbanity of New York City, Peyton becomes the appointed and, importantly, *female* voice through which Styron articulates the despair of a young America raised in war and faced with a new world order while simultaneously being thrust into stereotypical roles from previous generations. My intention in Peyton's section is to chronicle *in detail* the chronotopes of Styron's careful presentation of her new sensibility as it inevitably clashes with those of her parents and with others who can relate to her only on *their* terms and not on *hers*. In feminist dialogic terms, Peyton is unable to communicate her "internal dialogic" directly to other characters, although she does achieve an understanding at the close of her "monologue" and her suicide certainly gives expression to her troubled life; in fact, the novel is all about *why* she commits suicide. As Dale Bauer points out, a female character experiences the dialogic which can reaffirm her as a speaking subject which in turn contributes to her "coming to consciousness" or growing self-consciousness (Bauer

1988, x). Further, this growing self-consciousness "in the final analysis, always leads us to *class-consciousness* (77) and evaluation. Unfortunately for Peyton, her internal dialogic confronts repressed feelings which overtake her fragile stabilty and self-concept. But Styron does not allow her voice to be lost, although she is a member of *his* "lost" generation. Indeed, Styron holds up for critique Peyton's entire society, her "interpretive community," as it ponders her suicide: "Within the [text], the interpretive community is often the site of repression, subversion, marginalization, and *suicide*" (xiv; italics mine). In this sense, the dialogic of the novel enables the reader to examine (and interpret) interpretations of Peyton.

To achieve a careful reconsideration of this process of interpretation, we must, as Michael Holquist explains, pay special attention to the chronotopes (time-space) or "the dense particularity of our everyday lives" which are an integral parts of Bakhtin's dialogic approach. The basic scenario for linguistic interchange involves two people "talking to each other in a specific dialogue at a particular time and in a particular place" (Bakhtin 1981, xix–xx). Further, "each of the two persons would be a consciousness at a specific point in the history of defining itself through the choice it has made . . . *in this specific exchange*" (xx; italics in original). "Language, when it *means*," explains Holquist, "is somebody talking to someone else, even when that someone else is one's own inner addressee" (Holquist xxi), as is the case in Peyton's "monologue." For Bakhtin, a "general" language does not exist, that is, a language articulated by a general voice apart from the specific, particularized context of the immediacy of utterance (Holquist and Clark 1984, xxi). Detaching oneself from the immediacy of the "social situation" leaves one bereft of the true nature and evanescence of utterance, of the articulated sound which inheres in the basic orality of language (Ong 1982, 7). If we ignore the conditions of utterance, "all we have left is the naked corpse of a word" (Bakhtin 1981, 292). Language is, in this sense, a "living, socio-ideological [and] concrete" *process* of achieving meaning for the individual consciousness (293), and in my close examination of Peyton, I endeavor to regard novelistic discourse as such a process of voicing.

In his presentation of the voices of Peyton Loftis, Styron portrays one of the most effectively drawn American heroines by a male author by problematizing the efforts of various interpretive communities as they attempt to "explain" her. She is one of those American heroines who "force the polemic to be a communal property rather than an internal one," in Bauer's terms (Bauer 1988, 5). Styron's use of Peyton's voice, his *ventriloquating* her inner dialogue and speaking *through* her in the Bakhtinian sense (Bakhtin 1981, 299), enables Peyton to become what Bauer refers to as "cultural capital": "a way to work within the dominant, prevailing values by subverting them consciously, *by seeing through them and articulating that unveiling*" (Bauer 1988, 5; italics mine). She is seen simultaneously as a "lamb" slaughtered in the terrible urban American landscape and as a whoring wife-nymphomaniac preying upon men, dangerous to know. That Styron chose a complex and deeply troubled young woman to voice his vision reveals, I am convinced, the formation of a sensibility more egalitarian than most, a sensibility more attuned to the concerns of his times. The importance of observing in detail Peyton's discourses—and even the particular *dates* of those discourses—is primarily that *her interior voice* is articulated by Styron, her exact contemporary. Because all language is "inherited" in the Bakhtinian sense, the inner speech of Peyton reveals her author's which itself is "a product of his entire social life" (6). In her investigation into the voices of selected American heroines Bauer has observed

the process by which alien or rival social languages are excluded or silenced . . . [and how] historically divergent voices are made uniform, a process which leads to a central, dominant ideological stance—to closure. In this way, the author orchestrates his or her themes, through the interrelation of voices, their contradictions, their juxtapositions, their exclusions. (6)

Even if Joan Smith appears to identify Styron's fiction as "fevered imaginings" or as lethal male sexual fantasies (Smith 1992, 137), we need to observe closely how Styron is able to communicate his vision by *ventriloquating* a woman's voice, *from within* that "dense particularity" of self, a self which he moves "beyond the atomic self or body into the larger discursive corpus" (Bauer 1988, 6).

The portrayal of Peyton Loftis in the novel begins with Milton's reference to her as "our daughter, not just mine" (LDD 10) in his grief-stricken state as he, Dolly, and Ella await the train carrying Peyton's coffin. Ella sobs on the train platform and is actually the first to call Peyton by name. "Train gonna come soon. Peyton comin' on de 'leven-fo'teen. Po' precious lamb" (11). As such a sacrificial lamb, the very image of helplessness in the animal kingdom, Peyton takes on early in the novel a particular quality of a lost and innocent voice of a victim of the complex circumstances which eventually culminate in her suicide. In fact, it is not until the last eighty odd pages of the novel that Peyton's own unfettered point of view is offered. Her section reveals, in a stream-of-consciousness flow of prose, many details of her life, but in an at-times cryptic, self-referential mythology populated with bird and clock images set against the background of a sweltering August day in New York City—at the beginnings of the atomic age in 1945.

Helen's is the first point of view from which we see Peyton when she is but four or five years old. Peyton's shrill childish cries are recalled by Helen, "The bees, Daddy, the bees!" (LDD 26), when the child is described as a giggling, beautiful little girl, bubbling with excitement about her foray into the woods. But Peyton is also seen as squirming already under Helen's attempts to comb her hair; she is impatient and must be told to "keep still." The Polish housekeeper in the "bees" scene remarks further that Peyton "is spoiled already" and that Helen should take care with Peyton. However, the stern Polish mother of five does admit that Peyton is "a nice little girl" who is "pretty" (27). Pretty and precocious, she has the very evening before crawled to her mother in bed and asked: "do you love me?" to which Helen cannot remember an answer.

The narrative's next presentation of Peyton is in her own letter to her father, sent just days before her suicide and written on her twenty-second birthday. Milton is waiting in a shabby restaurant as he reads the six-page missive, Peyton's voice from the grave. Peyton tells her father of receiving his latest gift of money with which she has bought a clock, two quarts of milk, and a Mozart concerto. She relates the story of her breakup with her husband Harry, her despairing regimen of wasted lonely days and nights in New York, and her recent loss of a job. Peyton writes that she has recently begun to think morbid and depressing thoughts which she tries to fight against but cannot. She feels a "black, terrible mistiness like the beginning of a disease" (LDD 35). Adrift, she explains that she is "drowning out in dark space somewhere" when the black moods descend upon her; then she sees "the birds." These birds, in addition to being a pun on Milton's mother's maiden name, Byrd, make up a motif Styron repeats throughout the novel—they figure in Milton's, Helen's, but primarily Peyton's experiences. However, in the letter, a heartrending cry for help, the birds actually mark the end of Peyton's lucidity and the beginning of her spiral down toward self-annihilation: "the birds are haunting me beyond all belief," she writes, once again, an instance of Styron's punning on Peyton's paternal grandmother's name; but then Milton

can read no farther because the letter becomes "crazy and confused" to him. In the letter Peyton also reflects on how she has
tried "to grow up—to be a good little girl" and this apparent contradiction of maturing only to be a good "little girl" is symptomatic
of Peyton's troubled mind as she tries to deal with what she sees
as a series of events in which she ends up walking "deeper and
deeper into some terrible despair" (35). Styron is obviously inter-
ested here in problematizing the roles young women inherited as
either whores or Madonna-like figures. The irony of Peyton's addressing her irresponsible father with her growing awareness of his
implied complicity in her crisis is striking. Finally, Peyton wants
only to have her father "say nice things" to her; she wishes she
could go home to Port Warwick even though she laments that the
family has collapsed. "We've all been so unkind," she writes in
powerful understatement.

The letter is, of course, significant for detailing Peyton's last
hours in expository prose and its brave attempts to record her
growing despondency and her increasing hallucinations, especially
the wingless birds she sees which are more fully realized in her
long interior monologue later in the novel. The letter serves as
a counterpoint to Helen and Milton's recollections as well as to
the observations of Carey Carr and Doc Holcomb. In the main,
the letter reveals that Peyton's alienation reaches a fevered pitch;
she maintains several times, with increasing intensity, that she
misses Milton, or "Bunny" as she has referred to him since her
adolescence. Peyton also explains how lonely she is without Harry,
but she does not mention her ongoing, purely physical affair with
Tony Cecchino, whose name means "magpie," another bird image
(Ratner 1972, 48) ; and in the stifling August heat of the city she
suffers from insomnia which is not helped by the cacophony she
hears from the street. Listening to the traffic of the city night,
she sinks deeper into despair over her seeming inability to control
her own compulsive behavior. But an overwhelming aspect of the
letter is Peyton's plea for answers, for guidance from a parent who
has surrendered his role in favor of becoming a "Bunny," almost
a suitor to Peyton and one who himself has failed to mature beyond
the vague yearnings he remembers from his own wedding. She
begs her father to answer ultimate questions: "Why did [Maudie]
have to die? Why do we have to die?" (LDD 36). Unfortunately,
Milton has been unable to construct for himself anything but cliché
anecdotes on the human condition, most of which he remembers
in times of crisis as coming from his father's own store of apho-

risms. Peyton expects absolutely no help from her mother and in the letter refers only obliquely to Helen: "What has she said?" (34).

Asking for help, she actually addresses Milton as "Daddy," especially when she repeats: "What's wrong, Daddy? What's wrong? Why is happiness such a precious thing?" (LDD 35). Above all, Peyton wants to "come home," but she makes it clear she knows she cannot: "I wish it were possible," she writes; and then her final plea, "Oh, Daddy I wish I could come home!" Ostracized by her mother, abandoned by her ineffectual father, Peyton tries one last time to explain herself, but her syntax, the cogency of her language, her voice, breaks down to confusion which Milton cannot decipher. Peyton has literally become "lost" to the reader at this point, lost because her words disintegrate off the page, followed appropriately by a dash, the typographic symbol for a sudden break in thought. But Peyton's dash points to oblivion: the loss of voice, the loss of Peyton's words which literally fall out of the text of the narrative.

Peyton reenters the narrative in Milton's memories of her when she is nine years old and announces to him that she is "beautiful" as she gazes into her toy mirror; Milton reflects that she is indeed beautiful and picks her up "with a sudden almost savage upwelling of love, pressing her against him" (LDD 42). The language is fraught with implications of an inappropriate intensity that Milton feels for the little girl; this quote could as easily refer to his feelings of lust for a grown woman, especially the "savage upwelling." Milton further muses that as he holds her tight "with wonder and vague embarrassment" he is "paying homage to the beautiful part of him, in which life would continue limitlessly" (42). As he holds her awkwardly against his chest, she brazenly calls him "stupid" and the rest of their interchange suggests as the Polish housemaid had remarked years earlier that Peyton is indeed "spoiled." Her father's attentions, in contradistinction to the way he avoids contact with his "failed" daughter, Maudie, exhibit his deep guilt feelings about his older retarded girl. "Until Peyton was born, bleak doubt assailed him" (46). And although Milton tries to assuage this "infuriate guilt" with inner protestations of love for Maudie, he admits to himself that she causes him "dreadful unhappiness," which is mitigated by Peyton's validity as a beautiful child. The clear distinction in the novel between Helen's child Maudie and Milton's Peyton highlights the intense polarization in the family. The dependent Maudie and the fiercely independent Peyton are set up in the novel to dramatize the family's fracture. Both parents seek to love and adore one child to the exclusion of the other, and, coincidentally, for the same reason: Peyton is bright, beautiful, and full of promise; Maudie is not.

This scene, when Peyton is nine, occurs during Milton's initial open flirtation with Dolly Bonner. It is the summer of 1933 and FDR is in the White House as Milton drinks himself through the disastrous day; in fact, alcohol figures largely in Milton's important scenes in the novel, up to and including Peyton's burial. In this case, Peyton and Buster, Dolly's hapless son, conspire on this day to tie and gag the helpless Maudie who, with ropes around her neck, her face turning blue, shrieks in pain and fear interrupting Milton's alcoholic fog. Helen sweeps Maudie up, viciously slaps Peyton's face, calling her a "little devil" (LDD 58). After peace is restored, father and daughter seek Helen's inner sanctum, and Peyton apologizes in the dark, stuffy bedroom. Helen also apologizes, and both weep as they embrace making "the soft soothing sounds two women make when they try to forgive each other" (60).

What can be ascertained from the scene is that Helen at least appears to apologize and then forgive Peyton in 1933, but a little later in the same scene she reveals that the only reason she stays on with Milton is Maudie; she does not mention Peyton, or say "for the sake of the two children" that she will remain in the marriage. Again, Peyton the gifted "beautiful" child is paradoxically ignored by Helen precisely because she is not crippled or retarded. This nine-year-old who quizzes her father on the meaning of the word "contraband," who punches her male playmates, and who is so pretty, grows into adolescence stressed by her parents' dysfunctional interplay. But is Peyton in this scene a little devil? More likely, she is a child seeking the attention her mother lavishes on her less fortunate sister, or perhaps Peyton is "punishing" Maudie for her infirmities which steal their mother's attention away from Peyton, and in this way Peyton can release her pent-up hostilities at being the perfect child. Yet at the very close of the scene, Styron has Peyton say not only that she is sorry for hurting Maudie, but that she feels that "Children should be kind to one another" (LDD 63). Clearly the reader is meant to see the correlation between this statement from the prescient nine-year-old Peyton and the twenty-two-year-old who laments in her final letter: "We've all been so unkind. I've been so unkind to people" (35). Peyton knows early on the value of kindness, kindness that she cannot seem to elicit from her mother or, finally, from herself for herself. She feels monumental guilt for not pleasing her mother enough, for her treatment—however childish—of Maudie, and for being beautiful and vivacious to such a degree that she beguiles her father, perhaps pushing him into a quasi-incestuous relationship with her. Under the weight of all this guilt, she is unable to build her own life. In her last letter she asks: "What have we done with our lives so that everywhere we turn—no matter how hard we try not to—we cause other people sorrow?" (35).

By 1939, Peyton is sixteen and heads off to Sweet Briar and a traditional southern girl's education; even though she goes off during the outbreak of World War II, her life and that of her parents seems little affected by global turmoil. At the country club party celebrating her birthday, Peyton is feted by the community at large as a young beauty and as a social success, but she will not enjoy her full measure of happiness. Helen has built up a crescendo of emotion since the 1933 revelation of Milton's flirtation with Dolly, and she is convinced that Milton has been carrying on an affair for the intervening six years. On this stage, set typically by Styron to be one of extremes of domestic happiness and turmoil, Peyton and Helen clash, predictably, when Helen discovers that Peyton has been drinking. Interestingly, Peyton is initially docile and follows Helen "obediently" as they enter the powder room where Helen dumps out the offending punch. It comes out, of course, that Milton is behind the whiskey-drinking, but Helen's punishment is still severe: Peyton must leave her own party immediately. Peyton is at first silent when she hears this, but she strikes her first note of alcohol-inspired defiance at Helen: "she raised her eyes, gave her hair a wild outraged toss. 'I despise you!' she said, and was gone'" (LDD 77).

Besides her first defiant act toward her mother, her sixteenth birthday also delivers the narrative's first detailed physical description of Peyton, which is from an anonymous point of view in the novel, quite like the voice that introduces the novel in the initial "Riding down to Port Warwick" passage.

> Her eyes were brown, always hugely attentive; like her mouth, they lent her face at once an air of thoughtfulness and of inquisitiveness. Her lips, which were just full enough seemed always slightly parted in a questioning way. . . . Her hair was dark brown and generally cut short so that it closely framed her face. . . . (LDD 78)

The narrative continues, adding that Peyton has lost count of the boys who had asked for her hand in marriage. And, significantly, she is seen in the party as addressing her father as "Bunny"; that is, more like a confidant, an intimate, than like a fifty-year-old father. Peyton also speaks of her feelings for her mother; she tells

Milton something about Helen that fills him with fear and dread: "It's absolutely a terrible thing to say and *I don't know how to say it* it's so terrible . . . but I can't help it, Bunny, I just don't love her" (LDD 80; italics mine). We should note here that Peyton does not possess a language to critique her mother's unmotherliness. Later, Milton asserts himself, after some more booze, and tells Helen that Peyton will stay at the party, only to have his inebriate teenage daughter ask him for a "big old sinful Packard convertible" in her best adolescent manner (91); but the scene is more like one between a *mistress* and an adulterous husband than a father and a daughter. Indeed, Milton calls Peyton a "goldigger" and refers to her as "baby," while she presses "a big smear of lipstick on his neck" (90).

But the night's revelries are not ended with this alliance of tipsy father and daughter against the teetotaling mother and wife. Peyton passes out of sweet sixteen innocence when she slips into a red lastex bathing suit, swims with an adoring boy, and unexpectedly happens upon the sounds of her father and Dolly making love in the golf museum of the club. She recoils in horror and seeks consolation from the boy (probably an autobiographical portrait-cameo of Styron himself; perhaps even the first appearance of Stingo in Styron's fiction) who sees her initial reaction to her father's tryst. This passage, related from the point of view of Peyton's young admirer, Charlie La Farge, is poignant particularly because of the heightened awareness the reader has of Peyton's sudden discovery, an awareness ironically unavailable to Charlie who sees only Peyton's "slick" young body. In fact, from Charlie's vantage point we see, in detail, how Peyton first tries to open the door of the golf museum and then listens intently at the door, hearing, we know, the sounds of her father's lovemaking. To Charlie, however, this scene of Peyton at the door with her head "cocked thoughtfully" is a "lovely thing"; and Charlie thinks only of kisses and love as he watches her. Peyton, on the other hand, has just realized the import of the sounds beyond the door, and she screams in sudden terror and tension as Charlie sneaks up behind her with a juvenile "Gotcha!" Charlie assumes, to his credit, that Peyton "must have seen or known something frightening and terrible" (LDD 95). She implores him to hold her close as she puts her arms around him and they lie silently in, appropriately, an "abandoned playground," for Peyton has just lost her innocence along with her Daddy, her "Bunny." She has also lost her meek acceptance of her mother's imperious demands. For the ensuing six years, until her death,

Peyton will not return home for anything longer than a brief vacation.

One such important visit occurs during the Christmas of 1941 when Peyton once again asserts herself. Milton describes her as a grown-up; she has let her hair grow, and it falls in "brown waves to her shoulders, somehow lending a new, saucy assurance to her face" (LDD 151–52). But this older Peyton arrives late and on her way to another Christmas Eve party, a fact that Helen finds objectionable, and thus mother and daughter are at odds again within minutes of Peyton's arrival. Another aspect that reveals itself in this encounter is Helen's jealousy of Peyton's effervescent socializing, a skill Helen has not enjoyed much since her marriage. At Peyton's sixteenth birthday party, Helen had declined dancing, bridled at light party conversations, and in general wished she was ensconced in her bedroom's quiet, dark safety. A bit of an agoraphobe, Helen is therefore resentful of Peyton's seeming breeziness with young men and with the party scene in Port Warwick. Helen remains in her room, and Peyton goes forth to cavort with her new consort, Dick Cartwright; in fact, Peyton takes on "the tones of Tallulah Bankhead" and makes a grand exit with her young man (153). Milton reflects that she is now a woman and that for Peyton "the age of eighteen was made for fun" (153).

The following morning, narrated from Milton's point of view, we see how intimate daughter and father are in their alliance against Helen; but there is something more to this arrangement than a mutual disregard for Helen's "severity." We also see in this scene how "lost" to both Milton and Helen Peyton has become. Her voice is suffused with the casual nuances of collegiate life and its value systems. Milton kisses his visiting daughter awake, "gently" punches her ribs, kisses her yet again, and spanks her across her "bottom" (LDD 155). Peyton breezily says that Dick is in love with her which causes in Milton a "sinking sensation" for he is in a sense a suitor for her affections. Peyton does kiss Milton on the mouth here, and he watches as she undresses: "fascinated and confused, he watched this woman . . . there was a final swift wriggle as the pajama pants fell from her waist" (156) After this bit of voyeurism Milton leaves, but only *after* Peyton yells at him over her shoulder, "Daddy, get out of here!" His mind is caught up in "the moment of excitement, confusion, whatever it was. . . ." (156). Significantly, in this passage we are exposed more to Milton's obsession with his daughter, one that has affected him before; but at this Christmas he appears more concerned with his sentimental notion of family harmony, and he suffers greatly when his optimistic bubble is burst by Peyton and Helen's squabble over Peyton's partying. During that Christmas dinner, tensions finally erupt and Peyton leaves promising Milton that she will never return. Milton kisses her in despair, and like a lover says: "Baby, . . . don't leave me. I love you so" (162). As Peyton and her beau drive off, Milton kisses her yet again, but this time through the car's open window which seems even to *him* "neither sweet nor proper" (162). Peyton's response to his farewell is a sad grin and a wink. The family's vicious alchemy of thwarted desires and expectations concludes that Christmas with Helen locked in her chamber, Milton retreating to booze and his appropriately named mistress, Dolly, and Peyton plunging with abandon into the "wild" life she later confesses to her husband Harry. True to her word, Peyton does not return until her wedding in 1943, and even then she does not stay one single night in her parents' home.

The intervening scene in which we see Peyton occurs when Maudie is in the hospital and eventually dies in Charlottesville in November of 1942. Peyton is attending fraternity festivities at the university with Dick Cartwright, and as she enters one party she is cheered as "the Body" and "Lover" by a crowd of drunken college revelers. She is, obviously, a big woman on campus: popular, attractive, outgoing. Styron's use of Peyton as a focal point for his presentation of his own generation's complex combination of aplomb and angst registers itself fully here in this scene of wartime decadence and despair. In the hubbub of the partying, we are treated to an omniscient point of view that zeros in on Dick and Peyton at the party. Dick praises Peyton with the usual devotion. "You look like a million bucks," to which Peyton lazily replies: "Money . . . that's all you know" (LDD 200). Dick also says, "I thought you were the Sweet Briar intellectual type with modern ideas," which means for him "free love" (201). But Dick's insistent question: "Do you love me?" is evaded by Peyton entirely; her relationship with Dick, although it has been solemnized by a "pinning" also seems doomed precisely because of Dick's fawning adoration and Peyton's apparent weariness with such attention. Just as Dick has finished asking yet again "Do you love me?" Milton stumbles in after a drunken and disastrous time at the football game searching for his Peyton; the father has usurped the boyfriend's role, and Peyton once again becomes wife-daughter.

At the hospital Helen condemns them both, but as usual she is more severe with Peyton. In her fury and frustration Helen lashes out at her daughter's attempts to comfort her. "*You* . . . don't whimper at me. You're half the cause. Remember when you let

[Maudie] fall?" (LDD 214). As the person responsible for finally getting her wayward father back to the hospital in the first place, Peyton reacts in horror as Helen continues: "You don't care. About anything. And is that why you kept your father away from here all day? Guilty? You with your whoring around and your drinking" (214). Of course, the narrative reveals that Peyton is no whore; in fact, she has had no sexual experience with her fiancé. But the structure of the novel heightens the dramatic tensions of the moment and Peyton does not/cannot explain because Helen immediately turns and leaves the waiting room. Peyton apparently leaves with Dick in a desperate whiskey-fed attempt to find solace in sex, which parallels her father's similar behavior with Dolly.

Thus for Peyton, sex becomes a coping mechanism she has learned from her father, a mechanism she uses to deal with her mother's rejection, for Helen refuses even to let Peyton see her own dying sister and ascertain how much of the illness has been "made up" by Helen. Helen intensifies this punishment with her pronouncement of Peyton's share of responsibility for Maudie's condition, a punishment that Helen must feel will be very effective on Peyton. Unfortunately, the verbal abuse Helen throws at Peyton for supposedly dropping her sister "on purpose" years before takes on an intensity far beyond what Helen could have imagined: it becomes part of Peyton's great burden of guilt from which she eventually frees herself by suicide. Helen's overwrought accusations intensify the tiny bruise—which Maudie did not feel, ironically—into a fatal injury to Peyton's self-esteem.

The final grand scene in which we find Peyton attempting a reconciliation with her parents, especially her mother, occurs at her wedding in October of 1943, about a year after Maudie's death. After casting off Dick Cartwright and Virginia for New York City, Peyton returns to an elaborate ritual set up by Helen, as we discover in Helen's interior sections, to show the community once and for all that "Helen Loftis was a good mother, a successful mother" (LDD 261). Still, Peyton spends the night before her wedding at a friend's instead of with her parents. This telling detail is passed off by the guardedly optimistic Milton as a way Peyton has of making her "homecoming an easy, gradual thing" (239). But Peyton quickly disabuses Milton of his naïveté and tells him twenty minutes before the ceremony that she is simply playing "the good sweet role" of a prodigal daughter (255). Once again Styron utilizes Peyton to comment upon the vagaries of an American culture in transition during the war. Even the Tidewater communities were under the attack of the easy casualness of sexual relationships and of the prosperity born out of the multifarious arms and supplies mercantilists. Indeed, Milton has found her, dressed in her formal wedding gown, "sitting alone reading a world atlas and looking beautiful and somewhat bored" (249). She reiterates that she has always wanted to be "normal," and that her father should cease his "sentimental slop" and not "smother" her (254). Peyton also narrates through Milton's point of view her life during the past year when she "lived like a tramp" although she didn't write Milton of these times, sparing him these lurid tales. Peyton explains, however, that her wild life was miserable. "I tried to pretend that I liked these new people, any people at all, but I didn't. I don't even guess I liked myself" (250). She admits to Milton, "Here I am trying to be sober and sophisticated and modern and I feel like I was twelve again and back in dancing class" (251).

In her critique of herself, Peyton succeeds where her parents fail; she is of a "lost" generation that perceives all too clearly from whence they came. She is of Styron's own generation, which was forced by global conflagration to question the fragile notions of humanity that their parents had promulgated. Peyton sees with the clarity of her generation the absurdity of the social facades built up by her parents. Her doom also resides, however, in this very realization. Peyton is aware of the "insanity" of her family, but for all her knowledge and insight she cannot help herself. She cannot work her way past the injuries she has suffered from her mother's pointed "fixing" of guilt upon her, nor can she recover from the excessive devotion of her father-lover. She is trapped, as she says, in the "sweet role" of the prodigal, sweet but deadly and defined by guilt.

Before the wedding itself, Peyton and Milton drink whiskey, fortifying themselves for the ordeal they envision awaits them. The Episcopalian ceremony is in "fine style," as Milton sees it, but he is swept up in a tide of random thoughts that alight on Peyton as she stands before him during the ritual. Milton describes her "solid curved hips" that have obsessed both Helen and him, and he thinks, "the flesh too, the wet hot flesh, straining like a beautiful, bloody savage" (LDD 258). Styron quickly shifts the narrative to Helen's thoughts which reflect her "profound and unalterable loathing of Peyton" (261). The structure then switches yet again to a quasi-omniscient view that presents the wedding party and its center of attention. "Peyton, everyone thought, was so beautiful and so graceful. She smiled at everyone and introduced them to Harry, remembering the right names" (262). And so Peyton is, at this moment, a perfect success in her role; later, her uncle Edward describes her as a "honey" and a "little sweetheart," pointing out how Peyton and all the other nubile young women at the party are open to the "itchy reminiscent lust" of the older males in attendance (287). Styron here reveals how much the role Peyton plays—and the other young women will play, each in her own time—is really based upon a bankrupt patriarchal assumption that she will continue to be the ornamental but *impossible* iconic Southern woman: the kind of woman Helen, too, aspired to become.

The portrayal of such incongruities between reality and myth continue when later, during the small disaster of La Ruth's unwitting drop of a chain of hot dogs, Peyton is portrayed as in "lone command of the situation," although she is "tight" (LDD 272). Peyton hugs La Ruth and immediately alters the "colossal awkwardness of the scene." Predictably, in Styron's doomed atmosphere of the wedding, it is Milton's genuine outpouring of love for Peyton as he witnesses his daughter's inebriate cool that propels him into a real disaster. Suddenly overcome in his boozy state by love for Peyton, he finds himself kissing Peyton in front of the crowd "much more than a father." For her part, although drunk, Peyton pushes Milton away "furiously," angrily saying. "Don't smother me, Daddy. You're crazy! What will people think!" (272) Again predictably, because of this push, Helen resolves to "fix" Peyton. "Now she gets drunk and lures him on with her sinful little tail twitching and then turns on him like a dog" (287). In spite of all the positive hopes for the wedding, this resolution to "fix" Peyton brought on by Helen's increasingly delusional behavior leads to a complete break when Helen attacks Peyton and Peyton responds in kind to her mother's physical and verbal abuse. Peyton again rushes out and, again, Milton smothers her in drunken kisses—on her hair, eyes, cheeks, and her mouth. She pushes him away—again—and leaves for the final time.

Taken from Harry's perspective, the section following the wedding elaborates on Peyton's state of mind as they wait to begin their honeymoon. Harry is presented as the sensible, sober *male* outsider who reports his take on the day and is more than a little taken aback by the venomous attacks Peyton hurls at her parents and even at him. Peyton gives her assessment of the family succinctly. Helen is beyond "redemption" and "beyond hope" since "the day she was born" (LDD 303). Milton she calls an "ass" because he has had good in him , wasted now that he is not "man enough to stand up like a man and make decisions and all the rest. Or able to tell her [Helen] where to get off" (303). Peyton then begins to rant that Harry has not helped her enough, protected her enough from her mother; the narrative's point here is clear: Styron is here underlining the temperament of both Helen and Peyton by revealing Peyton's own apparent paranoia about Harry's "disloyalty." Judith Ruderman explains that "What Peyton seeks is release from her mother; but ironically, she becomes as incapable of real love as her mother is" (Ruderman 1987, 43). Harry reflects that Peyton had not been "like this" in months: "he thought he'd straightened her out" (LDD 304). Harry "shuts off her words from his mind"; it is the only thing to do because there is "no truth to what she had been saying." He cannot combat "her frightful logic." Harry reasons further, "He thought he had it licked, too, this kind of perverse, crazy talk, and now he felt weary and sad and disappointed" (305). Styron thus forces the reader to compare Peyton's outbursts with Helen's previous apparent dementia. He also brings Harry into the comparison by suggesting that Harry's attempts at deciphering Peyton's moods mirror Milton's lifelong wrestle with Helen's "neuroses." The success of this technique lies in its drawing the reader into the text by carefully designing dialogue that echoes previous situations. The recurring passages of Helen's severity, Milton's boozy affections, and Peyton's pained withdrawal/banishment reinforce the almost Sisyphean pattern of the text. Like the characters, readers continually attempt to build an understanding or a union with the voices in the text, only to have that constructed dialogue challenged again and again as events evolve and understanding or even empathy becomes more problematic.

After the wedding, the next time that Peyton returns to Port Warwick is in a coffin and, in a sense, belatedly in the last letter her father receives and reads on the day of her burial. The novel, however, returns to Peyton by fleshing out two important periods of her life: the two years in New York after the wedding and the monumental day of her suicide. The section narrating Peyton's two years of marriage and her courtship with Harry before the wedding is chiefly told through Harry's perspective; in fact the last earthly picture of Peyton is mentioned when Harry views Peyton's New York City morgue photograph and identifies her. Harry's story also presents his first encounter with Peyton in the spring of 1943 at a Village party. He finds her drunk, aggressive, and argumentative, but she is the "most beautiful girl he had ever seen" (LDD 314). The next day they meet again and Peyton explains that she feels as if she is drowning, a sensation she describes again two years later in her letter to Milton. To Harry, Peyton appears curiously open and yet withdrawn at the same time. She is well-read, and she has a tendency at gatherings to lecture New Yorkers about their "bigoted" views of the American South. Peyton explains to these Northerners that the South may be filled with guilt—an important aspect of Peyton's own existence—but this is the "very tragic essence of the land" (315). Still, the South would eventually rise from its ruins and be a greater place for its ordeal. The New Yorkers take this as a romantic view of history, but Harry sees a "passion glowing in [Peyton's] eyes, and love" (316).

Harry's friends, on the other hand, see her as a "nice-looking tomato" who is "confused" but who changes for the better after a few weeks with Harry. Friends still warn him, though, that Peyton is "the dependent kind." After the wedding, Peyton reverts to her confused behavior, sees a psychiatrist, has an affair with a mystery writer, and eventually loses Harry as he moves out in frustration over her drinking and infidelity. Interestingly, our final view of Peyton in this section is from Lennie, an early critic of the "tomato"; it is he who comforts her after Harry leaves, and she appears "drunk, hysterical, and crying about drowning" (LDD 317).

The final, most important section describing Peyton is, of course, the seventy-page interior monologue reminiscent of James Joyce's "Molly Bloom" section in *Ulysses*. Peyton's monologue is likewise crafted to approximate the free-association of images, in this case the workings of the mind of a deeply disturbed young woman. The section promises much; if a reader can "solve" the relational puzzles of the section, much as a psychoanalyst examines the free-associating of analysands, answers to questions in the previously more straightforward and chronological—albeit couched in flashbacks—narrative can be found. In Styron's presentation of Peyton's last thoughts, we have the "actual" transcript of her mind's working up to a moment of importance. However, we meet in Peyton's interior the central problem of such a literary technique: the closer we appear to get to Peyton's mind as she grapples with her own hallucinations and delusions, the more we find ourselves groping at meaning and at the process of its construction. Indeed, Styron's involvement of the reader in the process of Peyton's journey toward suicide allows us to come dangerously close to "a sense of involved discovery which is closely akin emotionally to actual experience" (Law 1990, 53), but it is still an *aesthetic* experience, the purpose of which is ostensibly to focus our attention on the social conditions Styron views as contextualizing Peyton's voicings..

Peyton's "monologue," which is really in dialogic terms a *collection of voices* from Peyton's entire life and is therefore replete with parental and other significant voices as well as voices imagined, serves to collect several motifs that define the character's reality. One of the more important details "on" her mind during the passage is her menstrual cycle. Throughout, she is suffering from severe cramping that at times incapacitates and exhausts her on a journey to find Harry and to ask for forgiveness. When the cramping strikes, Peyton describes "claws" that attack her insides; the cramps make her feel as if she is "all womb again" (LDD 321). In this fevered pitch of menstrual pain and hallucination, Peyton leaves her apartment with her clock, which she dreams that she can enter and drowse inside, a "womb of brass," safely inside and outside of time itself. Melvin J. Friedman has made much of this clock image in the soliloquy; in fact, he relates the section to the work of Virginia Woolf as well as that of Joyce, especially Woolf's *Mrs. Dalloway.* In both Joyce and Woolf, comments Friedman, "the use of clock images bears a relation to Bergson's theory of psychological time" (Ratner 1972, 49). Peyton is also accompanied by her flightless-bird fantasies that are related to her feelings of guilt; she feels the birds' presence when she recalls events like her adultery with a mystery writer. As she travels New York City by foot, train, and taxi, she meets a cast of city characters who help her and eventually direct her to Harry. Along her trek, she has a few drinks in a bar, and as she tells stories to men trying to pick her up, she discloses to the reader that "Guilt is the thing with feathers" (LDD 335), and thus is she plagued with her "birds." And, as part of his ongoing critique of both his society and even its young iconoclasts like Peyton, Styron has her recount another startling comment Harry made to her: "You're a Helen with her obsession directed in a different way" (337). Again, Styron raises the question: What must Peyton do to escape her mother's (and her father's—in fact her society's) legacy to her?

In terms of feminist dialogics, the reader is exposed in this "monologue" to a cacophony of dialogues, so the Modernist term of *monologue* itself, as just suggested, appears to be inadequate to describe the reality of the multivocality of Peyton's inner *voicings.* Styron uses this section to inject pertinent biographical and emotional information into the narrative stream as it appears to occur to Peyton herself, but the structure of the text suggests that Peyton "hears" the details, the voicings, more than she observes them linearly. To use the puzzle metaphor again, pertinent pieces are presented in associational patterns and the reader fits them into an understanding of the text and therefore of Peyton and her family. Harry's sudden, inspired comparison of Peyton with Helen, then, is related to us as it occurs to Peyton, and we recognize the inherent truth of Harry's observation in light of other comparisons of the two women. It is precisely the "monologue's" effect of being simultaneously within and *without* linear, syntactic logic that allows it to interrelate fragments of consciousness unhindered by "normal" restrictions of chronology and logic. At one point Peyton reflects, "Oh, God, I must die today, but will I not rise again at another time and stand on the earth clean and incorruptible?" (341) Clearly, she hopes to be another kind of "bird" (from a family of "Byrds"), different from her wingless, flightless birds of guilt which she associates at times with both her mother and her father. She wishes to rise, Phoenix-like, from ashes of her life and be newborn, free from her unbearable guilt feelings.

When Peyton finally meets Harry, she is distraught and tries desperately to explain herself to him, but is able only to plead while she thinks, "I have not fornicated in the darkness because I wanted to but because I was punishing myself for punishing you" (LDD 359). Peyton's severity, unlike Helen's, is inner-directed and therefore lethal to herself. She continues to ponder what she really wants to say to Harry: "not out of vengeance [unlike Helen, again] have I accomplished my sins but because something has always been close to dying in my soul, and I've sinned only in order to *lie down in darkness* and find somewhere in the net of dreams, a new father, a new home" (362; italics mine). In this eloquent and wrenching passage, Peyton discovers her true motivation: her search for renewal, redemption, salvation. But she has not found solace in dreams or sex, and now she begs Harry for yet another chance. *Even at this stage,* he gives in to her. He is, in effect, seduced by her obvious delirium, but she pulls back archly and claims that Harry has never understood her or tried to see her "side of the matter" (362).

Once again Styron hurls us back from the edge of understanding: Why does Peyton, at the very moment of achieving forgiveness, choose to aggravate the situation by becoming argumentative with Harry who is the very soul of charity at the moment? Analytically, we can see this juncture serving at least two purposes in the narrative: first, the reader sees that Peyton is truly doomed at this point. Second, the reader can see a repetition of the same behavior exhibited by Helen who hurled just such objections at Carey Carr when she railed against men during Peyton's wedding party. So the scene brings the reader a sense of art, of repeated themes and carefully chosen motifs. But it also suggests that a complete, thoroughgoing understanding of human behavior and motivation may be beyond the exercise of analysis. In the novel itself, Harry reacts to Peyton's reversion by throwing her out, and once outside, she throws her clock into a drain, ridding herself finally of her dream of nesting safely in the clock; she is moving beyond time.

Finally, Peyton begins her last trip to the building from which she will jump, thinking as she goes that Milton will understand her going: "undivorced from guilt, I must divorce myself from life" (LDD 364). As she walks to the subway, she calls to the birds haunting her steps; she tries to shoo them away, only to hear passersby giggle or claim that she is drunk. The birds come on, anyway. She pauses to reason that she has rejected Harry, and "by that rejection making the first part of [her] wished-for, yearned-for death-act. . . ." (365). As she climbs the stairs of the open loft building, she thinks, "only guilt could deliver me into this ultimate paradox: that all souls must go down before ascending upward" (367). She reaches the top floor, strips off her clothes, and carefully rips up her silk dress and throws it into a trash bin before she entreats her flightless birds to fly with her, "ascending my flightless birds through the suffocating night, toward paradise" (368). Her last words address Milton. "I am dying, Bunny, dying"; and then, "naked, clean if sweating, just as I had come," she leaps.

Because Styron refuses to allow Peyton's voice to be silenced, he has designed her "monologue" as a means by which she might become a "maker of meaning" rather than a mere "sign" or "bearer of meaning" (Bauer 1988, 3). Bauer's further insight is instructive:

> When women step out of their traditional function as sign; when they refuse the imposition of the gaze; when they exchange their sign-status for that of manipulator of signs, they do so through dialogic polemics. And, at that moment of refusal, they become threatening to the disciplinary culture which appears naturalized. (3)

In this sense, Styron has become the "interpretive community" which is willing to listen to a woman's "alien and threatening discourse," as Bauer puts it. Another important apect of this moment or chronotope in the novel is that Peyton, like Edna Pontellier, sees her plunge off the tenement in Harlem as promising "a moment of pre-linguistic wholeness" which Bauer explains as a moment "when she does not have to struggle in the social realm for possession of her own voice" (xvii). Edna hears the sea's "voice," but Peyton hears her mother's voice injecting "propriety" and social strictures into this final moment; Helen's voice here reinforces the failure of Peyton's community to hear her as something other than a defined entity in the patriarchal whole. Peyton's failure, like Edna's, is her suicide which ends her internal dialogic and its eventual growth into a externally voiced and ongoing "subversive dialogue" with the privileged patriarchy that has defined her.

Of the two parents, Helen is the final one to speak of Peyton in the novel. After Milton's attack upon her at the funeral chapel, Helen says, "Oh, God, Peyton. My child" (LDD 370). But the final mention of Peyton in the entire narrative comes from the mouth of a black servant, just as the first naming of Peyton came from Ella. La Ruth, to whom Peyton had been so kind at her wedding, moans, "po' Peyton, po' little Peyton. Gone! Gone!" as she grieves after Daddy Faith's service. La Ruth is quickly chastised for her grieving by Sister Adelphia who sniffs, "Ain't you been baptized, sister?" (381). And so it is that Peyton whose last cry was for her own faithless Daddy is mourned at Daddy Faith's revival gathering.

Peyton's soliloquy, which can be seen in dialogic terms as a multivocal re-presentation of her mind, what Wayne C. Booth refers to as Bakhtin's discovery that humans are by nature "constituted in polyphony" (Booth 1982, 51), raises other questions, however, about the true nature of her relationship with her "daddy." As has been discussed in brief earlier, clues are dispersed throughout the entire narrative and deserve attention as well, although in true modernist fashion Styron refuses to assemble them for the reader; indeed, a number of hints and innuendos succeed in obfuscating and clarifying simultaneously. The relationship between father and daughter is set forth as being obsessive from the very beginning when Milton reflects that "Until Peyton was born, bleak doubt assailed" him concerning his "infuriate guilt"—a term reminiscent of Faulknerian stylistics—about Maudie's infirmities (LDD 46). He heaps upon his beautiful child love, grateful love, really, for her sound, beautiful body and sharp mind.

The incestuous character of the father-daughter relationship can be found with some regularity in brief snippets of flashback in both Milton and Peyton's narrative sections. One scene has Milton daydreaming on a Sunday morning when Peyton is nine; he has been drinking, and his mind wanders as he argues with Helen about his drinking: "He and Peyton . . . they would be together in the warm house" during the coming winter's frost (LDD 50). Milton doesn't envision sharing this sunny winter day in the future with Helen, but with his bright and beautiful daughter. Later, in 1942, he dreams of Peyton and himself on a ship: "Beside him at the rail Peyton turned to face him, lips upturned for a kiss," but the kiss is interrupted in the dream by an icy blast of air, and he wakes feeling shame (177). This dream also projects an image of Peyton going off into the cold dark arctic barrens—a premonition of her suicide.

At least two other scenes portray definite sexual arousal but are frustratingly hazy due in part to Styron's presentation of these flashbacks as repressed memory-feelings. Peyton explicitly tells Dick Cartwright that she and Milton have a "Freudian attachment" (LDD 224), but it is not quite the socially acceptable Electra complex that Peyton seems to invoke in order to minimize the relationship in Dick's eyes. She also refers to Milton as a "demonstrative old bum" a few times, especially when he kisses her "much more than a father" (247); again, she is minimizing. In one of Milton's embedded flashbacks, the threat of Milton's "unnatural" attentions comes to light. At Peyton's wedding Milton recalls a walk they took to a church belfry when Peyton was a little girl; ironically, he recalls this as her wedding ceremony is in progress and after he has been ogling her hips in her wedding dress. In the belfry of long before, however, Peyton, frightened by the loud bells, cries and Milton soothes her fears and kisses her. This scene may also be the source for the "birds of guilt" that haunt Peyton's suicidal mind; up in the belfry, beneath its eaves "sparrows scuttle in their nests and fly off with a raucous sound" (277). The birds may have been associated with her father's frightening behavior. As he soothes her, Milton's heart begins to pound and he kisses her again, "in an agony of love," but he does not know "why she should push him so violently away with her warm small hands" (277). Clearly, her "violent" push indicates that Milton's kisses are perceived by little Peyton as unusual and frightening; further, his denial of knowing why she should push him away suggests that his is an obsession beyond his rational control.

In Peyton's own interior "monologue" there is more detail suggesting Milton's at times uncontrollable attraction for her. She was the "spirit of light" in a school play, she recalls, and her costume was a silver gown "that you could almost see through"; then Milton took her "in his lap and when [she] jumped up [she] saw his face: it was red and tense like a baby's when it goes off in its diapers" (342). Milton's apparent ejaculation seems clear, although it does not, necessarily, lead directly to a conclusion that he sexually abused his daughter; from the text it appears inadvertent.

Even though these two clear references of Milton's arousal for Peyton as a child seem the result of proximity and not some conscious pattern of abuse, still he does fit the profile of a man led by incestuous urges, especially when he has been drinking. Peyton has certainly been aware on some level of her ability to arouse her father to ejaculation, and it is quite possible that her own guilt feelings surrounding her sexuality have been influenced by the trauma she felt when she was dressed as "the Spirit of Light." Peyton certainly exhibits some form of trauma as she trembles with "dread and guilt" when she feels "hot" during an examination by a gynecologist who refers to his probe as "a naughty leetle instrument" (LDD 331). Her guilt feelings may indeed stem from an actual molestation, and she may blame herself for her father's behavior. It is not unusual for victims of molestation to blame themselves; it is also not unusual for their mothers, especially if the victims are girls, to deny that the abusive actions are indeed taking place. It is a commonplace that the mother of an abused girl will blame her for being too provocative, and deny that the father could be initiating the sex act. Helen's "poor Milton" excuses come to mind here wherein the father is seen as helpless before Peyton's beauty and precociousness, an idea supported by Helen's own insistence that Peyton seduces Milton, actually "lures him on with her sinful little tail twitching" (287). At least in this sense of active denial and subsequent transference of guilt, Helen is in an incestuous triangle. Behavioral pathology aside, the text's clues are enough to confirm the possibility of abuse caused by one parent and exacerbated by the other. It is no wonder that at the close of her short life Peyton longs to arise like a Phoenix: "will I not rise again at another time and stand on the earth clean and incorruptible?" (341).

That *Lie Down in Darkness* presents a rich panoply of female characters is obvious; that the novel was written when Styron was in his early- to mid-twenties deserves constant restatement. His method of unflinching exhumation of past guilt, despair, and lost hopes for his female characters, especially Helen and Peyton, involves the reader in a demanding investigation of sexual taboos and the cultural limitations of women's experiences. The novel, as Bakhtin explains, is by its very nature inclusive, and it is this that allows Styron the freedom he needs for a dialogic "rhapsody" in which female voices react candidly to their circumstances within the largely patriarchal society of America in midtwentieth century. Charles Schuster explains that for Bakhtin, the novel is "the dialogic made textual"; and further, "Novelistic in this usage becomes a descriptive term denoting texts saturated with ideological content, filled with voices, engaged with other speakers, heroes, and listeners as speaking subjects" (Schuster 1992, 190). In this sense,

Styron's work is a critique of his time, not a slavish panegyric of life in the southern United States. He structures his novel in a series of meticulously detailed and described flashbacks to give context to people's lives, particularly women's lives; clearly, he lets the patriarchy speak, too, demanding that the reader enter the text and make yet another discourse out of the at-times disparate cacophony of voices. As Bakhtin writes, "form and content in discourse are one, once we understand that verbal discourse is a social phenomenon" (Bakhtin 1981, 259). Styron's critique can most demonstrably be read in passages like Milton's reflection on Helen. "Here was woman, with a capital W, tricky and awful, inconsistent as the weather" (LDD 89); or in young Charlie La Farge's Stingo-esque mind-set. "He also gave women a great deal of thought . . . his real and only desire was to lose his virginity. Breasts, legs, thighs, and other things filled his mind with constant fleshy images" (92); or even in Carey Carr's rather more textured description of his wife's "brittle way she had, combing her blond, lovely hair . . . with that brisk, self-assured, woman-of-the-world gesture which he never dared tell her really set his teeth on edge. . . . Adrienne who was really quite gentle, steadfast and full of the warmest and sweetest passion" (105). In this, Styron investigates scrupulously the underpinnings of male assumptions about women in his society as well as women's visions, voiced and otherwise, of men. Some critics may question Styron's technique as mere chauvinism masquerading as inclusion, but Bonnie Kime Scott's point about a supreme modernist like James Joyce is instructive and sheds light on Styron's own "writing of woman":

> A troubling possibility is that Joyce's writing of woman still serves a male author's ego, proving he can move into "other" forms. On the other hand, if the move is made, not in the spirit of epic conquest, but as wanderer-gatherer and re-viewer of writing, we would wish for more male writers who will follow in Anna's [Livia Plurabelle] wake. (Scott 1987, 129)

Clearly, however, William Styron has produced in his discourse on the Loftis family a work in which "[e]very language in the novel is a point of view, a socio-ideological conceptual system of real social groups and their embodied representatives" (Bakhtin 411). As Dale Marie Bauer has written concerning the suicide of Zenobia in *The Blithedale Romance*, Styron, like Hawthorne, has Peyton "finalize" her own self-consciousness, "rather than be reduced" to the patriarchy's categories (Bauer 1988, 23). Peyton's death forces her parents and those who knew her to focus on the contradictions in a society that values her as a commmodity but cannot seem to accommodate her as she struggles to achieve her own self-definition away and apart from her family, her husband, and her lovers. But as Higgonet has discussed as length, suicide does not diminish a character's voice in literature. Peyton's act indeed sets up the entire discourse of the novel and the revelations that are realized by each character in the community of voices that re-present Peyton and are themselves re-presented in the narrative's voices. As Bauer has written about Zenobia, "the novel cannot silence [Peyton's] oppositional force precisely because her discourse grounds the narrative, gives it its edge and reason for being" (23).

In the end, Peyton, like Zenobia, commits suicide as a way of finalizing her desire to remain *unenclosed* by the language of the patriarchy. Indeed, Peyton's last linguistic act is to shrug off the notion that she must be "proper," that she must be the Southern "lady" supposedly represented by her mother. Peyton's reply to that final recollected fragment of her mother's opprobrium is: "I say, oh pooh. Oh pooh. Must be proper. Oh most proper. Powerful" (LDD 368). Peyton here employs suicide as a tool with which she can "rise" like her "birds"—if only momentarily—above the din of patriarchal definitions which become all the more insidious when they are recalled in her last moments as fragments of her mother's disdain. As Bauer writes, "self-violence is a subversive strategy against a culture which has interiorized violence" (Bauer 1988, 50) and internalized violence in this case has surely been at the center of the society in which Peyton has lived, defined as it is externally by a world war. Styron emphasizes just this point as he has Peyton kill herself just after the mass death of the first atomic explosions in Japan. Peyton's suicide, which is really a form of gynicide taken as a last resort by one bereft of a community and cast off by a succession of supposedly "responsible" adults, male and female, "makes explicit," as Bauer explains, "as no discourse can, [the] myth of individual freedom" (50). Peyton leaps from the pretense of a society heavily invested in its notions of "liberal progress" even as the atomic bomb vaporizes the "bland humanism" underpinning the power structures of those who created such a weapon and introduced *communal* annihilation (50). Such resisting voices as Peyton's, however, reaffirm the notion that dialogue never "dies." Styron's voicing of Peyton's literary suicide is a metaphor for her "refusal to be conscripted" into the patriarchy's "proper" hierarchies. In Bauer's terms, Styron's "artistic will of polyphony" forces Peyton's suicide and suffering from an internal dialogic into a literary and therefore interpretive dialogue.

3

Yet Am I His Creature Still: The Women of *Set This House on Fire*

> [T]hat that God . . . will not looke upon me now, when, though
> a miserable, and a banished, and a damned creature, *yet am I*
> *his creature still,* and contribute something to his glory, even
> in my damnation. . . .
>
> —*Set This House on Fire,* epigram from
> John Donne's "To the Earle of Car-
> lisle"; italics mine

ALTHOUGH Styron's second major novel was not received in this country with the same accolade that greeted his first, *Set This House on Fire* excited praise and extended commentary in France two years after its 1960 debut. In America, the book's sagging sales caused it to be remaindered by its publisher in less than a year, but in 1962 Maurice-Edgar Coindreau, William Faulkner's first supporter in France, translated the novel as *La proie des flammes* (Ruderman 1987, 9). The French reading public was prodded to reinvestigate Styron's *Lie Down in Darkness* with the result that he came to be regarded as a major author in France as well as in the rest of Europe; in fact, his first novel appeared on an official list of required English readings for all French doctoral candidates during 1973–74. Styron was then the only living author on the list, joining at the age of forty-eight the company, at least in spirit, of Shakespeare, Hawthorne, and Poe.

Inasmuch as the novel chronicles somewhat seamy social events that occur during the forties and fifties in both America and post-World War II Allied-occupied Italy, Styron's most vehement critics suggested that the work was anti-American in an extremist form. It is worth noting that 1960 was also the year Leslie Fiedler published his *Love and Death in the American Novel,* a study which concluded that only Gothic fiction could hope to capture and "best express an American nightmare" such as the one enacted in

77

Styron's novel. According to Marc L. Ratner, Styron's work fulfills Fiedler's prescription in the "exotic and Gothic setting" of Sambuco (Ratner 1972, 71). In choosing to focus on the political commentary by a few characters, almost all critics of the early sixties ignored the portrayal of relationships between the sexes in the novel. Indeed, not one critic has come forward to discuss the overwhelming acts of violence and threatened violence aimed at women portrayed by Styron as a symptom of the social pathologies of the times. Louis D. Rubin, Jr., almost alone in his praise of the novel, claimed that it surpassed Styron's first as a presentation of American values and as the complex relationships of its characters. Rubin notes that the novel completes the "symbolic journey begun by Peyton Loftis in *Lie Down in Darkness*" (Rubin 1981, 101). Even after three decades, informed and careful critics like John Kenny Crane are not quite so sanguine about the novel as was Rubin. This chapter reevaluates the problems raised in the novel about the ends of fiction in terms of how it portrays women in the midtwentieth century both before and after the debacle of the Second World War.

As such, the novel should be seen as an exploration of the language of males as they recount tales of violence against females they have known or whom they themselves protect *and* attack verbally and physically. Styron lays bare the inner feelings of men who, although they may believe themselves sensitive and open to the struggles of women, are in reality accomplices in the violence and abuse aimed at the women in their lives. *Set This House on Fire* is in fact the first of Styron's novels that delves so deeply into a dialogic presentation of male-directed first-person points of view, chiefly those of Cass Kinsolving and Peter Leverett.

In examining Styron's novel, it is useful to remind ourselves that a common tool used by feminists is an assumption that language, as Sheila Rowbotham explains, "is part of the political and ideological power of the rulers" (Rowbotham 1973, 33). In an important work on the subject of male power structures and language, the British feminist and linguist Dale Spender argues that "society has been constructed with a bias which favors males; one of the basic principles of feminists who are concerned with language is that this bias can be located in the language" (Spender 1980, 14). To see that the use of English, and by extension for this novel, Italian as well, has literally been "man-made," according to Spender, is to observe that language is still "primarily under male control" (12) and as such needs reevaluation in terms of feminist concerns. As Angelika Bammer reminds us, the power of cultural conservatives like E. D. Hirsch should not be underestimated, especially when they refuse to acknowledge the changes that have been accomplished in the last decade thanks to feminist cultural activism. In fact, in his *Cultural Literacy: What Every American Needs to Know* (Hirsch 1988), Hirsch "not only has no reference to sexism, he leaves out feminism entirely" (Bammer 1992, 264). Similarly, Jonathan Culler has criticized the absence of even the mention of feminist criticism in another critical work, Frank Lentricchia's *After the New Criticism.* Culler writes, "Lentricchia's decision to ignore feminist criticism . . . casts doubt upon his claim to historical understanding and his authority to criticize others for their lack of it" (Fuller 1982, 42). Judith Fetterley underscores the importance of raising such an important point for literary studies. "Thus men, controlling the study of literature, define as great those texts that empower themselves and define reading as an activity that serves male interests, for regardless of how many actual readers [and scholars] may be women, within the academy the presumed reader is male" (Fetterley 1986, 150).

Peter Hitchcock identifies one benefit from the "bankruptcy" of conservative thought: "it continually reveals the ideological underpinnings of its own position while claiming that ideology has gone the way of the dodo" (Hitchcock 1993, xii). Bauer comments upon this conservative, authoritative strategy further by arguing that novels like Wharton's *The House of Mirth* show the difficulty female voices encounter when they attempt to engender themselves contrary to the expectations of "bourgeois authority." A community's power over its constituents rests primarily in its threat of exclusion; this authority in turn determines "what the community can or cannot incorporate" (Bauer 1988, x). Elizabeth Meese argues that such communities, constituted to ensure basic conventions of interpretation, are indeed chiefly exclusionary and andocentric, when they reject feminism's validity; in this sense, "interpretive community" becomes "authoritative community" (Meese 1986, 8), and the phenomenon of *feminisms* as casualties, to use Elizabeth Ermarth's term, can be observed along with the marginalization and resultant silencing of female *characters* in American interpetive communities. What is even clearer, Bammer insists, is that "language is a cultural institution to which our affiliation is not optional. . . . Indeed, we are unthinkable without language; our very sense of self—our identity as individuals and as members of whatever communities with whom we choose, or are assigned, affiliation—is constructed and experienced through language" (Bammer 1992, 238–39). As such, then, the languages of male authors offer particularly inviting opportunities for a study of patriarchal assumptions and interpretations of women as these assumptions are revealed in the inner "monologues" and other discourses of male (and to some extent female) characters as they delve deeply into their own actions and attitudes toward the women in their lives. As M. M. Bakhtin theorizes, every speaker is an ideologue, and every utterance is an ideologeme (Bakhtin 1981, 429); that is, each utterance is steeped in ideology.

Styron's second novel offers a critique of patristic ideologies in the Gothic landscapes of Sambuco, Italy, and the environs of New York City and the American South. The overarching subject of the revenge extracted in the tale of Mason Flagg's murder and the rape and murder of Francesca Ricci, however, remains the possibility that even "informed" men can and do abuse women. For all its attempts to reify the events of one tragic summer night in Sambuco and bring them into a clearer light of understanding, the novel cannot resolve the specter of gynicide which can be seen as a direct effect of patriarchal notions of women as commodities, as "romantic" or familial property over which the males in their lives have had absolute sway. Styron offers a dark portrayal of male domination that critiques the very explanations offered by the males involved as they make their cases, as their voices enter into what Bakhtin refers to as the *carnival* of dialogism. For all of the violence portrayed in the novel, the voices of the women so abused are indirectly presented and heard (if not fully understood by the male characters), and they suffer in silence no more. In this, Styron does continue the vision he began in Peyton Loftis's story; the extra dimension here is a novel use of partially comprehending male points of view to present his concerns. No female interior "monologues" are presented, so the reader hears the voices of beaten and abused women through men who themselves are implicated in the system which allows and even encourages violence against women.

As a novel that describes in grisly detail the victimization of women at the hands of violent men, *Set This House on Fire* may indeed be one of the first modern narratives that so openly investigates the subject full in the face of the supposed "good life" midway through the American century. Of paramount importance among the victims, however, is the Italian peasant girl, Francesca Ricci, whose brutal murder follows quickly her rape by the wealthy sociopath Mason Flagg. It is worth noting here that she is killed by another Italian whose previous murder of his own sister was ignored largely due to a prevailing conviction that the murdered woman was a peasant and therefore not worthy of a full-fledged investigation; in addition, the excuse is given that the first murder took place during the war when one peasant woman's death, even one the result of a vicious beating, was not important. The war, arguably a worldwide paroxysm of male domination and violence, was the overriding concern. So two *gynicides* result from a male-dominated police force turning a blind eye to the suspected but never investigated male "town idiot." But the explanation by Luigi, the apparently thoughtful and benevolent Italian cop, fails to deliver the reader from the mystery: Why did Saverio, fifteen years before he ended Francesca's life in a rain of bone-breaking blows, beat and then murder his own sister? The failure of the authorities to recognize the seriousness of his original dementia implicates them in the second murder, although they are content to blame the American Mason for Francesca's death because, as Luigi reveals to Cass at the close of the novel, there is no need for the populace to learn that the murderer is still in their midst in the person of the blank-minded, and therefore in a sense, guiltless, Saverio.

The Italian patriarchy has failed in its social contract with the peasants of Sambuco here: the authorities demand fealty and obedience and in return promise to provide security, but the male figures of authority in fact blame the female victim, battered Francesca, for parading her "piece," her "crack" before an American (STH 467, 476). The story in this novel is a midtwentieth-century version of a male system of power, and one of its most infamously cynical ploys is to censure victims whom it has victimized itself. The novel raises concerns, however, about the assumptions that portray Saverio as a dumb animal who kills Francesca in a blind reaction of animal fear: to say he is not guilty of premeditated murder or that he is feebleminded merely aggravates questions about the patriarchy's ability to control any raging male from terrorizing women or even other men; we must remember that one of the supposed sensitive and most sympathetic of the male characters, the artistic and well-read Cass, is guilty of premeditated murder, *and he killed the wrong man.*

The novel is, in effect, a tale of Gothic revenge enacted upon Mason by Cass for Mason's rape and assumed subsequent murder of a virgin, a valuable and even mystic commodity in the acquisitive world of male patriarchy whose continuance depends in large part upon the orderly succession of property rights from one generation of male power brokers to the next. The total control or at least manipulation of the value of women's reproductive activity is responsible in a large way for Cass's murderous mistake. In fact,

Cass himself reveals that his main motivation for seeking out and then killing Mason resides in his drunken conviction that Mason had really raped *him* when he raped Francesca. Later he adds: "Who knows why he did it? Because her beauty and her innocence drove him crazy? Because he knew *she was mine?*" (STH 444; italics mine). Not only does Cass feel a need to minimize even his beloved Francesca's suffering by suggesting that Mason was out to avenge Cass's growing independence, but he also reveals the true nature of his rage at Mason: Francesca was his. Francesca is Cass's *property,* his model, his Dream Girl, and Mason rapes her in a bizarre *property* dispute (indeed, Francesca can be seen as "property" more directly in the way Cass uses her as a "prop" in his painting and in his own drama of self-destruction) in which one male destroys the other's property so as to deny him its use. In fact, Cass goes to great lengths to explain himself to Peter on this point, and his listener accepts all without offering judgment, a device Styron uses to bring the reader's own judgment into the textual discourse. Cass says that he would find no peace until he had confronted Mason; he wanted his "pound of flesh" (445). "It was all I wanted—this you must understand—and it was not much, or so it seemed to me; nothing would right his wrong or restore Francesca's loss . . . *for the sake of my manhood alone,* or what was left of it, for the sake of whatever notion of honor I still honored, I knew I had to have . . . some token. . . ." (445; italics mine).

Thus even sympathetic white males from the powerful American society of which the poor Italian peasants can only dream are debased and lost in a property dispute, or, worse, a dispute in which Francesca is sacrificed for men's absolute need for a sense of control over her sex and her image as a vessel of purity, a sad comment on their inability to articulate their interiorization of the monologism of patriarchal control. They do not develop a meaningful awareness of their predisposition to *dominate* women as part of their attempts to define themselves as men. So it is that the reader can see Styron's novel as a serious examination of the victimization of women by closely examining the text to reveal how, even at the very moment of their much-vaunted and ritually revered defence of the supposedly weaker but adored female, even in this their most mythical moments of devotion to the female, males consider their own selfish motives of "honor" and property rights first. Cass sees himself and not Francesca, in the end, as a victim of Mason's rape; Cass sees *himself* as the victim, even though he explains how he encouraged Francesca's continuing pilfering of Mason's supplies, an act that eventually leads Mason to "discipline" her by raping her.

As yet another party whose complicity in the novel's tragedies becomes more and more clear, Peter reveals that, although Cass protests vehemently that he "wants to know," it is only after much initial evasion that he relates the events which had transpired that summer evening in Sambuco. Cass's confessions perhaps temporarily validate Peter's internal conviction that he was no more than an "observer," but they also allow him "to view recesses" of himself that he had "never known before" (STH 433). Knowledge of what transpired is the grail of this experience for Peter, but it opens him up to scrutiny as a character whose purpose is not to understand human nature, but to "view" his own self in an almost narcissistic fashion as merely an uninvolved *spectator* of the morbid events he had at the time been only dimly aware, or so he claims. Questions arise about his so-called humanitarian motives: Why did he not wait for the two days it took Cass to return to his family after Francesca's death? Peter claims he was looking after Cass's wife and children, and yet he leaves after only one day. Why does not Peter react more vehemently against the beatings to which he knows Mason subjected Celia and Rosemarie? Why does he quail before the wealthy Mason even as his inner rage against Mason's cruelty is at its zenith? And why after the passage of two years does he locate a man he barely knows but suspects of murder? Peter's efforts to find an explanation for the events in Sambuco (and yet maintain a lack of self-awareness about his own interiorization of male dominance) are also complicated attempts to vindicate himself and mitigate his own complicity in those events. And if these suppositions are true, the entire discourse of the novel is an intriguing example of patriarchal handwringing that is symptomatic of deep and abiding convictions of guilt over the gynicide of Francesca as well as the *psychogynicide,* or psychic death-in-life, experienced by the other female characters in the novel who are abused either physically or verbally: Wendy, Celia, Poppy, and Rosemarie.

One can feel guilt for *not* acting against an injustice. The guilt feelings expressed by Cass are indeed as selfish as Luigi, the amateur philosopher and newly appointed police sergeant, claims in his apologia for the failures of the "fathers" to save Francesca. Guilt is a sin, explains Luigi, especially when it is as self-serving as it is appears to be for Cass. "You *sin* in your guilt!" (STH 494). As Styron has us observe, even the most stalwart defenders of the innocent are themselves irredeemably bound up in the patriarchy's domination and definition of women's roles. Cass's defense of Francesca has its roots deep in *his own* needs and not in some altruistically benign love for charity and the human race.

According to dates Peter gives here and there in the novel, the action surrounding Mason's death in the narrative takes place in Sambuco during July 1955. The earliest scenes in which women are portrayed occur, however, in the early forties and they involve the lives of both Cass and Peter. Peter explains how he met Mason, who is one year older than he, at a small boarding school on the James River in Virginia. Mason's wealthy parents had moved to Virginia to set up lives as ersatz country gentry, but Mason had been a careless, reckless student and thus ended up in the crumbling school where he meets the middle-class Peter. Peter recalls one particular day during which he, Mason, and Mason's mother, Wendy, sail about the river and laze off the shore of Yorktown in the spring of 1941. Peter's slavish devotion to Mason's persona as a wordily adolescent is overshadowed only by his dumbstruck attraction to, and fascination with, Wendy, then a thirty-five-year-old woman devoted to her son primarily because her rich husband has abandoned her for other, younger women. Wendy's portrait reveals Peter's sentiments about motherhood because he never discusses his own mother at any length, unlike Stingo who is haunted by his mother's accusing gaze. Peter marvels at Wendy's "flaxen hair brushed with electric perfume" and her "inch-long vermillion fingernails": "these were attributes I had never connected with mothers, who in Port Warwick tended to be portly and subdued" (STH 77).

Wendy seems to him a "fantastic apparition, irresistibly, almost alarmingly beautiful." But her devotion to her son, which has strong hints of the incestuous attraction that Milton Loftis has for his daughter Peyton, startles Peter, especially when they address each other in lovers' terms of endearment. "I love you, angel," says Mason to his mother, and she calls him "cheri" and "darling" (STH 72). Peter describes Wendy as a dipsomaniac who is "blank and lovely" as they sail, and "svelte and nimble" even though she consumes a half-dozen martinis. "Wendy-dear," as Mason refers to his mother, is the first "lady lush" Peter has seen, and he is further confounded by her relating to him in Mason's company that her husband is "seeking another woman's bed" and therefore Mason is "the only thing she [has] left on earth" (77). These secrets fall on his sixteen-year-old ears only to leave him "flabbergasted and depressed" because heretofore Peter had enjoyed a blissful ignorance about the troubles of married women and "had lofty southern notions about ladies at the time." With her "adult" but drunken conversation, Wendy beguiles the young Peter with her lectures to Mason about sex, "her gorgeous hair flying out behind her in streams of undulating gold" (77). He is further mesmerized by their colloquy and their intimacy. "Mason, unperturbed and elegant in a camel's-hair jacket beside his mother, would turn his luxurious profile toward her from time to time and lightly peck her cheek, the two of them lost in tender banter, gazing long at one another. . . ." (78). To young Peter, Wendy appears as hardly a mother at all, "but some grown-up Dulcinea possessing both sexual allure and incalculable wisdom" (79). On the day that Mason must tell his mother that he has yet again been expelled from school, this time for fornicating in a church with a poor oysterman's half-wit daughter of thirteen, Peter sees her total collapse contrasted with the power of her husband; he begins to appreciate the power of the male.

At Mason's disastrous birthday dinner party, Wendy's drunkenness spurs her to reveal her own childhood and to contrast her father—Daddy Bob—who looms large and benevolent and "wonderful" in her memory with her diminutive financier-husband who refuses to get her the horse she so desires. She advises Mason to be, in effect, a copy of her own idealized father figure. "Always be good, my adorable one, always be bright. Manly. Proud and poised. You're all Wendy has. Remember? You see, you're the bright star in my crown" (STH 83). Wendy continues to praise her father's old Virginia ways: "Daddy-Bob had a heart as big as all outdoors. . . . Parties. Dancing. Moonlight sails. I mean it was a—a way of life that was—oh, free and wonderful" (85). In the face of the reality of her ruined marriage, attributable to both her husband's supposed infidelity—although he is at home that night when she suspects him of finding other, younger women—and her own alcoholism, Wendy escapes into the dreamy memory of her "coming-out" party, only to have her booze-ridden haze suddenly undone as the oysterman comes to the door ready to beat Mason for debauching his thirteen-year-old daughter. Male authority asserts itself as the senior Flagg orders the burly but grieving father out of his house with promises to pay for the sins of his "contemptible swine" of a son. Wendy, who appears more shaken by her husband's actual presence in the house than by the oysterman's entrance, is told in no uncertain terms that her husband will go where he wants, when he wants. "It will be that way, do you understand? It will be that way" (92). And he adds that it will be that way as long as she is a "common drunk" and a "moron"; with this, he strides off in his pajamas," a short little man, stiffly erect" who leaves in his wake "the strange girlish scent of gardenias."

Wendy is not seen again in the novel except as a historical footnote that Mason adds. In 1943 Mr. Flagg dies, leaving his son $2 million and releasing his wife from his stern displeasure. She purchases the forbidden horse she so desperately wanted to fill out her dreams of her past with Daddy-Bob, and she takes on a Belgian "boyfriend" who is seventy and who teaches her about Zen and the art of archery. "Poor Wendy," says Mason; "What with that spooky Belgian and that horse and all that sauce she'll end up for certain in some laughing academy" (STH 133). When Mason tells Peter of these events, it is spring of 1951, ten years after the debacle of Mason's seventeenth birthday; Peter does not comment upon Mason's account of his mother, but he is clearly beyond seeing her as "the most glamorous mother on earth" as he once had (80).

Cass Kinsolving's first detailed portrayal of a woman is his account of a sixteen-year-old Christian fundamentalist whom he attempts to seduce only to find *himself* seduced and quickly brought to orgasm. In early 1942, a seventeen-year-old Cass sets off to get a "piece of nooky" in the furor of the country's war-fever. As he tells Peter of Vernelle Satterfield, his first sexual partner, he exclaims: "Listen! This has a whole lot to do with it all" and proceeds to relate how he walked around and around in his pin-striped suit, a gawky big-handed farm boy who wanted sex, but who did not have the five dollars to buy a prostitute's "favors" (STH 259). He meets Vernelle, "all brown hair and round young breasts and soft contours and rose-gold Botticelli flesh" (261) and talks his way into her room, rhapsodizing about her "plump knees" and "silky crossing and recrossing of her legs" which turn him into "one solid sweaty torment" (260–61). What is really important for Cass in retelling this story, however, is his appreciation of its "sad nostalgic glamour" that makes this "loutish seduction of an adolescent" into an important moment "surrounding her, the clouds of time through which she bore like a pair of chalices her witless carnality and her innocent love of Jesus" (262). Cass is here relating Vernelle to his later infatuation with Francesca, who is likewise voluptuous and pious and "innocently carnal." Cass's point enlarges as he comments upon the "mood" of those early war years when millions of men and boys "prowled" the streets in an "endless, endless search for girls." The mood lingers, Cass explains, "in the heart of a whole generation . . . behind it all, shadowing all of it is the memory of the time when all the lovely girls had vanished from the land. The time when *only the whores were abroad*. The whores and Vernelle

Satterfield" (262; italics mine). For Cass, Vernelle is a touchstone for his lost innocence and for his subsequent plunge into the carnal oblivion of the war as a soldier and lover of "whores." Ironically, his description of his encounter with the "virginal" Vernelle is itself not the seduction of an innocent girl, but of *himself,* the innocent boy. She calls him "lover boy" and groans, "Dawling, what took you so long?" when he finally puts his arm around her. She was, Cass says, "Not a treasure of the Lord, but a junior-sized harlot!" (264). She drags him to her bed, urging him to hurry lest her aunt return too soon, but with one single caress of her hand, she brings "the divine spirit" flowing out of him: "Why you pore silly," she says.

Both Cass and Peter are disabused of culturally constructed notions of the virginal and the wisdom of glamorous siren-mothers, respectively. Yet Cass never ceases to be hounded by his search for the innocent girl-woman ideal until he finds Francesca; Peter, meanwhile, pursues the wisdom he imagined Wendy had personified, and he continues to seek it in cajoling Cass into ever deeper soundings of his murder of Mason. Styron's unveiling of these early and meaningful scenes in each man's adolescence allows the reader to contextualize later events and share in their confessed search for themselves in the story of Mason's death. The startling reality brought out in these revelations is that the men are themselves defined by their own cultural definitions of women as sacred or profane mercantile articles: sacred mother turns out to be slattern-drunk and virginal Christian becomes wanton "harlot." Clearly, the reality is that patriarchal definitions of women's roles are wanting and present unrealistic, essentially dehumanized portraits of both Wendy and Vernelle. Cass has been seeking the purity he has been acculturated to expect, represented by Vernelle's supposed virginity, but his first sexual encounter shocks him with the realization that women, even the fundamentalist Christian Vernelle, are carnal underneath the mythic patriarchal facade erected for women which either denies their sexuality by defining them as pure virginal vessels, or reduces them to the polar opposites in the market of sex: whores.

Adding to the irony of Cass's memory of his encounter with Vernelle, however, is his avowed determination, in spite of his desire to worship purity and virginity, "to try *anything short of rape, and even that,* to enter this pure undefiled vessel of the Lord" (STH 264; italics mine). Cass in his ruminations about the times of war and whores misses entirely the point that men decide which women are whores and which are not; men pay women for their sex and thereby determine the market for services rendered. And even if there is no money exchanged, women like young Vernelle are perceived as whores ironically because they want sex with the men who want sex with them. Cass's own complicity is revealed and opened for critique: the reader sees the observance of the ageless double standard of sexual behavior for women codified by men in order to define women's sexuality and their societal value, and thus exercise control over them. Cass's disappointment is not with his own duplicitous expectations of a virgin whom he himself has a right to despoil as part of some ancient patriarchal rite of passage, but with his failure to lose *his own* virginity with another virgin. His disappointment is in his failure to consume, to take her innocence as some talisman of his male power over her. Instead, she exerted power over his sexuality by exhibiting a carnality with which he had had no experience. Thus begins his early dislike of women who are experienced, who are not childlike as Poppy is. Early in his life, then, he was shocked that women were like *him*. Since Vernelle, his orphaned existence has been punctuated with drawn-out searches for purity in art and life in foreign lands that finally culminate in Sambuco and cause him to kill Mason, the quintessential American, for committing precisely the same crime he would have perpetrated upon Vernelle: consuming an innocent, beautiful female totally, by means of rape if necessary. In this, as Styron surely wishes his readers to see, Cass shares aspects of Mason's view of women as objects; in this sense, Cass is a *bohemian* representation of this ugly side of the American male.

The New York City scenes in part 1 of the novel, which are related by Peter to Cass two years after the events of Sambuco, reveal more of Mason's treatment of the women in his life, as well as Peter's "observer" status. Peter contextualizes his meeting of Mason after a ten-year hiatus in their "palship" in the spring of 1951 by prefacing the story of that brief interlude with Mason's wealthy bohemianism. "He was the world's worst liar. He *hated* women. . . . Yet he was great fun to be with sometimes" (STH 130; italics mine). The apparent contradiction between Peter's genuine dislike of Mason and his gee-whiz admiration of Mason's wealth and self-confidence signals Peter's own complicity in the attitudes for which he criticizes Mason. Peter himself lives a rather shabby existence as he prepares for his agency job in Europe. "I became wholly unkept, and was sour and spiteful to the girls I tried to pick up in the Village hangouts" (132). In fact, just as his eyes meet Mason's for their first meeting in ten years, he confesses that he was especially "burdened with mean-spirited lusts" (132). Still, the "older" Peter, whose frame narrative is the transcendent present of the novel, as John Kenny Crane describes it, does view his conduct in those days as "regrettable," and he claims no sense of nostalgia for his lack of fastidiousness, much as the elder Stingo laments his slovenly habits in *Sophie's Choice*.

When Peter meets Carole, whom he mistakes for Mason's wife, he describes her as "a hefty, good-looking girl with milky skin and a rich, contralto, barrelhouse voice and elliptical green eyes that mirrored almost nothing save an imperturbably confident passion" (STH 134). She is from Greenpoint, Brooklyn, and depresses Peter about Mason's choice of mates; thus is Peter rather snobbishly dismissing Carole and her origins as being beneath those of Mason, but he cannot help feeling "a bachelor's itch and envy over what [Mason] had acquired otherwise" (135). Again the spirit of male mercantilism enters through Peter's narrative; he sees this woman as the kind of property Mason seems to acquire effortlessly. Carole is also portrayed as a drunk who laughs easily at Mason's "droller-ies." Mason himself writes her off by referring to her as "Baby" and confiding in Peter that "the kid's bobo for flowers." Later at a party Peter meets the real Mrs. Flagg, although at the moment he is unaware that she is Celia Flagg. He is aware of her as "a stunning girl with soft coppery hair" who has a warmth and gentleness "that seemed to radiate from her as she moved." She possesses a voice "devoid of flim-flam" with "warm and womanly intonation" (143). He is immediately attracted to this new prospect and is determined to meet her, continuing his "prowling" for women. But in the crush of the party she is lost to him. He laments that she is "lovely" but will never be his, so he decides to leave and continue his melancholic preparations for Paris. As he leaves he interrupts Mason in his lovemaking with Carole in another room, "naked as pullets and frenziedly abed, locked in that entangled embrace all pink flesh and pounding posteriors" (145). Still thinking Carole is Mason's wife, Peter leaves insulted by what he sees as Mason's staged showing off of his wife, only to encounter Celia again, described as "a little doll" by one of Mason's sycophantic friends. "She was a flute-sound, a bell, a reed; Carole was a moo" (145).

Peter's subsequent memories of the week he spends with Mason and his women in New York City center upon the reflections he has when he thinks of two photos from the period: one of the "dazed and voluptuous" Carole preparing to kiss Mason at some wild Village party, and the other of Celia gazing at Mason "seeming ready to give him a roguish nibble on the cheek" while they lounge on the rooftop of Mason's apartment on a sunny spring day. Peter rhapsodizes about Celia's lovely face but also describes the string of women that Mason procured for him: "each night (and there were at least five of them) brought me a different girl. And they were all brainless, beautiful, and willing" (149). In this paradise of male libidinal craving, Peter admits he had never experienced so much "consecutive sex" of such variety in all his life. "I had become the crown prince among his freeloaders," as Cass later characterizes his dependence on Mason's largess. So although Peter expresses mild disdain for Mason's double life with Carole at wild early morning bohemian parties, he himself is more than content to have Mason pander to his carnal desires.

Peter also experiences Mason's extensive erotica collection, itself a textual presentation of women and sex, and is made privy to Mason's theorizing on sex as "the last frontier" (STH 151). The older Peter does not mention that Mason, in his reveries on the glories of sex, fails to acknowledge women's sexuality. "In art as in life, Peter, sex is the only area left where *men* can find full expression of their individuality, full freedom. Where *men* can cast off the constrictions and conventions of society and regain their identity as humans" (151; italics mine). Women, apparently, can find no such release as Mason claims for men; but the reader is forced by the lack of commentary from the older Peter to see Mason's rambling theorizing for what it is: an attempt to validate his own *nouveau libertinage* by alluding to de Sade's work as unheralded genius. And, of course, one is forced to ponder the begged question: From *what,* or more precisely *whom,* does Mason feel "Man" needs the Freedom of "orgiastic purgation"? Mason speaks passionately of the improper "bottling-up" of sexual urges which doom "Man," whom he sees as a "thinking biological complex" suffering from the "anguish and misery" of the "evil in the fruitless repression of sex." But just as Mason's pornographic collection reduces women to mere arms and legs in a Swedish orgy photo or obviates the necessity of women in sex altogether by showing a man copulating with an ostrich, women do not enter into Mason's theorizing on the rejuvenating aspects of sex. In reality, Mason appears desperate, and irony of ironies, passionate in his desire to escape from women with his pornography; indeed, later Peter learns that Mason has not had sex with the Celia—who "stuns" Peter with her attractiveness—for two years as he dallies with his porn collection and with a string of "moos" like Carole.

Although Mason mouths some avant-garde ideas about the dangers inherent in sexual repression, his own apparent inability to develop a meaningful sexual relationship with Celia reveals the emptiness of his own understanding of repression. Mason speaks of the "cleansing aspect" of the orgasm "at least among those humans who have been bold enough to break convention," but he himself does not break convention, but rather reinforces the most strident convention of sexual politics: the subjugation of women to the sexual needs and desires of men. Women for Mason become nothing more than a means by which men may "free" themselves to live more "fully" in some nebulous shallow Utopia of group sex and anonymous orifices (STH 152). Mason appears to want freedom from women *as people*. Peter himself begins to chuckle at Mason's vehement presentation of his ideas, and he tells Mason, "You seem to want to turn [sex] into a cult, and a gloomy one at that." In response Mason calls Peter "the squarest of the squares" and shields himself behind the hip rhetoric of the time, using language as a buffer between himself and the world. Still, Peter admits in the narrative that he too longs for "orgiastic purgation" and once again finds himself dutifully following Mason like some acolyte to a sexual guru (153).

When Peter eventually does attend one of Mason's "orgies" where marijuana-smoking participants share each other's wives or dates, he is, curiously, shocked and even repelled at the reality of sex-swapping. His own "date," Lila, a "ripe and amiable" stripper "dug up" for him by Mason, is from the beginning far more knowing and dubious about "the setup" than he is, even though Peter earlier dismisses all his dates during the time as a half-dozen or so "brainless" if "willing" girls. Peter also refers to Lila as his "barometer": a "big healthy girl with a fine elastic bosom; she had been around and there was no nonsense about her" (155). Lila does not like "dirty talk" or group sex, and so they both leave for what Lila calls "something good and private." His own description and affectionate portrait of Lila gives the lie to Peter's claims that the women he enjoyed were "brainless"; in fact, if anything, Peter admires Lila for her perspicacity at the party, but he cannot refer to her, in the end, as anything more than a stripper with whom he has had a "full night." She is a professional "body" for him to use for his own "orgiastic purgation."

Significantly, Peter never relates the details of his own sexual encounters in his narrative, never actually describes a satisfying, meaningfully "orgiastic" experience with any woman. Similarly, Cass cannot recall an "orgiastic purgation" with a woman; indeed, he relates no tales of sex with his wife Poppy at all; instead, his most enticing stories to Peter are of Vernelle the evangelical non-virgin and her opposite, the Madonna-like Francesca. In neither of these stories does Cass speak of the power of the orgasms he enjoyed; he prematurely ejaculates with Vernelle, and Francesca remains a tantalizing vision, posing for him in the nude, a "prop" always fresh and virginal, but always a love unconsummated. In a sense, Cass's image of Francesca is like Mason's own fictive, if spicy, "revelations" of his rendezvous with the exotic and passionate Serbian teen he claims to have romanced during the war: both are fabrications. Therefore, both Peter and Cass, like the wealthy and handsome Mason, can be said to flee from the reality of women as people, as sexual beings with voices of their own—not mere "texts" upon which men may "write" or, more properly, "*in*scribe" their own definitions.

Mason's focus on the orgasm reveals his, and by extension his society's, preoccupation with male sexual satisfaction with women as helpmates and intermediaries for men on the way to "orgiastic purgation." Instead of achieving a sexual unity with a partner, Mason is doomed to exploit his power over women as he tries again and again to dominate and finally rid himself of them. Styron's presentation of the incongruities between Mason's theories of sex and his relationships with women allows the reader to assess and evaluate male presuppositions about sex and female sexuality, especially those assumptions that not only omit women from such theorizing but portray women as a means by which men may escape, paradoxically, from women. Kate Millet's *Sexual Politics* makes a similar point concerning D. H. Lawrence's "sexual religion" in which sexuality is separated from sex. Millet writes that the priests of sex in "The Women Who Rode Away" consist of "supernatural males, who are 'beyond sex' in a pious fervor of male supremacy that disdains any genital contact with women" (Millet 1970, 290). Mason also recalls Millet's characterization of Henry Miller whom she sees as a male author whose "most original contribution to sexual attitudes is confined to giving the first full expression to an ancient sentiment of contempt" for women (309).

Like Stingo's ménage à trois with Nathan and Sophie, Peter joins Celia and Mason for a brief triangle in which he plays the part of the young man who has fallen for the woman of a friend in a "distant hopeless way" (STH 157). In his description of the perfect memory he has of Celia, Peter comments on beautiful women as a class. "She had dignity, too, and that kind of radiant poise, so rare in beautiful women, which comes from the consciousness that *one's beauty is meant to please men, and not oneself*" (157; italics mine). In this, one of Peter's more condescendingly chauvinistic remarks, we see patriarchal assumptions at work. Peter further comments that Celia lacks even "the small streak of bitchiness that even the most angelic of women can muster, given the provocation." With reasoning such as this, Peter concludes that Mason may have indeed been "driven" into Carole's "swollen embrace" by Celia's "decency, generosity and goodness" (157). Even in the late fifties, when the supposedly older and wiser Peter is reporting the stories of Mason and Cass and the women in their lives, he blames Celia for Mason's reckless and pseudointellectual plunge into sexual experimentation, yet another example in the text of the novel of blaming the victim for her own victimization. As the story unfolds, we find that Peter tries to validate his claim by describing his final encounter with Mason and Celia before he leaves New York.

On the morning before he embarks for Europe, Peter learns that Mason has savagely beaten Celia, smashing a plate on her head. She has run to Peter for succor, but as he reacts to Mason's "foulest of all foul sins," she retreats back into defending Mason's actions by claiming that he does not beat her often. Peter offers the reader this "sage" male response to her claim: "you either hit your wife often, or not at all" (STH 161). Peter sees Celia as "a flower upon which has been impressed the print of a dirty boot," and he comes very close to exclaiming his love for her, something, again, Stingo will do when Sophie is beaten by Nathan. In fact, Celia reacts by telling Peter that she loves Mason desperately, that she is "mad" for him (162). Peter hears in her voice a "preposterous, avid, debutante tone" which he finds repulsive, but he nonetheless listens devotedly to her continuing defense of Mason as a driven visionary whose search for truth demands of her certain sacrifices which she feels it necessary to make. Celia offers a rationalization for her acceptance, even her complicity, in Mason's frequent debaucheries. "But after all, he was a man, and a different kind of man, too. . . . He was an adventurer in the arts, a discoverer, and he just needed to have this kind of release, that's all" (163).

She further claims that no marriage is perfect, and even though she has no real friends, she has learned a great deal from Mason, especially about music. She explains that a wife should defer to her husband, because "it was the husband who was the—well if you want to call it that, the guide. It was his career, not hers that really mattered" (STH 164). True to his concern for presenting the period, Styron reproduces in full the rationalization for the domination of women in midtwentieth-century America, but he heightens the poignancy of the scene by having the desperate, bleeding, "perfect" wife Celia pleading the case before the reader's transparently limited and unreliable witness, Peter.

Styron's presentation here emphasizes the sheer power of the social strictures on sex roles over people, even educated and informed and wealthy women who can easily avoid the more repugnant aspects of chauvinism by virtue of their favored positions in that society. A cliché of recent social commentators, the denial exhibited by Celia in the midst of her "battered wife" speech is especially powerful in raising the reader's awareness of the duplicity of a culture that demands submission to male figures even to the extent of radical self-abnegation. "He can do anything to me . . . anything at all! I'm just mad for him." When she admits Mason's refusal to make love with her for two years because he does not want children, Celia collapses into a "babbling" state. At a nearby hospital, the staff sedates her: "she would pull out of it in a while, they said" (STH 165). And with this understated note, Peter leaves Celia, never to see her again, never to inquire about her again, and, for all his professed "devotion" and caring, never even to speculate upon her fate again. In dialogic terms, as a voice in the novel Celia speaks loudly and we learn later that Mason and she are "splitsville," and thus we can conclude that somehow Celia saw through Mason's false visions and found her way out of his definition of her.

As for Carole, we see her again briefly as Mason bids farewell to Peter a few hours after the encounter with Celia. She is described as having" a forlorn, distraught look on her creamy face . . . as if she had just stopped weeping and was about to begin again" (STH 168). But Mason moves her "briskly aside" and "chews" her out in sight of Peter, who longs to escape the situation; Carole collapses and gazes up at Mason "in dismay, with piteous amazement," and then runs away in a "sinuous, big-hipped retreat down the corridor, keening like a Hindu, sending through the bowels of the ship ponderous, contralto moos of despair" that bring people to look curiously from their cabin doors. After violently ejecting Carole, Mason shifts smoothly into his charming style and laments to Peter: "Women! . . . They're like cannibals. Turn your back and they're ready to eat you alive" (169). Mason complains that Carole has "the rag on," and is therefore "moon-struck" and incapable of rational thought. He minimizes her feelings in the extreme as he proceeds to elaborate on his point about women's anatomy. "It's the worst thing about women—that really screwed-up plumbing of theirs. *A big jumbo sewer flowing through the Garden of Eden* "(169; italics mine). To this Peter makes no reply nor does he mention Celia's suffering, even though he has left her in the hospital but scant hours before, her head beaten and her mind tranquilized. Peter's docile "yeah" is augmented by his own sarcastic inner judgment of Mason's diatribe as "poetry." Mason's position is extreme enough that Peter implicitly recognizes it as the supreme "poetry" of sexism: the reduction of a woman to her reproductive cycle, the classic male reductio ad absurdum.

Mason attempts to placate Peter's concerns about Celia by anticipating his objections and blithely passing his "women troubles" off as some kind of common male problem that will actuate a bonding pattern; he also denies he has ever beaten Celia before. "Oh, Peter, women! Sometimes I think I'll switch to beavers. Or moose. Or Rotarians. I don't know. Or maybe go back to Merryoaks and have Wendy rub me down with Baume Ben-Gay" (STH 169). This last desire to revert to the lover-mother he has back down in Virginia is another clear indication of Mason's inability to enter into an adult relationship with a sexually mature woman. Just as obvious is his attempt to deal with his own impotence with his wife; unable to perform sexually with her, he instead dominates by beating her. It is clear that this is a means of silencing his wife, and yet, as Dale Marie Bauer has explained, the repressed voice of the female finds its way into the text, in Celia's case through Peter's testimony about Mason's flagrant abuse of her. Bakhtin's observations of the power, the force of "novelisation," explore the ability of the novelistic discourse to achieve in its penchant for verisimilitude an inclusive "voicing" of all levels of the social hierarchy. This voicing of the voiceless is further explored when, during Peter's only reprimand of Mason during the entire New York scene, he is himself suddenly led to an outburst ordering Mason to "lay off" Celia. But this is tempered immediately by his inability, like the abused women in the novel, to speak further to Mason in a tone of rebuke: "For a moment *I had no words*" (172; italics mine).

In terms of feminist dialogics, Peter's incapacity here to voice his concerns can be read as a comment on the power of patriarchy over the language; Peter literally has no words with which to reprimand Mason further. He has been in such a position of abject fealty for so long that he cannot conceive of words to express his criticism of Mason's behavior and therefore the moneyed patriarchy of which Mason is a member. And the moment is an important one because, after a breath, Peter continues, but "more amiably" even though he has caught Mason in lies and seen the results of his beating of Celia. Peter amicably tells Mason that "we're all a bit neurotic" and implicitly takes on the position of the battered *wife* by trying to buoy Mason's feelings of inadequacy. As soon as Peter backs off from his confrontational tone, Mason begins to take on the persona of a wounded friend and elicits from Peter pity for the lost little rich boy he has become. At the close, Mason rewards Peter's loyalty with a wad of French money. The money further emphasizes Peter's problematic relationship with Mason: by accepting it, he validates Mason's assumption that he would take it and that both would thenceforth be united in some male sense of shared pain and shared riches, of which women are tangible, if difficult, trophies of accomplishment.

Peter finds it difficult to chastise Mason because he is himself heavily invested in the rewards/spoils system of the patriarchy: he will enjoy the women and life-style Mason's money will buy for him in Paris. Feminist dialogics argues that silence is not empty narrative "space"; it is, rather, filled with material meanings. In this case, Mason appears to become the outward manifestation of Peter's own deep impulses, impulses that even include Peter's probable desire to be seduced by Mason. In an earlier passage, the older Peter relates how he has wondered about a homoerotic connection between Mason and himself. In the passage, Peter claims his sensitivity opens his mind to such a possibility, but he has examined Mason's "allure" for him from "all angles" and found that although his attraction is "tainted enough," it is not "flawed by that complication" (STH 136) of a homoerotic attraction. What *is* flawed is Peter's implicit complicity in Mason's world through his acceptance of the definitions it perpetuates with regard to women.

During the period between Sambuco and his New York adventures, Peter explores France for one year and Italy for three, a period extending roughly from spring 1951 to July of 1955. The women that Peter meets and describes from this time are not people that seem important to him. In fact, Peter spends more time depicting his neighborhood near the Circo Massimo than the women in his life during these four years, yet the last single day he saw Mason alive elicits from him a five hundred-page text. That aside, Peter's women in Italy (he mentions none from his year in France) include "two or three girls": Ginerva and Anna Maria as well as "a junior from Smith College with wonderful black eyes," all of whom shared evenings with him of whiskey and music while watching Rome "spill out" beneath "in a luminous frieze of rust and gold" (STH 20). The Smith junior leaves just days before his July trip down to Sambuco, "spirited aloft on the first west-bound plane by her mother" who had "sensible plans" for her daughter. Peter reckons that it was all for the better that he and his "Smith girl" parted; the core of their romance, "love in the eternal city," had by that time "become worn down by time and familiarity" (23). Such is Peter's complete albeit brief catalog of his encounters with women in Europe.

Cass Kinsolving's time between his New York experiences and Sambuco are detailed much more completely in the second part of the novel, which is essentially from his point of view but reported in quotations by Peter, much as Stingo relates Sophie's recollections. Cass meets Poppy, née Pauline Shannon, his Irish Catholic wife and "scioness of a large Delaware family" (STH 252), in New York shortly after the war in 1946 or 1947. He relates that it was "love at first sight" (253), and Poppy was on her way to "flunking out of her first year at Vassar, not because she's dumb, you know, but because . . . she was a little what you might call ethereal for that kind of setup" (253). They lived "in a drab little apartment on the West Side" where he worked at becoming a painter and Poppy worked at a Catholic youth club. At the time, he had dreams of married couples, not of Poppy and himself, but of other couples: "mainly just these brave and pretty girls, and the brave boys they married, all hurried toward the same weird impossible destiny" (447). He has a "very sorry vision" of them as "Young lovers, stardust—piled up through the unimaginable centuries"; he clearly sees his and Poppy's synchronicity with the rest of the new generation of Americans starting married life after World War II in the American century, parents of the "baby boomers."

Cass moves his family to Paris in the spring of 1953, just after his fourth child's birth, and the family settles into a haphazard existence among the expatriates and artists, where the family lives more or less hand-to-mouth on Cass's disability checks and Poppy's trust fund income. A year later, Cass endures an epiphany of sorts that begins with a banal day's worth of children's screaming and Poppy's continued failure as "the world's most catastrophic housewife" (STH 252). In the late spring of 1954, he throws Poppy and their four children into the Paris streets while he is in the throes of "a perfect alcoholic fog" (254). To his credit, an older, wiser, and totally sober Cass of September 1957, two years after the Sambuco disaster, explains how Poppy brought to their relationship a "strange blend of childish wisdom and elfin charm" and that she is "the pride and joy and despair of her husband's life— sweet-souled, generous, loving" (252). Poppy is described as not much "bigger than a mouse, with the baby in her arms, hustling down the street . . . all of them heading for God knows where"

(255). Cass, meanwhile, experiences a Bergsonian moment, a "bone-breaking" moment of "loveliness" which seems to transfer all sordidness and shabbiness into a "divinely crystallized" conception of self-release in which he embraces "all that was within the street and partaking of all that happened there in time gone by, and now, and time to come" (257). The irony of this moment of great selflessness is that it occurs during his utter and completely selfish act of abandoning his own family and thrusting them into the streets of a foreign city. But as Cass discloses, the fantasia of the "moment" of rapture is a "fraud" (267). His euphoria is chemically induced, and he is in "real danger" at the time, as a woman friend of his exclaims when she sees him later on the streets. The woman is a "whore," as Cass describes her, but "she was a nice friendly girl" he has had a night with after an argument with Poppy. Cass tumbles deeper into despair after the meeting because she brings back to him the guilt of his night with her: "the sour sheets and the whorish counterfeit lust and myself slobbering and humping away while Poppy lay home weeping" (270).

After wandering Paris streets, he returns to his apartment, "safely back in the womb" (STH 272) only to plan the murder of his family by gassing them in their sleep and by finishing them off with a claw hammer he takes to bed with him. When he awakens, Poppy is there, sleepily berating him for his long hair, but betraying no sense of bitterness. "I hope you feel better today, darling. You certainly were cranky yesterday. I do hope you feel better" (277). Thus does Poppy enter American literature as perhaps the most understanding and forgiving wife in recent memory. Cass does not kill his family, but as Poppy "jabbers" on, he declares that they might have to move "on down south" to Italy in order to recapture the "divine spirit" that has eluded him.

The challenge in evaluating Cass's portrait of his wife Poppy is his revisionist history as he tells and retells the details Peter so wants to hear. In dialogic terms, Cass recapitulates or "engenders" himself—that is, he reveals *and* discovers himself—as he adjusts his discourse; Poppy's *voicing* in the novelistic discourse challenges Cass with her sheer ubiquity, which he becomes more and more aware of as he re-presents events and other voices in his evolving polyphonic view of the events leading up to Sambuco and after. At the time of his deplorable behavior toward Poppy, he is anything but understanding of her problems as she rears four children in poverty in foreign lands and without assistance from him. His self-destructive drunken behavior leads him twice to contemplate the mass murder of his little family, in spite of the total support his "childlike" wife heaps upon him—even after his dramatic throwing of them into the streets. Another complication is his revelation of his rapture in which he achieves a kind of phony release—akin to Mason's ersatz "orgiastic purgation"—but which is not connected in any direct way with the life he supposedly shares with Poppy and the children. His "moment" is qualified by its context, a context he labors to build for Peter's, and more importantly for his own, edification.

Cass continually assures Peter that he has learned the error of his drunken self-destructive ways and no longer abuses but rather much more fully appreciates Poppy. For all that both he and Peter continue to refer to her as a "child" and "childlike" throughout the narrative. "She was like a pretty child" (STH 285) who has a "rosy little face" (284); in fact, Peter's first description of her is as a "girl" standing by the side of the road, "her thumb out, hooking for a ride" (37). Peter describes her further, "Hardly larger than her little children, and so resembling all three that she seemed like their big sister" (38). Cass criticizes her teaching of the children even as he praises her: "Had it not been Poppy who had brought them presents, who had cared for them and watched over them, who in her *aimless and scatterwitted fashion* had nonetheless taught them everything they had ever known. . . ." (289; italics mine). Admittedly, when he looks back and comments, he confesses the error of his ways and his abdication of parental responsibility in his quest for his "divine spirit." But after the terrors of the children's scare with scarlet fever, when he writes about his wife's body as she swims in the Mediterranean, she is still described in diminutive terms that underrate her courage and tenacity in the face of his own dark personality. "Poppy, wet, brown, slippery-looking in a polka-dotted Bikini the size of an eye-patch, would call from the foaming shore: 'There's Daddy! Cass, come in and take a swim!'" (291).

In a journal entry that recounts the family's near tragic illnesses on their journey south, Cass summarizes a discussion he has with Poppy about the children's quick recovery and in the process he comments upon his marriage. He refers to Poppy as "the wicked little nymph," returning to a rumination he had in Paris about her ability to seduce him into procreating and forcing upon him the role of a pater familias, a role he does not handle adroitly. By blaming Poppy's effect on him—a variation on Celia's "mad" passion and love for Mason—for his woes, Cass repeatedly falls into the trap of assigning someone else the responsibility for his adult life. Cass's account of Poppy's serene faith that her children would survive is one of admiration and perhaps even jealousy for that serenity, and thus Cass concludes his relationship with her is "all harmonious dis-harmony." He "blows his top" when she affirms that she was never as worried as he was about the outcome of the children's illness: "why I had FAITH, that's all, silly" (STH 294). With that, Cass launches into a tirade on the actual cause for the children's recovery: penicillin and seventy-five thousand francs worth of medical care, but Poppy will have none of it; she merely yawns and calls Cass "an intellectual bully which is about the only polysyllabic phrase she knows" (295). The interchange is worth remarking, for it exemplifies the difficulty inherent in Cass's assessment of his own marriage and therefore the reader's ability to gauge what at times appears to be an abusive relationship. The journal entry is from about eleven months before the disaster at Sambuco, but even then Cass is able to draw some conclusions about his relationship with Poppy: "What can you do. She gives & loves & I take & thats that" (295).

During the Holy week of 1955 in Rome, where the family settles for seven months, Poppy is in an intense stage of religious activity which "reached a kind of peak of fervor" on Holy Thursday as she dashes off to the Stations; while there she picks up an American couple who come back to the apartment for a meal. Cass argues with the couple about religion, gambles with them, and eventually throws them out in a blind drunken rage that leads him into the arms of yet another prostitute who steals everything he has except his spectacles. In this "dark night of the soul," he dreams of a girl whose voice is filled "with liquid syllables, remote, importunate, and ripe with the promise of love," only to be carried away before he can find the girl, who remains a mysterious disembodied voice (STH 311). He awakens screaming that God does not exist and that "He is dead!" Poppy, the devout believer, comes to save him from his latest debauchery, of course. Cass makes up a fantastic lie about his being mugged by "Somaliland Negroes" which she seems to believe; she has arrived to bring him back to the family, appropriately, on Good Friday. Later, the girl in the dream will appear to Cass in Sambuco in the young virginal form of Francesca Ricci.

Cass motor scooters to Sambuco three days later and embarks upon another drunken binge after his months of sobriety in Rome. Desperate and driven on by his great "thirst" for insight and "the wretched grape," Cass winds up in the local jail and is explaining himself to the magistrate as Francesca is brought in for stealing. She is eighteen, barefoot, and wears moth-eaten clothes, but even n her shrieking self-defense Cass can see only "how extraordinarily beautiful" she is. Cass immediately wants to "clean her up, make her happy, and press upon her lips a full and passionate kiss" (STH 326). He aches "to make sure that the rest of her body measured up to her legs which were perfectly formed though like her face smeared with reddish dirt." The local police sergeant insults her and calls her a slut; predictably, Cass becomes enraged, pays her fine, and barely escapes further consequences himself, but he has made a decision to move his family to Sambuco and to the spring air of the cliffs overlooking the sea—and his Dream Girl.

In their final scene before Sambuco, Cass and Poppy argue over his proposed move to Sambuco; she is more than a little weary of his roaming, but she is resigned to his actions. The scene also reveals how absolutely dependent upon Poppy's money he and the children have been. Her four-hundred-dollar trust fund check has arrived month after month and provided him with the freedom to live his artist's bohemian existence and to indulge his various fantasies of seeking the "divine spirit." But her inattention to a string of urgent letters demanding her decision concerning a real estate deal back in the states results in a cancellation of their monthly windfall, and Cass is beside himself in rage. It goes without saying that his own inattention to the details of his household is not criticized, so Poppy receives his barrage of fury as he insults and degrades her intelligence. "Why by damn, Poppy, you haven't got the brains God gave to a mushmelon!" (STH 335). He also calls her a "living, breathing, walking prefrontal lobotomy." He then suggests that they can pawn her wedding ring for the cash to get to Sambuco, but this is an indignation she will not suffer. "Go take a shit in your bleeding hat, you filthy misbegotten prick!" she tells him. In feminist dialogic terms, Poppy here is nothing if not a resisting reader within Cass's text. As such, she is what Dale Marie Bauer refers to as a Bakhtinian "fool" whose naïveté enables her to question the assumptions of the patriarchy (Bauer 1988, 11). The case for Poppy is, however, complicated by her strong Catholic faith from which she extracts her unshakable belief in a benevolent patriarch of patriarchs. As Poppy assimilates Cass's language, as she has with "prick," she appears to accommodate his ideology and yet confronts him with her own emerging self. Poppy can be seen, then, as a resisting reader inside Cass's narrative, of whom he is constantly aware as he talks with Peter in the frame narrative. Poppy articulates her own ideology—faith—as she takes on aspects of Cass's language. Indeed, he is at first paralyzed by her language, and for a moment he is "crushed": "He tried to touch

her shoulder, trying to get close to the mystery of her decency an
her sweetness, but she shrugged him away" (336). But, typical o
Poppy's indefatigable spirit of reconciliation in the face of any ad
versity, the next day she is chirpy and ready for the new adventur
south. "Oh, Cass, it's going to be dreamy!" she says.

So it is that Cass takes his children and his child-wife to Sam
buco, but the revelation of the line Poppy will not cross, the pawn
ing of her wedding ring, is an instructive comment on the languag
of disagreement that Cass and Poppy employ. Up to this point i
their nine-year-old marriage Poppy has clearly never used profan
ity; when she does, Cass asks her where she learned such talk
"Where do you think I learned them from, you dumb bunny," sh
replies. As I noted briefly above, Poppy uses Cass's language i
this extreme moment because she has no language of confrontatio
of her own, and he is shocked perhaps more by being exposed t
his own vehemence than the words she speaks, for they are literall
not Poppy's words at all. In feminist dialogic terms, she has assim
lated the language of the oppressor precisely because she has n
such vocabulary of her own as a Roman Catholic wife/mother
child-lover. We may surmise from his reaction that when he "fell"
for Poppy, it was for her innocence and vulnerability as well as fo
her vivacity of spirit; it is thus logical that Cass is faced with hi
own complicity in his wretched state, and so he is driven furthe
into an escape into booze and into the dream of an ethereal unio
with another "innocent": Francesca. Like Mason and Peter, Cas
cannot face the reality of his own involvement in the process o
his life; like the other two men, Cass is trying to escape from a
real relationship with a woman into a dream-state wherein he ma
be "free" from the demands of the consequences of his sexuality
his family. Similarly, neither Peter nor Mason are able to establis
meaningful relationships with women who are more than simpl
"willing" playful sex objects. Poppy may possess an excess o
selfless blind faith, but Cass's excessive selfishness and narcissisn
contribute to his horrific experiences in Sambuco every bit a
much as Mason's sadistic prodding.

What may be termed the climax of the novel, more of a "how
Cass did it" than the "whodunit" of an actual murder mystery
unfolds along the cliffs of Sambuco, and Cass himself, through hi
transcriber, Peter, adds to the portrayal of the women present a
he interprets their voices. Chiefly, we hear Mason's last mistress
Rosemarie, and the details of the violence against Francesca. Othe
women in the Sambuco setting include the shallow movie-star fe
males, Poppy again, and the peasant women that cause Cass dis

comfort as he tries to escape from the realities of human existence in his alcoholic haze. The sight of the burdened peasant women "in rags, ageless, their skin stained the color of walnut . . . carrying on their backs loads of brush and fagots which would have burdened down a strong man or a small mule" (STH 341) send Cass into a reverie that "distresses" and eventually haunts him.

In a dream, Cass conflates an image of a dog crushed by a bus accident into an image of a woman similarly crushed and pleading to be killed so that her pain might end: "the head of a woman, this scrawny peasant woman with the fagots. Somehow she had turned into the dog" (STH 357–58). She cries out to be released from her misery: "Liberatemi!" A man's voice answers her in Cass's dream. "I'm trying! I'm trying!" Cass identifies this as the voice of God, "who in His capricious error had created suffering mortal flesh which refused to die, even in its own extremity" (358). Cass explains to Luigi that God "is beating us, yet mercifully," but an explanation of his feelings eludes his own capacity, and once again Cass bolts for a haven which he finds in another desperate drunken romp through the hills surrounding Sambuco.

The image of a woman as bearing the weight of the fagots and Cass's merging of that image with that of the crushed but living dog crystallizes Styron's portrayal of the condition of women in the more "advanced" patriarchal society of the United States, as well as under the even more intensely exploitive practices of the patristic hierarchical structures of Italy. To intensify the plight of the poor peasant women of southern Italy who are regarded as little more than beasts of burden by even the thoughtful cynic policeman Luigi, Styron has Mason and Rosemarie arrive at the very moment that Cass is retelling his dream of the dog-woman to Luigi. Mason arrives in his huge maroon Cadillac with Rosemarie at his side: "the tall blonde called, sidling out of the car, 'tell him to bring the green hatbox fehst'" (STH 355). The terrible juxtaposition of the lives of the peasant women and this vision of American opulence proves too much for Cass.

Francesca is again brought before Cass while he is in this state; she wants to be his housekeeper because her sick father and desperately poor family need the tiny sum Cass can pay her. Cass recalls her from the jail episode, and he realizes that this "slim, full-breasted" innocent in oversize man's shoes may push him over "the bleeding edge" of his sanity (STH 361). But he cannot resist her, and he hires her just as he realizes Mason's growing attention toward her youth and beauty. The competition between the two men over this young woman begins as Mason initiates his usual reduction of the female into catagories of sexual attractiveness. "Now that looks like real tail," he tells Cass. Indeed, Cass himself has just been told by Francesca that she will also pose for him if he needs her: "I know you are an artist, signore. I could pose for you well, and do anything—" (390). He initially refuses her services as a "prop," but eventually she does pose.

While Cass is feeling his gorge rise at Mason's male badinage, he himself has been indulging in keen observations of Rosemarie's anatomy; both men define each of the women in terms of sexual accessibility and attractiveness. Cass tells Peter that Rosemarie is "a great blond undulating hunk of sex, that wonderful Rolls-Royce of a humping machine" who "bubbles" when she speaks to him, although he concentrates on "those beautiful knockers" of hers (STH 381). In fact, Cass lapses into another paragraph of description as he relates her attributes. "All that flesh! That tremendous heaving wonderland of a groaning carnal paradise! To think that that great walking Beautyrest of a woman was all wasted on Mason. It's enough to break your heart, even now" (STH 382). Even after all the chaos and drunkenness and murder, Cass is still fascinated by Rosemarie's flesh. The duplicity of his own feelings is clear, if not to him: he is suddenly enraged by Mason's leering at Francesca, even though he himself has been engaged in the same sort of wool-gathering himself over Rosemarie. He feels he must protect Francesca from the corrupting American who has his own "humping machine." Cass does in fact launch into a tirade against the commercial patriarchy of America which he sees as the degradation of teachers and "men of mind and character" (397; italics mine); but of course Cass's ability to observe the inherent chauvinism in his own views eludes him and serve to remind the reader of the mixed contexts of Cass's era.

Cass will later claim that although he was sorely tempted to make love with Francesca, he never did. "I wanted to, God knows. So did she, I know. We would have, sooner or later, I know. But we never made love" (STH 439). He explains that it is not his wedding vows that stop him; he is "too far gone to worry about a thing like that." Cass postulates that "maybe it was her beauty— this sweetness and radiance she had which made me simply want to contemplate her . . . the thought of knowing her, *of possessing her, of loving her utterly and completely* became a kind of daydream which was all the more glorious because of the anticipation" (439; italics mine).

Here we have the crux of the matter: Cass finds in Francesca the innocence and purity of form and substance that he has felt bereft of for so long, and he needs to possess it—that is to say *possess her*—as a kind of rejuvenation of his own internal *musa*. But just as Celia had claimed she loved Mason "madly," Cass insists he felt a spiritual joy for Francesca. "I loved her *crazily,* it was that simple—the *bleeding beginning and end* of the matter" (STH 440; italics mine). When he posed her, she "wasn't in the least self-conscious . . . she'd settle down and grin a bit and then look gravely out to sea." He sketched and she "chattered" away until he had to stop and they walked away, "wrapped around each other, shaking with desire" which was never consummated. So Francesca remains for Cass the Dream Girl whom he can never live with; she becomes the apotheosis of women for him, a Madonna figure whose blessed innocence is sacrificed to Mason who is in turn sacrificed for the sins of "Man" against women in Cass's attempt to expiate his own guilt and complicity in the "Gweek"—the innkeeper Windgasser's term—tragedy at Sambuco.

In fact, Francesca is violated by three men on that terrible night. Cass violates her peasant life by giving her a vision of art and an impossible romantic love; he may indeed be the proximate cause of her rape because he advises her to steal from Mason which in turn gives Mason a pretext for using rape as a punishment. Saverio gropes after her in his dim, clumsy, but violent and therefore frightening way, and although he does not rape her, he beats her senseless, unaware a few hours later that he has killed her, according to Luigi. Mason's rape of Francesca, which is followed by his attempt at another, more "romantic" penetration—based, presumably on the wildly erroneous male assumption that women "want" to be raped, is not in the least one of his "orgiastic purgations"; it is merely the logical extension of his role as a powerful male: he defines Francesca's value to him as "tail," as a human reduced to an animal appendage, and rape as a *legitimate* rite of excercising his power over her. As the owner of the property she has pilfered—a few groceries for her starving family—he claims the rights of his maniacally androcentric worldview to mete out the punishment *he* deems necessary. He violates her basic human rights as he violates her body. But for Mason, Francesca deserves her fate because *she* has violated the hierarchical rules that demand she "hand over" her body for his use—and do it *willingly.* She is sacrificed to his notions, which were clearly influenced by his autocratic financier father, of the preeminence of male sensibilities.

Back in Charleston, two years after Francesca's rape, her subsequent murder by the half-wit Saverio, and Mason's own murder, Cass recalls the "delectable morning" that followed his "dark night of the soul." As young Stingo experienced a morning "excellent and fair" after Sophie and Nathan's suicide, Cass discloses how he finally returned to his wife after the murderous events; Poppy is without her sublime assurance this time. She confesses that she had been "worried frantic" at Cass's disappearance after the killings. Again he tells her "some sort of lie" and, again, she begins to yawn and lies back against her pillow and announces, "Well, as usual, I don't understand about you . . . but I'm very glad you've come back" (STH 500). The implication Cass seems to be drawing is that Poppy will never be able to comprehend the wretched state he was in. But Poppy had known about his attraction for Francesca and that it had carried serious implications for them all. It is important to note the implications of Poppy's apparent ease in accepting Cass back, in spite of her own suffering during the tumultuous events of the previous three or four days. The absence of her voicings on the matter does not, of course, mean that Poppy has indeed "accepted" Cass back *as before*.

The novel's primary perspective is that of males in crisis with their worlds, and not that of the women in their lives. It appears that Styron encourages the reader to accept these males as Poppy apparently does: not quite understanding, but placing their actions in a context which can explain aspects of their behavior if only in an oblique or reflected sense, as the readers are treated to Cass's nightmarish experiences through the medium of Peter's re-creation of Cass's eyewitness report. To Cass's credit, he does not claim any metaphysical insights beyond his assertion that he chose between being and nothingness only in "the hope of being what I could be for a time" (STH 501), which is a perhaps a rationalization reflecting his thoroughly modern frame of mind. As for his "sins," Cass refers to them with an equal sense of resignation that marked his story about the Negro cabin he wrecked with his racist boss when he was fifteen. "What I mean is that you live with it. You live with it even when you've put it out of your mind—or think you have—and maybe there's some penance or justice in that" (379). We may "accept" his hard-earned resignation as a rationalization, but put into a context of a patriarchal system of domination and subjection, Styron's main concern must surely be that even those males most concerned with the evils of domination and forced dependence are subject themselves to the assumptions of the patriarchal system regarding women and economically marginalized groups of people like the Italian peasants and the sharecropper blacks of North Carolina in the novel.

Although the story at the center of the novel is Cass's and, as

Gavin Cologne-Brooks writes (Cologne-Brooks 1987, 451), the novel is about Peter, I would argue that the overarching concern of the narrative's discourse inheres in the ways men define the women with whom they invest important psycho-sexual needs. Peter's shaky attempt throughout to define the events surrounding Sambuco and his own role in them are evidence of his belief in the "possibility of an ordered existence" (453), but neither he nor Cass and certainly not Mason seem acutely aware of the overwhelming way in which they take the women around them for granted or marginalize their experiences. On the other hand, Styron's presentation of his narrator-Peter has him emphasizing Poppy's importance in Cass's life overall. Francesca remains only part of a one-dimensional "midsummer dream" (STH 439) that, although he does not express it explicitly himself, Cass must realize is not the kind of life-giving harmony that Poppy can provide. Peter describes Poppy as being at Cass's side after each dark night of his soul, and as such she is "the true reason for Cass's salvation" (458). Poppy is a source of strength for Cass, ironically much smaller than the statuesque Rosemarie who can finally offer Mason nothing more than a face to slap and vent his frustrations upon. As it is, Styron even allows Poppy to pose a thoughtful question to the stridently anti-Catholic Cass. "Maybe if you had some of that religion you'd be happier" (STH 284). Poppy is the only one in the novel who consistently retains her faith in Cass; and although Cass does not become religious in Charleston, he does have another baby by Poppy, and he does cease his self-destructive drinking, events which reinforce Poppy's role as care-giver.

Another point of view sees the successful characters in the novel as learning the value of "transference," of the ability to empathize with the suffering of others. John Kenny Crane observes just such a tendency in Alonzo Cripps, the movie director in Sambuco (Crane 1984, 111). It is he who sympathizes with Peter about the Luciano de Lieto accident; and it may be that it is also Poppy who first learns of the accident from Peter, but she carries transference one step further by taking the poor Italian's view, a position that Peter cannot stomach in his own sea of self-pity. Mason, of course, has no regard for the feelings or even the suffering of others and ignores not only Peter's stories but even excludes the input of Rosemarie and the worldly Cripps.

Perhaps we may see Poppy and Mason as opposite poles on a spectrum of empathy, but this ability to transfer oneself into the world and emotions of another demands that solitary, predatory natures become less so; thus it is in the spirit of Bakhtinian carnival that Styron's novel includes an interplay of voices that help break down monologic, patriarchal views of female characters. Francesca may be sacrificed, yet another victim of gynicide, as Dale Marie Bauer concludes of other women in American fiction, but her voice's violent end does not conclude our awareness of her importance in the text of the novel or the intertextuality of her society at large. The sheer drama in Francesca's memory of her fatal attack is, of course, supplied later by a male interlocuter, but its intensity offers a harrowing scene and reveals the kind of horror she endures at the hands of her attacker who epitomizes patriarchy itself: "she heard herself shrieking, unaware now that this was Saverio, or anyone, aware of nothing save that the whole earth's *stiff, protuberant and insatiate masculinity* had descended upon her in the space of one summer night" (STH 477; italics mine).

The passing of time has brought about a gradual change in the critical reading of Styron's novel that signals a growing shift toward an awareness of the importance of both women's voices and their silences. In Marc Ratner's 1972 study of Styron's novels, he writes that "Poppy is no help with her childlike faith, and Cass is intelligent enough to realize how inadequate her innocent belief would be for him" (Ratner 1972, 82). Behind Ratner's assertion is the contention that Poppy's faith—which he marginalizes by referring to it as "childlike," a ploy Peter and Cass also use to belittle her in the narrative—is not as significant as the spiritual angst Cass feels as a male artist seeking inspiration. I would argue, to the contrary, that Cass is more likely seeking a Dream Girl with whom he can escape from the world of "poopy" diapers and dirty dishes: diapers of *his* children and dishes with *his* dirt. Implicit in Ratner's critique of Poppy's faith is his dismissal of her true importance in Cass's struggle. After all, she is not holding Cass back from his quest for the "divine spirit" he believes he so desperately needs; she supports his struggle to the exclusion of her own desires. Finally, Ratner's study flatly *ignores* Cass's own mad delusions that he should murder his whole family and then commit suicide, an idea he has in Paris and again after he has murdered Mason. "I sat there, wondering if now at last wasn't the moment to take Poppy and the kids in a single swift hell of blood and butchery, and be done with it forever" (STH 490). It may better be asked or at least discussed why some male characters appear to desire not only suicide, which can in certain circumstances be seen as heroic, but also the murder of their families. How is Poppy's faith "inadequate" before this terrible male death wish, this recurrent motif of a male predilection for gynicide?

A more recent book-length study on the canon of Styron's works by Judith Ruderman argues that Poppy attributes the children's survival of scarlet fever to a miracle, "for she is a woman of tremendous faith," while Cass on the other hand, ironically, "thirsts for God [Cass's "divine spirit"] with a spiritual need so deep that no man-made potions can slake it" (Ruderman 1987, 59). In this reassessment, Ruderman points out the validity of Poppy's life-world and her experiences. And as for "childlike faith," Cass's blind groping south, always south, for some undetermined "inspiration" seems more "childlike" than Poppy's. Poppy may be a "disaster" as a housewife to the males in the novel, but none of the males who proffer such an opinion takes over the changing, feeding, washing, and shepherding of the four Kinsolving children. Just before he ponders mass-murder, Cass sees Poppy asleep: "she stirred, still asleep, and then buried her head in the pillow with one hand crumpled beneath her *like a child's*" (STH 489; italics mine). Cass may describe Poppy here at the close of the novel as a sleeping child, ignorant of the mayhem about her and in need of protection, but can his sudden mad desire to kill his whole family a moment later be seen as more attractive than her adult and fully responsible, grown-up concerns for her children's welfare? Cass is the willful, escapist child-man, if there needs to be such a label assigned at all.

The implicit insistence in such critiques as Ratner's gives tacit approval to the notion that childcare is somehow less valuable or fulfilling than more "artistic" endeavors, but the outcome of the novel suggests otherwise: is it a "good" thing for Cass to have bludgeoned Mason to death and escaped justice? Has all of Cass's self-inflicted, self-pitying, self-torture and two years of adultery, alcoholism, and even contemplated mass-murder all been worth it for Poppy and the children? Ruderman points out: "What one learns from Cass Kinsolving is that he, not Mason Flagg, has been his own worst enemy: 'Kinsolving pitted against Kinsolving, what a dreary battle!'" (Ruderman 58).

The novel's implicit critique of its male characters extends to Peter Leverett who has known all along that Mason could inflict harm upon women, and his denial extends to his conviction that Mason was not capable of rape. And so he keeps mostly quiet about Celia in New York and doesn't speak up when Mason strikes Rosemarie in Sambuco. It is not surprising, as Ruderman notes, that Mason reports that Wendy, his mother, likes Peter "precisely because he kept quiet about what he observed" (STH 62). And if Peter abets Mason in his rape of Francesca by keeping quiet when he knows what the scratches on Mason's face are all about, then he also aids Cass in his murder of Mason because Peter is the only one who sees the desperation in Cass and knows about the threatening note. In the end, we can see that Ruderman's analysis of Poppy is more inclusive and contextualizing than Ratner's. Although she is not the "stunning" and eventually courageous Celia who jettisons the sadistic Mason, Poppy is vindicated in the end. "Her sticking it out with Cass . . . appears foolish by any standards of reason or intellect; *but these are not Poppy's standards*" (Ruderman 1987, 68; italics mine). And if the novel says anything at all about the standards of male reason and intellect as exhibited in this discourse, it is that they are self-limited, cruel, almost devoid of human empathy and transference with regard to women.

"If Poppy is not voluptuous Francesca Ricci," writes Ruderman, "she is nonetheless Cass's wife, whom he loves, and her pregnancy [at the close of the novel] is both a sign of that love and hope for the future" (68). This hope is a long way from the cynical, insulting, reductionist view that Mason Flagg suggests to Peter in which women are portrayed as running "sewers" with vaginas; most troubling is Mason's prurient reference to the vagina as the "Garden of Eden" which he has decided he may violate at will (STH 169). As we have seen, Mason has learned to view women as property, "pieces," "cracks," "sluts," and "tail," all of which are procured much as he arranges for his American goodies from the PX in Naples. What we learn from Mason is the horror of domination and how a self-righteous patriarchal system can allow and even encourage men to trivialize other human beings into body parts for manipulation and domination. Even Marc Ratner agrees that we may see Styron's own role (and by extension those of his characters, especially the women) as that of an "artist in bonds in a false society" (Ratner 89). The falseness of such a society is evident in its promises for freedom and salvation for men only, as Mason's "orgiastic purgation" theory purports. John Kenny Crane accurately concludes that Styron is not, therefore, anti-American or' even anti–Italian, in *Set This House on Fire,* but that his work is "more *critical of the times* than of America" (Crane 1984, 113; italics mine).

Styron's portrayal of women as people duped and victimized by patriarchal ideologies inherent in pre-and post-World War II America and Italy, is chillingly clear. It is a woman who appears as the symbol of suffering in Cass's horrific dream in which God beats her, but "mercifully." Because Styron presents women as beasts of burden for the world, as the care-givers for the world's children, and as men's inspiration for beauty and art, women's voices appear in the novel to bear witness (and children, of course) and in effect direct the discourse of the narrative. In a feminist dialogic sense, readers must take up the text of *Set This House on Fire* and make sense of it, of its particular social, cultural, and historic events, and respond as participants in its carnival of voices. As Bauer writes: "Interpretation is an act that is always interanimated with other critical discourses and other ideologies, including those of sexual difference" (Bauer 1988, 15). In this way, it may be possible to see Poppy Shannon Kinsolving as the hero(-ine) of this male narrative, in spite of her role as a "deficient" housekeeper who leaves "poopy" diapers on an unswept floor; her resilience leaves Peter and Cass, finally, contemplating her as an adult human being and not as a child.

In a Bakhtinian sense, because the novel by the very force of its power to appropriate heteroglossia must re-present the voices of women realistically (even in the carnivalesque atmosphere of Sambuco), it cannot fail to reveal the underlying patriarchal suppositions active not only in the two American expatriate narrators, but also in the initially monolithic sententiousness of Luigi and therefore the Italian patriarchy. The egregious gynicide of Francesca in the novel serves to place the novel in the Gothic tradition, but it also points back to Bauer's point that women are "forced observers, coerced into passive roles because they are excluded by the conventions through which their voices might be heard" (163). Indeed, Luigi has to strain to hear Francesca's last gasps, and Saverio was, in his mind own mind, merely trying to quiet her down when he "accidentally" killed her—or, at least this is the gloss Luigi gives the events. We may see Francesca's gynicide as another ritualistic sacrificing of a female character whose fate has been engineered in some sense by the very man, Cass, who saw her as a Dream Girl. Cass's jealousy of Mason's easy manipulation of his several male status symbols (cars, position, money, and especially women) leads him to bring his Madonna into Mason's manic thrall. Mason reduces Francesca from a Madonna to a "piece," and eventually he dehumanizes her to a servant/woman slave "deserving" punishment/rape. In a very short span of time, Francesca embodies for various males the virgin, the Madonna, the tramp/slut/thief, and finally the silenced gynicidal victim, whose struggle and suffering is made intelligible by examining through feminist dialogics the "forms of women's oppression and silence" (165).

Styron preserves the male point of view in his narrative discourse of the novel; however, women's voices are behind the actual words that men report at the close in the remaining "letters" of the novel; women literally give meaning to the men's lives: Poppy will give birth again, Peter has met a woman and has mentioned her to Cass, and even hapless Luciano looks forward to being affianced. Indeed, the letter explaining the miraculous recovery of Luciano is written itself by a nun, so a female, ironically, has the final word in this male-centered text, although the resisting reader may not be predisposed to accept the account of the "good sister" without objecting to its obvious, inherent privileging of the patristic idea of the "miracle." Bakhtin's theory explains that, although women are silenced through gynicide and are "in fact made inarticulate, their voices still interanimate the male voices which remain the socially dominant ones" (Bauer 166). Carroll Smith-Rosenberg adds that "the dominant will never completely silence the words of the marginal and the less powerful, within as well as without class. Cacophony, although muted, will persist" and as such it will inform and inscribe the dominant structures of language in which it inheres (Smith-Rosenberg 1986, 36).

Although both the Italian and the American patriarchal communities may have failed Francesca and the other women who are brutalized, marginalized, or who are otherwise relegated to the limbo of psychogynicide, communities of readers employing feminist dialogics are able to reclaim these women's voices; "for it is a condition of every voice to depend on the dialogic situation" (Bauer 1988, 166). Even the individual, monologic voice is "a product of the social dialogue" and as such is a participant unwilling or not in discourse. In the narrative's discourse, Francesca's whispered explanations to Luigi about the true nature of her violation eventually free Cass from suspicion of murder and allow him to return, ostensibly, to a more meaningful existence with his wife and family. After he hears Francesca's words, Luigi is freed from his earlier conviction that peasants are "beasts" and that he himself was, like them, doomed to servitude. And Peter, when he finally learns the story of Mason's death, is freed from his need to confront Cass, although he never fully articulates an understanding of his own complicity in the tragedy. Finally, even though feminist dialogics allows us to perceive her material presence and importance in the discourse, Francesca is, nevertheless, a casualty, the kind of sacrifice who pays for the patriarchy's peace of mind in realistic fiction by men; as Elizabeth Ermarth writes, "the formal consensus [of the novel] contains her only at the cost of her life" (Ermarth 1983, 14).

4

Ye Shall All Bow Down to the Slaughter: The Women of *The Confessions of Nat Turner*

> Therefore will I number you to the sword, and ye shall all bow down to the slaughter, because when I called ye did not answer. . . .
>
> —*The Confessions of Nat Turner* (136)

THE barrage of critical debate that met the 1967 publication of *Nat Turner* has since abated and recently achieved a measure of clarity that transcends the concerns of those who have either praised the book for its deftly handled complexity or those who have bluntly dismissed the novel as a racist treatment of African-Americans and as an appropriation of their history. Yet critics have continued to ignore or to minimize the overwhelming importance of the female characters in the novel as well as the obvious examples of *gynicide* and *psychogynicide* in the narrative discourse. In fact, even some of those most sensitive to Styron's portrayal of the plight of women in the antebellum American South still prefer to regard the novel's main concern as that of *Man's* inhumanity to his fellow *Man* in the form of black slavery. By reapproaching the novel using assumptions based upon the work of Elizabeth Ermarth and Dale Marie Bauer's feminist dialogics, it is possible to examine the voices of the women in the novelistic discourse in a way that illuminates more closely and with greater sensitivity Nat's rebellion and its relationship to the patriarchal hierarchies and the discourse that empowers those hierarchical structures.

Particularly relevent to an historical novel such as *Nat Turner* is what Peter Hitchcock refers to as an important achievement in the work of M. M. Bakhtin: "he makes the utterance and 'utterance context' the focus of his translinguistics and thereby returns history to the center of analysis of linguistic systems" (Hitchcock 1993, 3). In this case, Styron's novel recognizes that women in Nat Turner's time were regarded as little more than chattel themselves, that they too were marginalized and their access to the language and patriarchal semantic authority severely curtailed. An approach to *Nat Turner* based on feminist dialogics examines the nature of the language the novel uses to portray women and the language women use themselves because "dialogisity is itself a measure of degrees of social struggle" (5).

John Kenny Crane argues that Nat Turner represents the "need of all humans to enslave other humans so that their own solitary expectations may be met in the face of Fortune's careless disregard of them" (Crane 1984, 57). Nat is seen here as a victim of history whose "forcing Fortune" lessens his own guilt over the killings he has unleashed in his insurrection. Like other men who separate themselves from their personal standards of right and goodness, Nat has to assure himself that he is correct and thus invents constructs that lend a "cosmic significance" to what is really "personal gratification" or at least a quest for this gratification (57). This suggests that Nat is ironically like the men who defended and enforced slavery and even like those who promulgated the Holocaust. "They heighten their solitariness and, by correlation, their division from *other men*" (57; italics mine). There is much to admire in Crane's point about the lack of transference or empathy as the "root of all evil" in the works of William Styron, but one is struck by the atavistic, even arcane use of "men" as a means of referring to all *people,* which is his true point, since in an earlier passage he had praised Styron's efforts to show how "all men and women" are enveloped historically "by their attempts to gain what they perceive to be their just desserts" (56). A Bakhtinian discussion of this analysis of a particular sign would comment on the way in which the sign's particular use is itself representative of social conflicts. As Peter Hitchcock comments, the "struggles over sign are not simply a reflection of the social, but as Bakhtin points out, they are a refraction—a mediation of social conflict at any one moment in history" (Hitchcock 1993, 5). Further, as signs mediate social conflicts and thereby provide access to the assumptions behind their use, such as the patriarchal systems that regard slaves as "animate chattel," readers are able to discern that "language is . . . a shared body of signs, but access to language and *semantic authority* are not created equally" (5; italics mine). Nat Turner's realization of this incongruity is a basis for his rebellion, but it also takes place because of Nat's own desperate determination to free and then enfranchise himself by violent means so that he may erase the patriarchy's *inscription* on him, actually in his own mind, as property. His determination is born out of his problematic existence both within and with*out* the worlds of black slaves and those facile managers of plantation domesticity, white women.

Robert K. Morris posed the question about the importance of women in the novel directly to Styron in an interview some twenty years ago: "Do you feel that if Nat Turner had 'found his woman' the slave revolt would not have taken place?" (Morris 1981, 40). Styron answered that Nat probably wasn't sophisticated enough to see the problem as other revolutionaries who "eschewed" women and sex; rather, Nat "unconsciously felt this would obstruct his own revolutionary impulse and idealism: that the cause had to be served by steadfast asceticism" (40). The trouble with Morris's question and the vague, evasive answer it provoked is that neither attend to the Nat in the text of the novel; if Nat is an "ascetic," he is one who is racked with tortured feelings about his "appetites." In the narrative discourse that is the novel, Styron presents Nat as a man whose very education, health, and even his early status as a "house nigger" are all the result of the attentions of women who themselves are chattel of greater or lesser degrees in the severely patriarchal system of the antebellum South.

As to the direct motivation for Nat's rebellion, Donald W. Markos postulated in 1974 that the sexual frustration Nat feels as a result of his inability, given his slave status, ever to "have" Margaret Whitehead is "the underlying source of motivation for Nat Turner's uprising. . . . Nat revolted to assert his manhood and his full dignity as a man" (Markos 1974, 53). Thus are women the alpha and the omega of Nat's journey from Turner's Mill to the executioner's gallows, but it has only been until recently that critics possessed the vocabulary and the awareness necessary to examine how women are not merely a backdrop against which the drama of the novel takes place. Indeed, women are the ones who give Nat his *voice*.

Women teach, inspire, and enrage Nat far beyond the male characters in the narrative; and, importantly, it is Nat's own desire to become a man who can, like the white members of the state patriarchy, "have" a woman, preferably a white woman in order to fulfill his fantasies. In this sense, Nat is not revolutionary with regard to women's roles in society: he wants the "freedom" to "own" his own woman. This ironic twist of the novel, that the slave wishes on one level to be able to have his own domestic "slave," that is to say a legal wife, is Styron's challenge to the reader. The Nat who understands all too well the debilitating aspects of enforced dependency and dehumanization as "animate chattel," a legal nicety that allowed the patriarchy to punish slaves on the grounds that they were in possession of "moral choice and spiritual volition" (NT 17), also says, "Lord, after this mission is done I will have to get me a wife" (281). Nat Turner is not a revolutionary in terms of women's rights; in fact, he tends to view women as objects of violent lust, a view that has been aided by his own sense of himself as property in the mercantilistic value system of a patriarchy which values his labor but not his humanity.

The fact that some critics have missed the point entirely about the central role that women play in the novel can be read in Laurence Shore's contention that "the murder of Margaret Whitehead is Nat's affirmation of his humanity; this act expresses his need to triumph over 'niggerness'" (Shore 1982, 98). How this can be so is amplified by Shore as he explains that, ironically, "this murder is also the point where Nat temporarily loses his humanity; he kills the person whom he loves" (98). Whether or not Nat Turner "loves" Margaret Whitehead is problematic at best, but surely to argue that Nat secures some measure of *humanity* by murdering her is fallacious. That Shore would argue the taking of a woman's life is somehow an essential step for Nat reveals a repugnant underlying assumption: that an act of violence against a woman is indeed a rite of passage by which a male or a male slave may enter into a fuller state of humanity. A more fruitful gloss on Nat's murder of Margaret may be that Nat needs, at this crucial juncture in the revolt, to reassert his authority over his troops, in particular over Will, who has himself been driven to acts of terrible violence against women and children by his enslavement. Victimizing others, albeit the more affluent, female victims of patriarchal systems, which surely is what the white women of the novel are, does not lead Nat to a fuller sense of "humanity," as Styron reveals in his narrative, however intuitively.

If Margaret's murder serves only as a means for Nat's attaining a kind of tentative "humanity" that is no more than a cruel copy of the power the white male patriarchy has over him, then Nat's rebellion is shallow indeed. Another critic suggests that Nat's pursuit and attack of Margaret is "a sexual encounter" because Margaret's arms are thrust "as if to welcome someone beloved and unseen" (Ratner 1972, 117). Just as the encounter is not the means by which Nat attains "humanity," it is surely not "sexual." Both of these critics seem unable to identify Margaret's murder as a murder of another human being. Ratner and Shore seem as caught p in Nat's masturbatory dream-visions of Margaret as he is. They o not see the eighteen-year-old woman as a human being, but as fantasy *vessel* for Nat's lust or as a means by which his may lose is "niggerness," his state of being mere property to the White 1an. In short, they see Margaret as Nat's psychological property; is as though his enslavement entitles him to abuse and violate a 'oman in order to prove he has the same physical power over a 'oman that a white man might have. In short, Nat is entitled to is gynicide.

In fact, Ratner's confusion over Margaret continues as he con- ludes that "Nat connects with *no man* really, except Margaret" 19; italics mine). Unless Ratner means to pun on the word "con- ect," since Nat does indeed "connect" with Margaret's head, the bsurdity of employing the generic "man" in this case serves to nderline how inappropriate are the conclusions behind such a tatement as Ratner's. Closer to the truth about the character Nat, s presented in Styron's novel, is that he actually empathizes or connects" with few people, and none of them are men, with the xception of Hark at the very close. If anything, Ratner's point of iew serves as a reminder of the validity of Elizabeth Ermarth's bservation about the troubling ubiquity and even apparent neces- ity of female "casualties" in realistic fiction written by males when e concludes, "If [Nat] loses his humanity in the course of that ebellion and destroys Margaret, he also regains through *her sacri- ce* his ability *to love as a man*" (119; italics mine). Ratner begs he question about what kind of man Nat becomes if he accom- lishes his transformation from slave to "man" by murdering an ighteen-year-old woman. Ratner, it seems to me, has missed a rucial point of the narrative: Nat has been so terribly dehuman- zed by slavery that he is forced into the situation of hating and hen, by the circumstances of the revolt, murdering the only oman he relates to in any meaningful, fulfilling way. Another orrific interpretation may be that Nat kills Margaret so that *no ne else* may have her, either. Evidence in the text suggests that Jat is threatened by Will who makes it clear that *he* will pursue Margaret—"Does you want her, preacher man, or she fo' me?" NT 335)—if Nat does not. In this sense, it becomes problematic vhether Nat chases Margaret to save her from Will's implied rape, o exhibit his bloodlust to his troops, *or* if Nat knows himself— ven in retrospect—that he *would* kill her when he caught her. It s nevertheless clear that Nat cannot have her and live as a white 1an, a "true man," in the society extant then, and in this sense is killing of Margaret *reinforces* the power of the patriarchy over him by forcing him into a situation where even as the *leader* of rebellion—a violent dialogic carnival—against that selfsame whit establishment that defines his worth, *he cannot have her.*

Although Donald Markos has suggested that Nat's motivatio for his rebellion is "sexual frustration," a more accurate explana tion may be found in Judith Ruderman's contention that "anothe motive for Nat's insurrection is sexual *repression*" (Ruderma 1987, 24; italics mine). As Ruderman states, Styron weave throughout the narrative the "motif of sublimated sexual urges a a primary component of the revolutionary impulse" (25). Instea of seeing Nat merely as an ascetic who "eschews" women an sex, as Styron contends in the interview cited above (Morris 40 Ruderman explores the repressed and therefore largely uncon scious aspects of Nat's narrative accounts of his sexual problems Gestures of pity from white women arouse in Nat almost "uncon trollable lust" which is "so inextricably bound" with Nat's "hatre of the kindly white and his view of sex as an act of dominatio and humiliation" (Ruderman 1987, 25). Because of his view of sex Nat allows himself only masturbatory outlet, except for his on very pleasing encounter with Willis, when they were both youn teenage men. Ruderman suggests, then, that Nat's murder of Mar garet may be in essence his revenge upon her for tempting him, minister and therefore a man of God set above the rest, with he young body, a body which he can never have as a white man coul in any case. Here we see the victim punishing another victim again but Ruderman goes further and suggests that by killing Margare Nat may be accomplishing his revenge upon Samuel Turner a well, "for both have tantalized him with dreams incapable of reali zation" (31).

How his religious beliefs further complicate Nat's attitudes to ward white women and sex can be seen in his rationalization—on of many—that he may masturbate weekly on Saturdays so long a that is the extent of his debauchery. After he has enjoyed mutua masturbation with Willis, he immediately baptizes the young ma and then himself, promising to sin no more. If he achieves suc excitement and physical pleasure with Willis, Nat reasons, how much more beguiling will sex with a woman be? Bernard Reit argues that Nat's fate is inseparably linked with the Bible, a chie instrument in the patriarchy's justification of its power over Afri cans, women, and other marginalized groups. But Nat's refashion ing of the Bible as a means by which he might eradicate hi oppressors and their "Godless white bitches" (Reitz 1987, 274) wh tempt him reveals his own repressed notions of sexuality as wel as his inability to see how, like his oppressors, he uses Christianity as "a tool for oppression" himself (478). In this, we see how "Styron makes us understand Nat not as someone standing apart but as an embodiment of his society and time. . . . Nat clearly reflects the notions and limits of the world he is part of" (479). Styron's Nat, in this sense, reveals in his repressed self, not an aberration, as Gray his first biographer would have us believe, but a man who identifies implicitly with contemporaneous views of women and religion. Ironically, the ideas of his Bible, which allow him to rationalize his role as an agent of vengeance for God, do not enable him to perceive how the Bible itself can be seen as a handbook for patriarchal exploitation. That Nat is not able to perceive this is at least partly the fault of the women who teach Nat how to read by using the Bible as their reading primer. For the most part, Miss Nell, Samuel Turner's wife, and Miss Louisa, their daughter, share in the promulgation of the patriarchy's defense of African slavery as well as the denial of basic political rights to women, regardless of race. It is important to reiterate a fact largely overlooked by critics: white women teach Nat Turner how to read, and thus they are the ones who literally *give him his words,* give him his Scripture—Nell actually gives Nat his own Bible—and in so doing engender in him the sensitivity which is so brutalized after he is sold from Turner's Mill (NT 126–27). Women also give Nat Turner the biblical cadences of his discourse. In fact, Miss Nell first teaches him the "great lines from Isaiah: *Therefore will I number you to the sword, and ye shall all bow down to the slaughter, because when I called ye did not answer*" (136; italics in original text). Women give him his *biblical* voice, ironically.

In the narrative, women are presented in Nat's confessions as a means by which he contextualizes his life. In terms of feminist dialogics, Nat is literally "engendering" himself as he relates the stories of the women who bore and raised him. Styron's Nat, then, becomes an intriguing example of what Bakhtin calls "ventriloquating" the voices that engender a narrator; Nat's discourse about his own engendering is not representative of Styron's own voice, of course. As Bauer points out, an author's style, "the author's choices and exclusions" articulate "the play of gendered voices" (Bauer 1988, 8). In this way, an author "transcribes" the language of the novel into a dialogic order, an order "which orchestrates the intentional theme of the author" (Bakhtin 1981, 299). In *Nat Turner,* one such theme is bound up, necessarily, in Nat's own problematic definition of himself as a black man with an interior voice of a white man, a voice engendered in him by his white women tutors.

Nat first describes his grandmother in part 2 of the novel, which is entitled "Old Times Past." Nat portrays her as a thirteen-year-old Coromantee girl from the Gold Coast of Africa, big with child from some anonymous black slave: "it is easy to see her as she squats beneath the live oak tree so many years ago, swelled up with child, panting in slow fright . . . a mouth full of filed teeth and raised tatoos like whorls of scattered birdshot on her cheeks, patterns blacker even than her tar-black skin" (NT 104). Nat has never seen his grandmother; she died almost immediately after giving birth to his mother, Lou-Ann, in 1782. His grandmother, named "Tig" by the Turners, had "been driven crazy by her baffling captivity"; so much so that when she is presented with her baby, she tries to "tear it to pieces" (105). It is precisely because his grandmother dies soon after the birth of her child that Nat's mother becomes a "house nigger" and thus Nat inherits the status of house servant, a position of relative ease when compared with the back-breaking labor of field or timber hands on even the Turner plantation. Nat laments that "nothing remains of 'Tig,' not the faintest trace" because the graveyard in which she was interred was plowed over as a yam field. Before the graveyard was desecrated, Nat used to "study" his grandmother's resting place, showing an irresistible interest even as a child in his origins: "there is a leftover savage part of me that feels very close to my grandmother," he confesses (106). Nat muses that it was strange "at age thirteen to ponder the last resting place of your own grandmother, dead at thirteen herself" (106).

Nat's mother, Lou-Ann, is brought up in the "big house" as a servant to the Turner family; she becomes a scullery maid and then a cook. Nat relates that she died when he was fifteen from "some kind of a tumor" when she was about thirty-three years old (in 1815); Nat himself appears to have been born on 1 October 1800; his father, also named Nathaniel, formerly the second most important butler-slave on the plantation, ran off to Philadelphia when Nat was very young, not because he wished to abandon his wife, but because, as Nat rather proudly relates, one of the Turner brothers slapped him across the face for being "impertinent" (NT 108). Nat's mother, whose voice narrates the story in "nigger English," as he calls it, tells of her sorrow: "ev'ytime I thinks of it my heart is near 'bout broke in two. Said he couldn' stand to be hit in de face by nobody. Not nobody! Oh yes, dat black man had pride, awright, warn't many black mens aroun' like him!" (109).

The most important scene that revolves around his mother chronicles her rape by the Irish overseer, McBride, which Nat as a young boy first overhears and then observes. Lou-Ann is warned that McBride is on a drunken binge, but she stubbornly refuses to escape and hide in the slave quarters: "dat man ain't no trouble. He gib me a bad time an' I smack him one wid dis yere kettle" (NT 117). Of course, McBride makes it clear that he *will* be trouble, and Nat listens from his safe haven beneath the house as the overseer threatens his mother with bodily harm if she does not submit to his "big greasy" (119). Nat scrambles into the kitchen and watches as McBride holds a broken bottle "like a dagger" at his mother's neck; Lou-Ann is beneath the large man as he fumbles with their clothes, dropping the bottle. "All at once a kind of shudder passes through my mother's body, and the moan is a different moan . . . and I do not know whether the sound I hear now is the merest whisper of a giggle." Nat sees his mother "embrace" McBride's waist with "her brown long legs" as the two of them are "now joined and moving in [the] same strange and brutal rhythm" Nat has observed in the slave quarters. At this, young Nat flies from the house out into a grove of trees, only to return awhile later to see McBride stamp off in a delighted stupor in which he dismisses the slaves from their labor for the day. In his haven under the house, Nat hears his mother's singing again, just as she had been before the rape: "I hear my mother's feet on the floor above, the broom whisking against the boards, her voice again, gentle, lonesome, unperturbed and serene as before" (121).

The scene, Nat's initial encounter with sexual intercourse, may explain, as Judith Ruderman claims, Nat's later repressed sexual feelings that link sex with violence, especially with regard to white women. Another troubling aspect of the scene is the way in which Nat, and therefore Styron, portrays Lou-Ann as "enjoying" at least some part of her rape by McBride; rape is, of course, an act of aggression and dominance, a physical assault, so how is it that Styron allows Nat to suggest that his mother "giggles" and "swiftly" embraces her attacker? The question is not addressed satisfactorily by James R. Huffman's arguments that Lou-Ann's reaction to her rape can be understood in terms of her limited "access to black men" or even because "she might as well submit since there is no way to avoid the rape" (Huffman 1986, 260). Huffman does argue, however, that the scene is still disturbing, and even if conditions may arise in which women may not only submit but actually respond sexually to rape, "the fact remains that Styron portrays black women only as sluts in the novel. There are no Miss Jane Pittmans or other strong, nonprostituted black women in the work, which seems at least an indirect distortion" (260). The critical question becomes, then, whose distortion is it? Clearly, given Nat's repressed urges that conjoin violence and sex, it is Nat whose memory chronotope portrays his mother as an iconic black woman whom he sees as a combination of confidence and wanton desire. The scene is also a suggestion that Nat has not progressed beyond the Oedipal stage; thus he desires his mother and romanticizes her rape as a sexual experience. But this perspective is not reserved for black women alone because Nat has white "mothers" as well. Styron has Nat view white women as lusty and wanton, even the virginal and unassuming Margaret Whitehead is described by Nat as being a "Godless white bitch" and a "wanton," reflecting his religious ascetic beliefs that sex is a degrading activity. It may well be that his mother's rape profoundly disillusions young Nat because he learns that white people are as sexual as black people. As Huffman explains, "Like parents, whom they substitute for, white people are not supposed to be sexual" (245).

The scene leaves Nat with a further problem, Huffman notes: Nat substitutes McBride for his own father figure and this creates a "great identity problem for Nat as Styron conceives him. Nat wants to believe he is white" (Huffman 1986, 246). Styron implicitly uses father figures or father substitutes and some aspects of the Oedipal phase to explain Nat's identity problems. Huffman concludes that the most crucial result of Styron's use of the Oedipal complex as it is presented in Nat "is one that may well affect both white and black people in the South: *the warped concept of women*" (246; italics mine). Huffman suggests that a parallel with Hamlet is useful; "Hamlet has two basic images of women; either they are totally chaste, or they are whores." Nat's religious views also contribute to his inner conception of women; because "bad" women are morally distasteful to him, Nat is aroused and excited by the "chaste image of white women" (247). It is this chaste image that Nat imagines he defiles in his masturbatory dreams about white women; and he also fantasizes that in each case he takes the white woman by force, as he had seen his mother taken. It is curious to note that Nat takes pains to mention pages after his mother's rape that McBride was later dismissed by Samuel Turner for his excesses with the slave population. "I'm fairly certain that the man, perhaps daunted by her basic unwillingness, never dared to approach her again" (NT 142). But this passage appears disingenuous, since McBride was not "daunted" at all by his first encounter with Lou-Ann; in fact, Nat describes the overseer as being very pleased with himself and uttering appreciative "God Blast!" ejaculations as he woozily lurches away from Lou-Ann's kitchen.

The other important women in Nat's life besides his mother, who dies when he is fifteen, include the Turner daughters and their mother Miss Nell who eventually teach Nat to read, his chief distinction among other blacks and indeed among quite a few whites throughout the novel. Miss Nell is described as "a patient, wispy creature who because of some private inner crisis had intensified her already fervid religious bent" to teach him the Prophets and the Psalms and the Book of Job (NT 136). Nat reflects on the generosity of this "white mother" of his often: "I breathed a silent word of gratitude to this gentle and motherly lady" who unbeknownst to herself has armed Nat with the rhetorical and intellectual weapons he would use effectively to plan and execute his rebellion against the duplicitous society of which she is an important member. But there is also a note of menace in some of Nat's ruminations about Miss Nell and her daughter Louisa as they catechizes him and drills him in the alphabet. Nat recalls them as "glossy-haired seraphs" with "soft tutorial murmurs"; yet he mentions that during the insurrection there are times when he "lingered on the memory of those sweet faces with a very special and *savage* intensity" (126; italics mine). Later, Miss Nell makes Nat the gift of a Bible with the admonition that he should "Heed this good book . . . happiness shall attend you wherever you go" (140). He receives it trembling with excitement, for he is in all probability the only "black boy in Virginia who possessed a book," especially *the* good book. In the bleaker moments of his life, Nat ponders this "gift" of literacy over and over; he wonders at times if the Turners' generosity is not more of a curse than a blessing for him.

Miss Louisa, the eldest of the Turner daughters leaves quite early in Nat's life and never returns, and so Nat is left in the hands of his "protectress, her Scripture-beset mother" (NT 143) who saves him from a terrible disease and tutors him. Miss Nell first conveys to him his "special standing" in the family when she personally nurses him through that dread illness by bringing him up to "an enormous bedstead with linen sheets" where he drinks water from "a tumbler held to my lips by soft white hands" (136). The same "pale hands" constantly reappear to cool his brow; Miss Nell's care for him also extends to her prayers that "poor little Nat" should not be allowed to die. In Nat's own words, he is "the household's spoiled child, a grinning elf" indulged by the family and pampered; later, he himself grows to look with contempt upon other blacks, and he even chases them away from the house with a "flourished broomstick" (137).

It is no wonder, then, that the Dream Girl inhabiting his weekly masturbation fantasies is a "nameless white girl" who has golden hair and whose lips he imagines half open with desire (NT 140). He has begun to feel the "pressures" of his "new manhood" but he is in an unusual position as a house servant in that he is almost totally ignorant of the "fleshly pleasures" other black boys enjoy with "the available and willing little black girls" (139). In any case, he is in a short time totally under the spell of the other Turner daughter, Miss Emmeline, a twenty-five-year-old woman who is rumored to have experienced an unhappy love affair. For Nat, she is an object of worship "with her lustrous rich auburn hair parted in the center and her dark intelligent eyes and the sweet gravity of her mouth which lent to her face such an air of noble calm." He considers her a "great beauty" (143), secretly watches her from his carpenter's shop while she works in her garden, and marvels at her "pure, proud, astonishing smooth-skinned beauty" (144). He claims that he learns later in life that such an infatuation for a beautiful white mistress is not uncommon for black boys; still, he views his adoration of her as "eerie, unique, and almost insupportable," as if he had been "afflicted at the roots of [his] soul by some divine sickness" (144). Throughout his adoration, Miss Emmeline seems "only faintly conscious" of his existence. After her tryst with her cousin Lewis, Nat's worshipful view of her will change.

In Nat's observation of Miss Emmeline's early morning rendezvous with her cousin, we see him again in his voyeur role, but this time his experience is almost totally aural. What shocks Nat is not her voice, but "the Lord's name in her mouth, uttered in a frenzy, the first time in my life I had heard blasphemy on a woman's tongue" (NT 146). After her calling out of Christ's name in the throes of sexual passion, Emmeline turns on her cousin and blames him for the encounter, although the narrative suggests that her contempt and bitterness is more a result of her own guilt feelings than her cousin's forcing her to a sexual act. She warns him that she will tell her father of his "ravishing" his own cousin if he touches her again or even speaks a single word to her. Lewis, in agitated tones, calls her his "darling Em" and claims that she consented to the act; she, however, is adamant, but her voice turns "raw" with despair: "Oh God, how I hate this place," she cries. "I would even go back to Maryland and become a whore again, and *allow the only man I ever loved to sell my body* on the streets of Baltimore," she continues (147; italics mine). Nat watches as she enters the dark shadows of the house and leaves her cousin to "slouch miserably into the night" (148). So affected is Nat by this event that his "entire vision of white women" is irrevocably altered; Emmeline's "glow of saintliness" dims and flickers out, and he replaces his Dream Girl with Emmeline: "whose bare white full round hips and belly responded wildly to all my lust and who, sobbing "mercy, mercy, mercy" against my ear, allowed me to partake of the wicked and godless yet unutterable joys of defilement" (148).

Nat's preoccupation with fantasies of defiling Em reveal him to be a very good student of the biblical messages imparted to him in his study: that women are the source of Man's damnation since the banishment from the Garden of Eden. Caught up in his severe, dichotomized images of the sacred and the profane, he reflects entirely on the patriarchal society in which he lives, although the paradox Styron presents us with is that Nat, a victim of white male Christian patriarchy, is himself held in sway by its power over his imagination. He so wants to be a white man, as Huffman points out, that he is blind to the inadequacies of the patriarchal version/ vision of female sexuality, and he falls prey to the division of women into either impossible divine being-images or "fleshly" whores. Emmeline herself falls prey to that particular distinction as she can see only one alternative to her terrible enforced celibacy at Turner Mill: she either stays and grasps at furtive, forbidden, almost incestual sex with her cousin or she returns to Baltimore for life as a "whore." In the antebellum South, there are no other alternatives for women of her class, thus she cries out in desperation that she hates not only her cousin, Turner Mill, and her life, but also God, and for Nat this is the ultimate blasphemy. What Nat fails to face up to in any meaningful way is his own "wicked" enjoyment of his carnal visions of Miss Emmeline; he chooses, like the good, albeit unconscious, consenting member of the patriarchal system that he is, to revile women for being less than the perfect images men have created for them in the first place. Nat blames Emmeline for being less than the Madonna figure he wishes her to be; in this, for all his vaunted sensitivity to the dehumanization of Africans at the hands of powerful whites, he is arguably as chauvinistic and sexist than his white masters. But his chauvinism is understandable for all that, given the society's emphasis on the power of white, wealthy, and wedded males.

The most important image of womanhood for Nat Turner, however, is that of Margaret Whitehead, whose very surname merges the purity of the image Nat draws of her throughout the narrative:

possessing, unlike Emmeline, her pure maidenhead as well as her fervent Christian beliefs in God's benevolence and charity, she is for Nat the apotheosis of women; indeed, Judith Ruderman goes so far as to describe Margaret as Nat's Beatrice who leads him up to Heaven in the final scene of the novel. The reader first encounters Margaret early in the narrative as the lawyer Thomas Gray, Nat's erstwhile confessor, rereads Nat's testimony back to him concerning the only murder Nat committed. The description of Margaret's death at Nat's hands in this passage is brusque and even banal: "on my approach she fled but was soon overtaken, and after repeated blows with a sword I killed her by a blow on the head with a fence rail" (NT 29). Later in part 1, Nat recalls how Margaret recited poems to him as they drove along the countryside in a wagon, and even in this early passage, Nat suggests in Margaret a kind of sexy wantonness that after close examination appears more a projection of Nat's own desires than a true indication of Margaret's behavior. He describes her as having "fine white skin, milky, transparent," images that suggest a kind of ethereal apparition rather than a flesh-and-blood woman (72). He characterizes her as having a "nose uplifted" and "the shadow of a saucy dimple in a round young chin." Her hair, in his reverie, has become loosened in her bonnet, "which all unconsciously lends to her demure and virginal beauty the faintest touch of wantonness" (72), an attribute which is itself all-important to Nat—as it is to other patriarchal males who desire to own the "innocence" of a young girl but who crave a "touch of wantonness," for the female must want to be "taken" by her man for the fantasy to be complete.

During the ride to the church where Margaret's brother will preach an obligatory sermon on the necessity for slaves to live in abject subjugation to their white masters, Nat is suddenly seized by an intense feeling for Margaret: "a bitter, reasonless hatred for this innocent and sweet and quivering young girl" (NT 74–75). He explains that he was baffled by his angry turmoil over "this gentle creature" since she is perhaps "the only white person" with whom he has experienced "even one moment of a warm and mysterious and mutual confluence of sympathy" (75). In his rage and confusion, Nat begins to plan out in more detail his rebellion, all the while conscious of his hatred of his own people; searching out Margaret in the church crowd later, he sees her caroling with her mother, "a radiance like daybreak on her serene young face" (84). It is at this moment, after gazing down on Margaret from the black section of the church, that Nat experiences a "wild, desperate love" for his fellow blacks. Margaret has somehow catalyzed his abrupt turnabout, but Nat does not dwell on it in the narrative.

On the ride back to the Whiteheads that afternoon, Nat overhears a conversation between Margaret and her mother that is particularly edifying to the reader, although Nat comments on it not at all. The topic is Richard Whitehead's sermon on the "natural" enslavement of Africans and the promise of total freedom in the next world as reward for loyalty and good service to the white masters of this world. Mrs. Whitehead holds that her son's sermon was "inspiring," but young "Miss Peg" says that the sermon is the "same old folderol for the darkies" (NT 85). Mrs. Whitehead is shocked, and calls on the name of Margaret's "sainted father" to shame the young woman out of her blasphemous opinions—an opinion that challenges the very root of the white establishment's biblical "justification" for African slavery. In dialogic terms, Nat is witnessing a "battle of languages," competing voices which articulate the structural hierarchies that make up his society—hierarchies based on gender, class, and power (Bauer 8). To Nat's surprise, Margaret's emotions overcome her at this point, and she sobs to her mother: "I just don't know. I just don't know." Mrs. Whitehead draws her daughter into her arms and comforts her by saying, "It must be a bad time of the month," and soon they will be home for a nice cup of tea to settle Margaret's apparent "hysteria" (NT 85). Styron effectively draws attention to Margaret's growing and troubled awareness of the wrenching contradictions the Protestant sermons of the era forced upon believers in the service of an all-out defense of the "special" institution of African slavery in the American South. A key aspect of the defense rendered by Mrs. Whitehead is that it calls upon the image of Margaret's deceased father as a "saint" who would scold her for her heretical comment on the transparency of Richard Whitehead's sermon; thus is the actual patriarch of the family brought into a discussion that assumes the justness of the patriarchal system of slavery itself.

In her response, Mrs. Whitehead attributes Margaret's growing awareness to a confusion brought on by the onset of her menstrual cycle, thereby giving voice to the myth of a woman's "hysterical" inability to "reason" during her monthly period. By assuming in his reader an awareness of the poverty of an assertion that Miss Peg is incapacitated by her period—that is, that his reader has a more modern perspective about women's reasoning abilities, especially in regard to patriarchal assumptions about the menstrual cycle—Styron evokes in this brief scene a wealth of qualifying, contextual perspectives. People like Mrs. Whitehead fervently believe in the inferiority not only of black slaves to white males, but also of the inferiority of white women to white males. Thus the system is able to perpetuate, with the help of moral instruction from women like Mrs. Whitehead, the myth of black inferiority as well as the myth of female inferiority by means of social censure and religious indoctrination. Styron here parallels the two classes of marginalized people in the Whitehead's wagon: Nat who wishes with all his soul to be white and Mrs. Whitehead who is a "consenting" member of the patriarchal system of reinforcement, keeping Miss Peg's "harmful" ideas in check by means of socially approved and therefore "moral" devices of opprobrium and marginalization that lead, ultimately, to a dismissal of Margaret's well-intentioned but only half-formed questions about the social injustices in her society.

Between the sections of the novel in which Nat relates his experiences with the Whitehead family, a scene occurs that is unsettling in its intensity but revealing in its compelling indictment of the antebellum South and the human toll of its "special institution" of African slavery. An elegantly dressed white woman from the North, from New Haven as Nat relates, appears on the streets of Jerusalem. Nat describes her as "an extremely beautiful woman of about forty, stately and slender" (NT 210); richly dressed and evidently an heiress, she is also rumored to be the fiancée of a notable local man who is himself one of the wealthiest landowners in Southampton. She encounters Arnold, whom Nat refers to as a "grizzle-polled old simpleton black," and although hers is a "voice clear, resonant, quite gracious and polite, in rapid yet pleasantly warm Northern tones," she is frustrated in her attempts to find her way or understand the "gabble" of Arnold's African accent. She suddenly bursts into tears and is shaken by "loud racking sobs." Nat explains that it "was as if something long pent up within her had been loosed in a torrent" (213). Nat himself is seized with "hot convulsive emotion" over what he perceives to be pity, "pity wrenched from the very depths of her soul"; the sight of that furious pity for the plight of all the Arnolds, all the Africans, that has so reduced this proud, stately woman from the North, causes in Nat "an irresistible flooding moment of desire" (213). This desire arises from his perception that the woman has divested herself of all composure, "exposing a naked feeling" in a way Nat has never seen in a white woman before. Nat appears to have forgotten his encounter with Miss Emmeline and her cousin Lewis when he was sixteen, although here he is referring to a public display before an attentive group of slaves. Nat confesses: "I felt myself burning for her. Burning!" (214).

Immediately, he has another rape fantasy in which he sees himself tearing at the woman's silk dress and exposing her "zone of fleecy brown hair" into which he longs to drive his "black self with stiff merciless thrusts." He admits that the "vision would not be mastered" or leave him alone this time. The woman continues to weep, and as she does Nat continues his fantasy of mounting her on the dust of the road, not for pleasure, "but only the swift and violent immediacy of a pain" of which he is the "complete overseer" (NT 214). The term "overseer" returns the reader and Nat to his mother's rape at the hands of McBride and reinforces Huffman's point that Nat's Oedipal fantasy is operative here: he has *become* the overseer who raped his mother, the man who had replaced his father as his father-figure. Nat longs for the kind of control he knows white men exert over slave women and he imagines over white women; he longs to be himself a patriarch. The slave wants to possess what the white master has; this possession of a woman will make him a man, or so Nat's desperate unconscious desires appear to suggest. He envisions the woman, once proud and white but brought low to the road in his reverie, crying out "in the wildest anguish" while he ejaculates "within her in warm outrageous spurts of defilement" (214). Just as suddenly, the woman ceases her sobbing, regains her dropped parasol, and in "a quick furious motion" shakes her head, "her pale and beautiful face tear-streaked yet no longer haggard with pity but quite proud . . . and angry." She then strides briskly down the street, "erect and proud" in the "resplendent silk of her dress."

Nat's "hot vision" dissolves almost immediately, and he later learns that the woman has left the town never to return. He searches his Bible for a "key" to the powerful emotions he feels about this woman from the North. "But the Bible offered me no answer" (NT 215). He does attempt to explain that the most troubling aspect of his encounter with the woman: that he feels his murderous hatred not as a result of a white person's cruelty, but after a moment of *charity,* vulnerability, and genuine pity. Nat evinces no perception of his desire to switch roles with the rapist overseer; nor does he seem aware of why he is particularly disturbed by a woman's pity. As a black man who desperately wants to enjoy a white man's sense of power and to identity through the control of others, his rage is aroused when he begins to perceive that his true station is below even that of a white man's woman. As a product of the patriarchal system in which he lives—and would like to join as a full member—he shares patriarchal views that women are the inferiors of men and are therefore prone to the kinds of sobbing outbursts he witnessed in this proud woman from the North. In Nat's by now seriously troubled mind, he sees the "pity" of a woman and her public show of emotion as outrageous insults directed at him and calling for some action on his part, but it is only in his rape fantasy that he can punish her for her folly of pitying and therefore insulting his manhood. It may not be too much of an exaggeration to suggest that vengeance against women is an important *motivating* factor for Nat's rebellion; such a motivation may explain, as Styron suggests, why the historical Nat killed but one person in the insurrection: a young white woman. For the Nat of the novel, however, Styron creates a context in which Nat's repressed sexual feelings are a basic component of his mysticism and his subsequent mission.

Nat Turner first encounters Margaret Whitehead when she is but thirteen or so—the same age at which his slave grandmother arrived at Turner's Mill, gave birth to his mother, and quickly died. His first reaction to the "young missy" is that she was "unsurprised" at his appearance at her door, "as if my skin had been alabaster-white," Nat relates (NT 256). Nat then also meets her brother who is an arch-defender of the patriarchical perogatives over slaves and women; in fact, Richard Whitehead recites the familiar circular argument against the very idea of a "darky minister"—that Nat has no degree in divinity—as "proof" for the inferiority of slaves. The same kind of argument directed against women, that they were not intellectually or, more importantly for patriarchal apologists, emotionally equipped to attain a college degree, had been eloquently rebutted as early as the 1790s by Mary Wollstonecraft. Nevertheless, because they were heavily invested, both psychologically and financially, in the belief of the inferiority of certain races of men and women of *all* races, patriarchs like Richard Whitehead reacted violently to arguments that suggested otherwise. Miss Peg, on the other hand, is described by Nat as being sympathetic even as a child, although it may be a bit of a strain to believe that such an enlightened young girl grows up in Richard Whitehead's home.

In dialogic terms, Miss Peg functions as a "fool" who naively questions the hierarchical structures of her patristic society and thereby opens the discourse to dialogic forces. The importance of such a character in the novel is explained by Bakhtin: "the very aspect of *not grasping* the conventions of society . . . not understanding lofty pathos—charged labels, things and events—such incomprehension remains almost everywhere an essential ingredient of prose style" (Bakhtin 1981, 402). On the other hand, Nat describes Mrs. Whitehead, the widowed head of the household as "an austere woman, very cool and withdrawn," but he adds that she is "completely fair and honest, and brooked no mistreatment of her Negroes" whom she regards in terms of their usefulness and ability (NT 260). Mrs. Whitehead clearly functions as a woman whose position of authority demands her strict adherence to the tenets of the slave capitalism of her culture; she is *not* a dialogic "fool" or naif. She is the very epitome of woman circumscribed by patriarchal power structures, but nonetheless a quasi-consenting ardent supporter of its strictures, *especially* with regard to Miss Peg's instruction. Mrs. Whitehead's voice, therefore, is like that of Helen Loftis who has also taken on the role of female supporter of the patriarchy in memory of her father. Mrs. Whitehead is also dedicated to the memory of a dead patriarch, her husband, whose ghost looms over her consciousness when Margaret naively challenges the slave system.

Later, after Nat has determined to kill women, children, and men in his uprising, he discloses that toward Mrs. Whitehead he bore no "ill will" (NT 265); he admits that she has been "ingratiating, even queerly tender . . . benevolent, in a roundabout way *downright maternal*" (265; italics mine). But she has never seen him as much more than a profitable piece of property, like "some miraculous wheelbarrow"; and for this, he condemns her with the rest. "Truly, that white flesh will soon be dead" (265). In light of Nat's encounter with the Northern Woman, however, we may observe that part of his vehemence toward Mrs. Whitehead is surely involved with his capacity for violent rape fantasies when he is in the presence of a woman with "power." In contrast, shortly after these thoughts, Nat draws up his "battle plan" and of the ten points he records in that plan, number eight stands out for this analysis: "Must sternly prevent violation of females. We shall not do to their women what they have done to ours. Also w'ld take up precious time" (267). This seemingly just if harsh text, a brief on behalf of power*less* and therefore more easily abused black women, is dramatically undercut by the last sentence concerning time; and given Nat's own violent rape fantasies, it appears as no more than an exercise in the denial of the cruelty he will unleash very soon. As Nat had been reduced to property and brutalized, he now reduces white people, especially white women with power whom he perceives as mere "white flesh" which must be exterminated.

Three scenes punctuate the relationship between Nat and Margaret Whitehead. The first of these occurs in 1830 about a year and a half before the uprising; Nat has been hired out to Mrs. Whitehead again, and he encounters the seventeen-year-old Miss Peg in the library as he works on bookshelves. She enters, wearing only a corset and ankle-length pantalettes uncovered by a skirt: she is searching for a poem by Wordsworth and is quite unaware of the frenzied turmoil she causes in Nat. He assumes that she is unconcerned about her state of "undress" before him because he is a "Negro" and "therefore presumably unstirred by such a revealing sight" (NT 273). "She is nowhere near naked," Nat explains, but her white pants "make her seem wantonly unclothed," and he is filled with a sudden confusion and "hot panic." He is barely able to control his rage: "How could she with this thoughtlessness and innocence provoke me so? Godless white bitch" (274). Again blaming the innocent, he watches her "firm young flesh" which is "nearly visible in a pink nimbus behind teasing cotton," and after she leaves, his rage continuing, he disingenuously claims, "I cannot tell why my heart is pounding so nor why my *hatred* for Margaret is, if anything, deeper than my *hatred* for her mother" (275–76; italics mine). Like Mason Flagg, Styron's other inveterate woman-hater, Nat voices his furious revulsion of females in terms of their body parts and blames women for their power over him as renters/owners as well as their power to arouse him physically in spite of his desire for ascetic "purity." In this, Nat's own voice as Styron imagines it merely echoes the Judeo-Christian patriarchy's definition of woman as the source of "Man's" downfall. We hear in Nat the paradox of novel: the patristic monologic discourse arising from the consciousness of the oppressed, marginalized, dehumanized black slave who, for all he has endured—indeed, *because* of it, continues implicitly to desire patriarchal power for himself.

The scene concludes with Nat still "thinking of those ruffled white pantalettes" and unable to articulate an understanding of his obsessional response to the young woman's attractiveness. Because he has placed himself above others as an ascetic preacher, he cannot deal with his own natural urges in any way except to heap scorn and blame upon the young woman. It may be that Styron's Nat cannot achieve the distanced self-reflection needed to see the nature of his obsession with blaming women for his own urges and thereby accept responsibility for them. Nat is clearly repressing when he says that he "cannot tell why" his heart pounds with excitement when Miss Peg is near. He has experienced arousal and employed masturbatory fantasies since his early adolescence and by his own account these fantasies chiefly concern

oung white women he wants to "defile." It appears, rather, that
is his rage at Margaret's *charity* that baffles him. But again it is
ne rage he felt toward the Northern Woman: Miss Peg insults him
y seemingly ignoring his manhood by appearing in the library
wantonly unclothed." Again, his rage is directed at her because
he reminds him, innocently, that he is a man without power over
omen. By her behavior, this white virgin has emasculated him,
nd she must be punished. In this sense, Nat Turner's rebellion,
s depicted by Styron, may be seen as an effort to establish a Black
atriarchy, exactly the kind of situation whites in the South feared
efore and after the Civil War. Given the evidence of Nat's indoc-
rination into the Judeo-Christian patriarchy, however, Southern
vhite paranoia seems excessive: Nat's patriarchy would be based
irmly on the mores of European white hierarchical systems; his
ision of a community "up north" is a version of benvolent patri-
rchy of Samuel Turner.

The penultimate scene in which Nat meets Margaret precipitates
discussion between them that Nat believes is a result of her
artless" innocence: she asks Nat if he would strike a white master
ack as Will had. No Negro, explains Nat, should be forced to
inswer such a question, "and because it was asked in such a spirit
of sympathy and innocence" he resents Margaret for it, but he is
inable to refrain from "stealing a glance" at her skirt drawn "tight
icross her thighs" and the "saucy tilt" of her chin (NT 295). But
Miss Peg pursues the matter: "if I were a man and a darky and I
vas abused like that by that horrible old Nathaniel Francis, I'd
ust hit him right back" (296). After being lectured by her on what
he would do, Nat, curiously, does not fly into a rage as he has
lone previously; he sweats and frets at her closeness, worried that
ie will take her and ruin his plans for the insurrection. In fact, as
hey roll along in the wagon, he admits that Margaret now fills him
"with boredom and lust" simultaneously. He realizes that he could
"ravish" her in the remote country on which they travel, and later
is they go for a drink at a nearby stream off the road, he is seized
by the same rape fantasies that plagued him earlier. Her breast
bumps into his arm and immediately a "voice" advises him, "Without mercy take your pleasure upon her innocent round young body
intil she is half mad with fright and pain" (302). Alternating Nat's
inner turmoil with Margaret's light and breathless recitation of her
nasque of Celia and Philemon, Styron energizes the scene: Phi-
emon, a convert to Christianity "holds his sword up in front of
Celia like a cross" and pledges his love; the scene will later be
played out to its fatal conclusion by Nat and Miss Peg. The juxta-

position of Margaret's recital of her masque of romantic, chivalric love in which her heroine swoons into an "eternity of love" with Nat's desperate struggle not to give in to the temptations of the Voice urging him to rape emphasizes the emotional intensity surrounding Nat just before the insurrection begins. The scene also explores the maddening complexities of relations between black people and white people, especially those who are in some way attracted to one another. But the scene does end with a chill sense of foreboding as Nat records that they left the stream and "a cloud passed over the day, bringing shadows and a breeze which teased the loosened, wanton edges of her hair"; for an instant, he sees Margaret "frozen in an attitude of stiff, still death" (303).

Their final scene together, of course, takes place at the Whitehead residence as Nat kills Margaret, finally. She is the only person he kills, and the description of his pursuit of her is surprisingly abrupt, considering its import for both the narrative and Nat himself. Nat chases her through the field behind the house, catching her as she begins to mount a fence in her bid for escape from the marauding band of slaves. His sword in his right hand, Nat comes upon her from the rear; she makes no sound except for her desperate breathing; she does not even turn about to face him to plead or speak: "our last encounter may have been the quietest that ever was," Nat wryly notes (NT 335). He plunges his sword "into her side, just below and behind her breast," and finally she screams and "crumples" to the ground. He does not rape her; this is not a "sexual" scene. He stabs her again, but must hit her with a fence rail to kill her—much as he had dispatched the turtle they had found fatally injured on the road during their last ride together. After the murder, he circles her body aimlessly, in shock and grief; he thinks he hears her voice at one point and also sees her "rise from the blazing field with arms outstretched" and reciting the lines of her masque. "Oh, I would fain swoon into an eternity of love!" (337). But she vanishes before his eyes and melts "instantly like an image carved of air and light"; Nat turns and rejoins his men.

The last image Nat has of Margaret appears in the final section of the novel in which he has a masturbatory vision of her. Her voice is "close, familiar, real" and for a moment he mistakes the wind against his ear for her breath. In terms of feminist dialogics, Nat can be seen here as once again "engendering" himself as he imagines Margaret; once again, a woman brings him to a re-birth, his final baptismal. The vision of Margaret brings him back to a relationship with God as well as with her. Feeling that he is "beyond fear," he searches his mind for an image of her face and her young body, "yearning for her suddenly *with a rage* that racks" him (NT 344; italics mine). The "rage" he feels dissipates as he ejaculates and imagines that "she arches against me, cries out, and the twain—black and white—are one." The motif "Surely I come quickly" appears in this passage and suggests both the second coming of Christ and the approach of the executioner, even as it constitutes a "bit of grotesque humor" on the speed of Nat's ejaculation (Huffman 1986, 258). In a more serious vein, the vision presents the religious/sexual encounter Nat has imagined with Margaret, "the first fantasy of a white woman in the novel that is not an expansive, desecrating forcible rape" (257). But Styron is not merely suggesting that a mystical interracial sexual union will indeed "join the twain." Ironically, Nat's killing of Margaret has indeed made it impossible for her ever to fall from the psychological pedestal of innocent, though at times "wanton," purity upon which he has placed her. Miss Peg can never be anything less than an ideal image for Nat. Although it can be argued that Nat kills her partially out of vengeance and partially out of need to show his men that he could kill a white person, he cannot kill his image of her white goodness; and filled with remorse, he later allows another girl to escape, an act that in all probability dooms the insurrection to failure because she warns the countryside of the slaves' movements (256).

Using Karen Horney's theory of anxiety neurosis as a base, Huffman builds a case that William Styron was surely aware of the Freudian elements presented in his novel, but Styron is not limited to a traditional Freudian orientation toward concepts such as the death wish and the Oedipal complex. Huffman explains: "These elements emphasize the *white patriarchal domination of American culture,* and may have caused much of the reaction of black critics to the novel. But Styron's intuitive grasp of anxiety neurosis shows that he went well beyond the tenets of Freudian analysis and the biases of a white Southern man in portraying the characters of the novel" (Huffman 1986, 259; italics mine). Still, Huffman admits that Styron may have gone "too far" in his presentation of a "pure image" of Southern women and a too sexual image of black women. For all that, Styron counters his excesses with other "contrasting" representations of black and white people throughout the novel. Styron's "intuitive grasp" of human psychology in this light validates his vision for the literary Nat and for the world the character occupies. The portrayal of Nat as obsessed with white women and repelled by black women, although one of the more controversial elements of the narrative, is not necessarily Styron's alone. Black authors have themselves written about the obsession and have suggested that black males have been acculturated to prefer white women. In any case there is a larger issue concerning the fact that the United States is "basically a patriarchal culture," the values of which are promulgated essentially by white men who still have pervasive control (247). As a product and an aspirant of the patriarchy, Nat worships and simultaneously hates white women, women he cannot "get inside," just as he cannot enter the white temple in his dream visions. Nat can achieve no status in the white culture and therefore he cannot achieve the necessary wealth and position with which he might have his own white woman. His deep internal repression derives from his sexual traumas as well as from his obsession with whiteness; he does not wish to admit his obsession because such a true realization would bring down upon him, and not God's call, the full responsibility of his actions, that is, his own *complicity*. Huffman expands this notion.

> Like the governess in *The Turn of the Screw,* Nat knows subconsciously that if his religious interpretation of his life is not accurate, then he must be mad. He avoids considering that possibility at all costs. (248)

Nat dares not explore the mystery of his dream of the "stark white building" on a promontory and as a result views women through a maze of oppression and suppression complicated further by particularly onerous forms of internal repression. "I know that to try to explore the mystery would be only to throw open portals on even deeper mysteries, on and on everlastingly, into the remotest corridors of thought and time" (Huffman 1986, 340–41). There may be, however, a danger in Huffman's gloss of Nat inasmuch as it appears in sections to be a delicately phrased argument carefully designed to imply that the victim may be more culpable than has previously been considered.

In terms of feminist dialogics, we can see that Nat is subject to the same sort of "misreading" of his culture that women characters can fall victim to in the process of a novelistic discourse. According to Dale Marie Bauer, such misreadings of the patriarchal consensus can lead, at the very least, to a form of psychogynicide, or psychic death-in-life. For Bauer, American heroines misread social codes, assuming the role of the "fool" or naïf, and although they misunderstand the monologue of the patriarchy, they open up a dialogue in the text and within the reader's own interiorized textual dialogue. When young Miss Peg accurately criticizes her brother's "darky" sermons, she is lectured by her aghast mother who initiates a defense by reviving the dead patriarch' s projected voicing of disdain. But the force of novelization in this sense employs the heroine's "mistake" as a device for calling into question the societal structures. In precise Bakhtinian terms, each speaker/heroine is an *ideologue,* and each utterance can be seen as an *ideologeme;* in other words, every word or discourse reveals the ideology of a particular speaker (Bakhtin 1981, 429; italics mine). Miss Peg voices a dissenting ideology of abolitionism and reveals to Nat that not *all* whites subscribe to the tenets of slave capitalism.

As a Bakhtinian "fool" in his own right, Nat misreads *himself.* Nat's confusion over his identity, caused by his literacy and exascerbated by asceticism and subsequent hallucinatory experiences of supernatural voices, problematizes the role he plays in the white community as well as his own African slave community. The situation "renders personal identity problematic" (Bauer 1988, 161) because Nat is a man in a patriarchal society that does not regard him as a man because he is not white. He is further alienated from his own people's voices by his interiorization of the Bible which he has accomplished linearly, not aurally, because he can read. In this way he is neither black-nor white-voiced. His is the dubious distinction of having a unique voice in *either* community. Under the white community's gaze, which is mostly disciplinary, Nat is forced to control his sexual impulses and conceal his hatreds so as not to give himself or his plan away, which further emphasizes his alienation. As a result, he falls into the trap of villifying all whites, including Margaret, whose innocent intrusions into his solitude he regards as attacks on his manhood; finally, his alienation leads him to sever his marginalized connections with the white patriarchal community altogether and to lead a rebellion that establishes a temporary brotherhood (a community nonetheless) of violence. For Nat it appears that the identity of a "murderous" slave-revolt leader—a clear, unambiguous voice of dissent—finally gives him a communal power base, however short-lived it is. Nat begins as a "preacher," the quintessential *voicing* man, and, as a result of his tortured and problematic history/identity, he achieves his role as a revolutionary leader which gives him, finally, a determined sense of self in his "mission." His voice is examined by the white courts and executed, but not before it brings to the monologism of slave capitalism a challenge it can no longer ignore. The patriarchy represented in the court that judged the historical Nat also appropriated his voicings in the person of Lawyer Gray whose

Confessions (1831) creates a voice for Nat and demonizes him, but does not *silence* him. To this day, the anxiety over Nat's voice is palpable. Styron's novel was published twenty-five years ago, but no film version of Nat's rebellion has yet been produced.

Styron's novel on the confessions of a black slave-revolt leader is a further indictment of the overarching patriarchal definitions of women as a class of individuals defined by the status of the males who control their economic and social lives. The gynicidal terror meted out by Nat Turner is, ironically, inspired by his frustrated desires to achieve status as a "real" man by possessing white women, the most valued of possessions in the white man's community and the most removed from a black slave's. In *Nat Turner* woman are presented as "creatures" who may be "beautiful"— a favorite descriptive of Nat's—but who are nonetheless almost completely circumscribed by the catagories and desires of white men. As a revolutionary, Nat is portrayed as a man often unsympathetic with the plight of black women, except that he refers to their rape by white men in his "plan of war." As for Nat's ability to sense the plight of white women, it is curtailed by the combination of repression and oppression which has determined his own self-definition. Even the white women themselves, except for naive Miss Peg, are largely unreflective about their unequal roles in white society. One woman, however, does rise above the fray to reassert her pride and depart Jerusalem. The woman from New Haven who is wealthy enough to reject a rich suitor and return North exhibits at least a measure of control over her circumstances and leaves the benighted South behind her. For all that, she contributes some spark to Nat's resolve as his manic mind continues to obsess about bringing a woman such as her down to the dust of the road: bringing her down because she shares in the bounty of a society that everyday emasculates and therefore violates him.

Women, even for the avenging angel Nat, are the first targets of retribution and blame and vengeance. In this we may see again the working out of Elizabeth Ermarth's thesis of female casualties in literature, especially realistic fiction by men. But we need not limit ourselves to the historical to find evidence of the marginalization and gynicide toward women; "killing," in the sense of Shoshana Felman's view that male critics often "kill" or reduce the importance of female charcaters in the process of their critiques, continues to insinuate itself into literary discussion. Samuel Coale's commentary on Margaret Whitehead is just such a recent (Coale 1991, 1991) critique: he marginalizes simultaneously the concerns of African-American critics about Nat's portrayal and Margaret's importance in the narrative discourse by claiming "the relationship does not appear to be as momentous" as others would have it. Coale bases his assumption on the observation that "Margaret and Nat encounter each other only four times in the novel," and that during the final time Margaret merely "pleads for him to finish his killing of her" (86). Yet later in his study Coale acknowledges that for Nat "it seems psychologically appropriate that forces of both desire and hatred should surge within him" whenever Nat encounters Margaret. Coale's reading/minimization of the importance of the only person Nat Turner kills—a white woman—is a poignant example of the Felmanian thesis concerning male critical marginalization of female characters; patriarchal assumptions, as employed by Coale, bear out Hitchcock's assertion that "the more meaning is stabilized or centralized in the voices of a few, the more it becomes centripetal or monological" in Bakhtinian terms (5).

Dale Marie Bauer's thesis concerning the marginalization of women's voices by the monologism of the patriarchy maintains that "[m]asculine self-identity is couched in terms of possession. . . . Children and property [like Nat] and wives carry a different value, but are all reduced to versions of the same" (Bauer 1988, 132). For all that, we find that women's voices, although restrained by the strictures of their patristic society, did in fact give Nat Turner his Old Testament voice. In this way does the patriarchy abide in the minds of the gender-oppressed only to be passed onto the race-oppressed. Jonathan Culler discusses this phenomenon: "The most insidious oppression alienates a group from its own interests as a group and encourages it to identify with the interests of the oppressors, so that political struggles must first awaken a group to its interests and its 'experience'" (Culler 1982, 50).

William Styron may be writing about a period in American history that concludes thirty years before the Civil War, but it is clearly his intention to portray that period through a projected modern sensibility in his version of Nat Turner. His portrayal of the antebellum South and critique of the patriarchal strictures it imposed on African slaves and white women alike must be read in terms of modern conditions relative to race relations and to the rights of women in the United States. Styron's "historical meditation" allows him to focus on historical dehumanization as well as the modern slaveries which male-dominated systems, in large measure through language, continue to manipulate and direct. As Peter Hitchcock reminds us, language is indeed shared, but *access to authority* in language is not created equally (Hitchcock 1993, 5; italics mine).

5

The Essential Region of the Soul:
The Women of *Sophie's Choice*

THE epigram by Andre Malraux that William Styron employs to open *Sophie's Choice* presents the problem of the novel succinctly: "I seek that essential region of the soul where absolute evil confronts brotherhood," except that Malraux uses *la fraternité* to apply to females as well as males. Sisterhood, as such, may be implied in the epigram, but it is not so translated, and so the quotation from Malraux itself duplicates dominant Western culture's tendency to use language that effaces the gender of female participants in the ongoing struggles of people to emancipate themselves from domination and oppression. Indeed, Malraux's epigram reflects the assumptions upon which most mainstream accounts of human history have been based, including the obvious predilection for seeing human experience from a male point of view. In Styron's novelistic attempt to understand Auschwitz, or at least to understand the limits of what can be understood about such an experience, a male author/narrator seeks the *region cruciale de l'âme* of a woman who survives the camp only to continue to suffer male abuse and eventually commit suicide, as yet another victim of *gynicide*.

In his determination to examine with great seriousness the regions of "absolute" evil, Styron in this novel continues his earlier concerns with fiction's ability to act as a useful tool for such exploration; further, his conviction that he himself may investigate the bases of a woman's experience of unspeakable horrors reflects what Richard Law refers to as Styron's refusal "to concede any privileged area to 'insiders'" (Law 1990, 47). Styron's approach, explains Law, may best be described as reverential; that is, the writer's imagination functions "in a saving way at the very margins of human experience" (47). The novel becomes, in short, redemptive in that it can treat even the most extreme, dehumanizing areas of human experience and thereby redeem human suffering from meaninglessness by that very exploration.

Several critics have found Styron's attempt ennobling but the results less than praiseworthy. Giorgiana Colville concludes that Styron's efforts in *Sophie's Choice* reveal his own attempts to rid himself of a dead mother and the attendant guilt he has felt about his relationship with her. In great detail, Colville chronicles Styron's negative portrayals of, and textual violence toward the women in *Sophie's Choice*. And to be sure, even the more "mature" Stingo/Styron narrator exhibits obvious anger toward his mother for being ill and toward Sophie for haunting him with her story, along with various antipathies for Leslie Lepidus, Mary Alice Grimball, and even Maria Hunt who are alternately described as "virginal cock-teasers" and "whack-off artists." As Colville not unreasonably summarizes, "Women were a deadweight. Stingo's fundamental desire is obviously to be free to write alone, away from Eros" (Colville 1986, 127). She argues further, "Stingo's triple fantasy in the New York hotel, in which he refers to Maria, Leslie, and Sophie as all being *dead*, clearly voices Styron's urge to destroy and kill almost every female character as a surrogate dead mother" (132; italics in original).

While I do not dispute the evidence of the dead women as a significant issue in the novel in terms of gynicide either in the form of physical death or psychogynicide, and even though Stingo/Styron's portrayals of women may be evidence of "black despair" over "emasculations" and "truncated passions," in my opinion they suggest another conclusion: Stingo's despair is primarily about his failures to achieve a union with these women, failures that spring from the taboos and social mores that alienate both men and women from one another and that pattern their relationships in terms of domination and submission. Stingo is angry, as I will show in some detail, at the *systems* that produce the situations in which he finds himself with women; that is, he critiques the "prevailing patriarchal consensus" that Elizabeth Ermarth writes of. Indeed, in a particularly risky intellectual move, Styron suggests women's own complicity in the formation and reinforcement of societal roles, a kind of masochism induced by the very patriarchal standards foisted upon them. In his suggestion that males and females alike share in the dehumanization of women and other purposely marginalized groups, exemplified in Sophie's tragedy particularly, we can see Styron not as a simple sexist or a misogynist, but rather, as Carolyn A. Durham has pointed out, as a novelist who explores sexism and misogyny without blaming the victims for their plight.

What Stingo seeks, in both his younger and older manifestations, is *communion* not domination.

Styron begins *Sophie's Choice* by foregrounding men, not women. The first brief line about a woman is Stingo's reflection that his father found him "difficult to handle" after his mother's death (SC 4). The passage suggests some of the trauma to come regarding his anguish over his mother by relating that Stingo's initial nickname of "Stinky" was awarded on the basis of his dishevelment and apparent "inattention to personal hygiene" after his mother's death. Later in the novel, Stingo will exclaim to Sophie that "Mothers and fathers—they're at the core of one's own life somehow. Or they can be" (462). In this way, amidst the tangle of even the elder Stingo's supposedly more reliable frame narrative, Styron lays down a detail that begins to define young Stingo's views of women. The technique lays open not only an important element of the psyche of both Stingos, but Styron's as well; the reader is asked to recognize the postmodernist self-awareness of an author *qua auteur qua* narrator and the resultant richness in the novel's range of voices. Styron invites a critical exercise in which readers may observe him *textualizing himself.* That is, Stingo/Styron constantly updates the reader about the process of both his human and artistic development, if they can be separated; indeed, the differences between the young and the old Stingo are a microcosm of the changes that Styron perceives to have affected the world during and since the debacle of World War II. A resisting reader might consider that the differences for women and other economically marginalized people are not in fact as materially realized or dramatic as Styron/Stingo imagines. Many of the power structures that the novel critiques in the era of World War II and its aftermath are still in place and continue to work against the empowerment of marginalized peoples whom Peter Hitchcock refers to in his *Dialogics of the Oppressed* as "subaltern" subjects, a term introduced by Gayatri Spivak (Hitchcock 1993, 20).

Other women enter the first chapter of *Sophie's Choice* via Stingo's merciless critiques full of "bitchery and vengeance," as he puts it, and directed at two hopeful authors: Edmonia Kraus Biersticker and Audrey Wainwright Smilie. The elder Stingo comments ruefully on the "bitchery" of the younger man, "Oh, clever, supercilious young man!" (SC 6). And Styron's point is clear: Stingo represents a young man of his times, chauvinistic dismissals of "scribbling women" and all. These reading reports reflect, however, as much Stingo's tormented mind-set as a drone in the "mammoth beehive" of McGraw-Hill than anything else. Yet another woman-image enters the chapter as Stingo periodically glimpses the "astonishingly well-proportioned blond wife" of a young "tweedy" man whose garden Stingo's tiny room overlooks in Manhattan. Stingo fantasizes further that he "fucked her into a frazzle with stiff, soundless, slow, precise shafts of desire" (11). This active fantasy life is brought on by his monkish existence at the University Residence Club, a seedy rooming house with an all-male clientele. The blond wife he christens Mavis Honnicutt and continues his fantasies until one evening she gesticulates toward his building; Stingo assumes, guiltily, that she must be referring to "all those creeps peering out at us"—thus the elder Stingo locates the younger successfully and ironically in his own text (15). It is precisely this relentless, self-effacing, running commentary of the elder Stingo on the younger's foibles that informs the overall concern of Styron's critique: a serious and self-conscious exploration of the period and mores informing his American narrator's secondhand, postwar confrontation with the horrors of Auschwitz.

Sophie is not even mentioned until Chapter 2, and Stingo does not encounter her physically until the close of the chapter which deals with the roots of Stingo's presence in Brooklyn and the money that supports him that summer of 1947. His paternal grandmother, "a shrunken little doll of an old lady" (SC 27), had a male slave who was sold after a scandal erupted over charges that he raped a white girl; the long-hidden money from the sale of this slave, appropriately named Artiste, is found and serves as Stingo's seed money for his project of writing a novel in New York. Stingo recalls how his grandmother, ninety when she told him the stories, regaled him with tales of her own two slave girls; this ancient grandmother from the distant southern past had a "sweet chirpy old voice" that finally gave out when the "gentle lady went to sleep" (28). With his symbolically tainted money, Stingo rents a room at Yetta Zimmerman's boardinghouse in Brooklyn, near Prospect Park, and encounters in her an "extraordinary broad-mindedness" toward sex that he assumes is the result of her "Old World appreciation of volupte" (35). Yetta's simple and direct approach to sexual encounters among her boarders is based on her strong feeling that her place is a place "for grownups" (34). Stingo appreciatively quotes her reasoning for allowing both males and females license to "entertain" guests. "And the same thing goes for the young ladies in my house, if they want to entertain a boyfriend now and then. What's good for the gander is good for the goose, I say, and if there's one thing I hate, it's hypocrisy" (34). Yetta's Liberty Hall, as she terms it, promises to allow Stingo to fulfill his long-awaited desire to end his virginal state at twenty-two; in fact, he comments that her broad-mindedness puts "the final seal" on his determination to live in the Pink Palace. It is Stingo's strong appreciation of Yetta's disdain for hypocrisy that informs the reader of Styron's own concerns with the moral and sexual hypocrisy of the period. Yetta, "a beaming Buddha," "squat and expansive" with a "porous spatulate nose" and "a slightly mongoloid cast to her cheerful features," voices an enlightened approach for this era toward her tenants' sex lives. "What I like is to see my tenants enjoy life" (34).

Because of Yetta's pep talk on her tenants' "enjoying" life, it is no surprise, certainly, that the young and sexually inexperienced Stingo expects a "summer of carnal fulfillment" (SC 35). At mid-June in 1947, he finds himself a "horny Calvinist" among the Jews in his neighborhood and in, so he thinks, Yetta's place. He hits on a scheme of copying down the names of the other tenants in the boardinghouse, especially those of the female tenants, and enjoys their marvelous linguistic variety. So it is that Stingo's first encounter with Sophie is a *linear,* even alphabetically visual, one in which he satisfies his "rapacious curiosity" by learning her surname, the exotic Zawistowska. Immediately upon this list-taking, Stingo is startled by the racket of two people making love with such abandon that he calls it a "jamboree" of copulatory exhortations (37). From a strictly visual orientation, he is thrust into hearing the couple whose female player turns out to be Sophie; but from the very first, clouds of foreboding gather as he hears the woman's voice grow "plaintive, defensive" and "shrill at moments as if in fright but generally submissive with an undertone of pleading" (38). A few moments later, Stingo perceives "the woman's broken sobs on the bed above" after the man's footsteps tramp off. Stingo has just been introduced to the tragic pattern of Sophie's life with Nathan, and it is barely past noon on his first day at Yetta's.

At this point Stingo assumes that Sophie as well as the other women in the place are Jews, an assumption which leads him to reveal his very first "love" had been one Mariam Bookbinder, a Jew and the daughter of a local ship chandler living in his hometown back in tidewater Virginia. Like other Southerners of "learning and sensibility," says Stingo, he responds well to Jews, and he recalls fondly six-year-old Miriam's "lovely hooded eyes" in which she wore even then "the vaguely disconsolate, largely inscrutable mystery of her race" (SC 39). On this note of condescension toward the Jewish "other," the reader is set to experience the unraveling of Stingo's preconceptions about his neighbors. He speaks with brusque Morris Fink, and the conversation turns toward the women of the place as Stingo tries to identify the woman whose voice he had overheard in the throes of both the zenith and the nadir of passion. Morris's summary of the women relegates all but Sophie to some animal form; one is a "pig"; another is a "dog." In fact Morris takes pains to discriminate among his labels: Astrid Weinstein is "plain" and a "dog," but she is no "pig," as is Lillian Grossman whom he also refers to as a *yenta,* even though it is *he* who is the gossip. Significantly, in Morris's pantheon Sophie is a "dish" and "the Polish broad" (41).

Another woman makes her way into Stingo's consciousness on his first day at Yetta's when he reads the news from home that Maria (rhyming with "pariah") Hunt has committed suicide. She had been a not-too-bright girl "beautiful enough to wreck the heart" with whom he had been wretchedly in love when he was fifteen. Maria is the model for a character that Stingo/Styron later evolves into an obvious version of Peyton Loftis, and it is her auspicious "arrival" that summer of 1947 which enables him to write his "guts out." The news of her suicide so strikes him that he is "stunned and horrified" and nearly faints (SC 43). In his father's letter accompanying a newspaper headline announcing Maria's demise, Stingo is given a précis of the plot line of the novel to come. Stingo will write *Inheritance of the Night,* an obvious parallel to Styron's story of Peyton in *Lie Down in Darkness:*

> Maria Hunt came from a tragic household, Martin Hunt a near-alcoholic . . . while Beatrice I'm afraid was pretty unremitting and cruel in her moral demands upon people, especially I am told Maria. (44)

Clearly we have Peyton, Milton, and Helen Loftis succinctly epitomized in their agony in this summary from Stingo's usually sententious father.

Maria/Peyton's arrival in Stingo/Styron's narrative at this point is further intensified by a dream in which Stingo fantasizes Maria's wanton desire to "fuck" him, only to be awakened rudely by the actual lovemaking noises of Nathan and Sophie, whom he refers to as "Fucking Jewish rabbits!" (SC 45). "Thus Maria Hunt," explains Stingo, haunted his dreams with such intensity that she was "bound up in the metaphysical," as indeed was Styron himself overcome years later by a dream of the woman who inspired Sophie. But in 1947, the only other dream that had produced such a reaction in young Stingo was of his mother soon after her burial. In that nightmare, Stingo saw his mother's open coffin and then her "shrunken, cancerous face twist toward" him and gaze at him "beseechingly through eyes filmed over with indescribable torture" (46).

It is in this nightmarish context that Stingo first sees Sophie, and he is immediately struck by her "distant" resemblance to Maria. Sophie is "not simply the lovely simulacrum she seemed to me of the dead girl"; Sophie's face is as he imagines Maria's must have been, "along with the promontory, grieving shadows of someone hurtling headlong toward death" (SC 46). The conflation of the narrative's initial characterizations of these three important women into a mere two pages dramatizes their significance in Stingo's life, a powerful presentation rich in ironic tension because the elder Stingo does not ruminate upon their staccato appearances. The reader must make the associative connection of the importance of these three women for Stingo, young and old. Importantly, Stingo first describes Sophie's voice as "plaintive," and later he observes, "There was something plaintive, *childlike* in her voice, which was light in timbre, almost fragile, breaking a little in the upper register. . . ." (47; italics mine). In describing her as childlike, he begins to move into a role of guardian and protector, especially because he has just seen Nathan verbally abuse her. In fact, Stingo confides, "I hungered so deeply to put my arms around her, to soothe her" (49). But his next thought is to *dominate*. "I would take over this flaxen Polish treasure where Nathan, the thankless swine, had left off" (49). Stingo reacts to Sophie the way men have reacted to her in her past: they wish to dominate her, and she will admit subsequently to Stingo her desire for this domination even if it is violent. Her father, her husband, Kommandant Höss, Nathan, and eventually Stingo all dominate and abuse her to a point where she believes that she deserves her treatment. She continually returns to the abusive male because she believes she cannot live without him; she has been defined for so long in a dependent role that it is literally true that she cannot live *as the Sophie she has been* without rejecting her life, which is what she does through suicide.

In Dale Marie Bauer's terms, Sophie's value to her society is precisely her role as an exploited object and "commodity." Lily Bart in Edith Wharton's *The House of Mirth* is affected in the same way by the patriarchy. "Lily's value is not intrinsic; it is an effect of social relations determined by a market economy designed for and by men" (Allen 1976, 95). But the sword of economic evaluation cuts both ways; Lily's mother dismisses her husband as soon as he has ceased to "perform his economic function" in the role of patriarchal provider. Indeed, Mrs. Bart exhibits what Mary Alen refers to as "misandry," but in this Mrs. Bart is reflecting the value system of the patriarchal consensus that eventually forces the character into the "necessary blankness" of marginalization that Allen chronicles in her study of women in American fiction 2). As a result of the father's bankruptcy, Lily's mother has to manage her daughter's sexuality as a commodity for the lucrative marriage market in the upper-class circles of New York society. Sophie is, of course, two generations removed from the times of Lily Bart's New York and even more distant from her in culture and experience, but she is similarly a casualty of the patriarchal system. Bauer explains, "The community requires a sacrifice in order to harmonize the disruptions in society and bring about a return to 'normalcy'" (Bauer 1988, 123). This "normalcy" is the overarching concern of the "will-to-monologism of patriarchal discourse" (Hitchcock 1993, 20).

Styron presents the deaths of mothers, wives, lovers, and daughters—females of all ages—as the result of male dominance or selfishness, an indication of the author's desire to give voice to the struggles and suffering of women; Styron's presentation of women's deaths is not, as Colville suggests, at base an unconscious desire to strike out at women. Styron's work, as argued by Carolyn Durham, calls for examination of the roles men have assigned to women in society and the ways those roles have been enforced by cultural stereotypes and rituals that have often precluded women's abilities to define themselves. His presentation of Stingo, an alter ego, as an oppressor in his own right further underscores his sweeping indictment of a ruthless, male-dominated society and the hideous fruits of such domination. One mother figure, however, appears to exhibit no hint of oppression; in fact, Stingo cannot recognize Mrs. Lapidus as a mother at all. Because she is the wife of a wealthy war-profiteer, she appears in the novel as the one woman untouched and even *enriched* by the horrors of the war. Leslie's mother is described as a "lovely amber-haired woman so youthful in appearance that she might easily have passed for Leslie's older sister" (SC 167). Stingo can scarcely believe that Mrs. Lapidus is a graduate of Barnard's Class of 1922, but his fawning admiration of her sophistication—reminiscent of Peter Leverett's early infatuation with Mason Flagg's mother—curiously does not lead him to any ruminations or comparisons with his own long-suffering mother or of Sophie's struggles. As a spouse of a member of the industrial-conglomerate class that can afford an original Degas, Mrs. Lapidus is sufficiently insulated from the privations of the world so that motherhood has not worn her. On closer examination, however, the character reveals how her wealth and social position have trapped even her in patriarchy's defining grip. Even though in the novel she occupies but a few lines, she has devastated Leslie's troubled psyche and becomes for her daughter an "ogre" who beneath the facade of sophistication punishes her daughter for masturbating when she is three, forcing the little girl to wear hand splints "for months as a prophylaxis against self-abuse" (SC 177). Styron's critique obviously includes not only men but also those women, an especially privileged few, who reinforce the strictures of the patriarchy as ruthlessly as their male counterparts.

The other important women in the novel consist of younger characters who plague Stingo's attempts to lose his virginity. That in large measure he sees these young women as obstacles to his carnal fulfillment is instructive at the outset. Maria Hunt, who has been discussed earlier, appears as another "phantom" woman from Stingo's past: his adolescent love-child whose suicide freezes her forever in his mind as a quintessential source of unrequited love. As it turns out, both Stingo and Styron achieve a literary, even *transcendent* union with Maria/Peyton in an interior "monologue" based structurally on a similar device from Joyce's *Ulysses* for characterizing Molly Bloom's mind. But Stingo's internal doubts about his ability to present the mind of a young Southern woman are worth observing. Although he exhibits at times cavalier over-confidence about his work in progress, *Inheritance of the Night*, young Stingo ponders his opus as he and Sophie ride toward an uncertain future after fleeing New York for his peanut farm in the South: "the tormented, alienated girl going to her lonely death on the indifferent summertime streets of the city I had just left behind" (SC 449). He experiences a "moment of gloom" in which he questions himself: "Would I be able to summon the passion, the insight *to portray this young suicide?*" (449; italics mine). Unsure of his capability of imagining the girl's ordeal, he is secure in the knowledge of the integrity of the work he is producing and allows himself to fantasize, with mocking self-recognition, about the reviews in which he will be celebrated for his as yet unwritten climax: "'The most powerful passage of female interior monologue since Molly Bloom's.' What folly! I thought. What conceit" (449).

This admixture of adolescent wishful thinking tempered by sober experience engages the reader's critical awareness and invites speculation on the complex intertextuality Styron has set up between the two narratives of Sophie and Peyton. In *Sophie's Choice,* there is no extended interior monologue from Sophie/Stingo; instead, there is constant vigilance to maintain the clear conditions f the storytelling: Sophie speaks to Stingo; he does *not* become er voice, he *transcribes* what he hears. But the point of his "relaionship" in this novel with Maria is his own admitted use of her uffering and suicide as a means of achieving his dream of being writer, a situation he will repeat by using Sophie's life as yet nother magnum opus, the very novel we are reading. Thus anther level of male domination arises from the narrative, and we re invited to speculate on the implied perversity of such a mind s Stingo/Styron's that seeks to tell the morbid tales of beautiful vomen and their suffering in order to arrive at some kind of "unerstanding" of the human condition as a whole. The difference etween the two narratives written thirty years apart is chiefly that he latter novel is postmodernist in its focus on the narrator's self-wareness of his previous text as he pens his present text. *Lie)own in Darkness* cannot, of course, have the self-referential qual-ty of *Sophie's Choice*. In the earlier novel, the young Styron/Stingo reates Peyton/Maria in an interior "monologue," but the elder tingo chooses not to duplicate this feat with Sophie—hence the lder Stingo's critique of his younger self's "conceit" at his confilence in producing a definitive interior "monologue" of a young voman. It is the conceit born of a sense of superiority over the voman, the "object" of the internal narrative, a superiority the nature Stingo rejects as merely another symptom of male domiance. Instead of dominating Sophie's interior voicings, he listens ttentively; his is not an attempt to "take over" and dominate her syche, but a desire to record her voice in its plaintive strains as vell as its husky sexuality.

Unlike Maria Hunt, the other young women in Stingo's summer f 1947 affect him in more direct and libidinal ways. Leslie Lapidus aunts Stingo in a different way than his mother did, but it is onetheless a determined haunting. After the emotional and for tingo physical buildup for his first "big date" with Leslie, which ollows immediately upon the heels of his meeting her on the beach, is wildly optimistic visions of "fabulous fucking" crash around im as he discovers Leslie's own particular traumata which com-lement, in a way, his own frustrations with sexual virginity. As e meets her parents and is exposed to the sheer wealth of her life, tingo's reaction to their life-style is a dumbstruck. "*Jesus Christ lmighty* was all I could think" (SC 165). His "stallionoid condi-ion" occupies his mind the entire evening as he attempts to get _eslie to go beyond vocalization and participate in lovemaking vith him; more than that, he also entertains blissful ideas of narrying a woman who would bring him both wealth and a sexual engine for satisfying his desires. "I would also be dishonest if I did not admit that to the sweet prospect of copulation there was added the fleeting image of matrimony, should it turn out that way" (166) in short, it is a young-man-of-the-province's dream.

A criticism of Stingo's dismissal of Leslie after one frustrating experience can surely be made on the grounds that for all his vaunted abilities to "imagine" the troubled mind of Maria Hunt and the horrors of Sophie's experience, he fails utterly to empathize with Leslie. From his perspective, his history has not been kind: he suffers "terribly" as "artful little coquettes" tease and manipulate him into priapic frenzies, all the while guarding the prize of their loins from him. He even goes so far as to characterize the girls of his adolescence as loathsome little vampires whose "counterfeit wantonness" was overcome by his own "almost saintly willpower" (SC 165). With this background, however rationalized it may be, we can understand his overreaction to Leslie's refusal to have sex with him when she appears to have "led him on." In a sense, the text's own "teasing" of readerly expectation exhibits Styron's mastery of the art himself; Stingo's account of the scene with Leslie is switched from apparent straightforward narration to a journal entry from the actual time of the "date." Using the voice of the younger Stingo's own 1947 words, the elder teases the reader into believing that an actual artifact from 1947 has opened, much in the same way Leslie opens herself tentatively to Stingo.

However, Stingo's honesty in his journal entry may be no more real than Leslie's apparent willingness to have sex, for he laments of his "desolation and letdown" such as he has never known before "or thought possible" (SC 174); such purple passages are entered without comment by the elder Stingo in order to involve the reader in the young man's fancy and his overblown sense of self. Startling in Stingo's revelations is his disclosure of a desire to "belt the living shit out" of Leslie; a dark side emerges from the sexual tension he endures, and he exhibits all the traits of the petulant young man. Even after her confession that she is a virgin and deeply troubled by even speaking of sex in spite of all her therapy, he can only chastise her more: "No offense, understand. But I think you're a very sick virgin" (176). So much for his empathetic powers with twenty-year-old women; indeed, he makes no effort to compare her "sick" virginity with his own dark desires to "fuck mud" when he heads off to Jones beach with Sophie.

In his journal entry, Stingo belittles her orgone therapy, concluding that all he received for his evening of troubles was a chance to feel one of Leslie's breasts momentarily. He never calls her back after the first date although he promises he will, and in this he again takes on the role of the male "cad." He refers only to the "torture she inflicted" on him when as the older, "wiser" Stingo he wishes her well. This scene with Leslie merely serves to reinforce the cliché/stereotype of the insensitive young man "on the make." The elder Stingo justifies this behavior by appending a projection of Leslie as a fifty-year-old sleek beauty by now sexually well-adjusted, but this egregious example of further chauvinism simply reinforces his younger incarnation's youthful callowness. As a further example of Stingo's youthful shallowness, we see him later boast to Nathan in a macho manner that he and Leslie were all right "in the sex department" and that he "got in" (182). The question still remains: Why did the youthful Stingo, full of a love for the battered and betrayed of the world, not lend Leslie Lapidus a friendly shoulder that summer? The answer is surely that he had some intuitive belief that Sophie would eventually turn to him; he saw the efficacy of attending to Sophie's needs. (In his own life, it is worth pointing out, Styron *did* marry the Jewish girl, his wife of forty years, Rose Burgunder.)

From Leslie, the next subject of Stingo's building scorn for young women is Mary Alice Grimball, who like Mavis Hunnicutt is assigned a name designed to evoke back-room male "good humor" the style of which Stingo tries on Sophie with his attempts to humor her with a joke about the "Mississippi" definition of a virgin: "a twelve-year-old who can run faster than her daddy" (SC 491). Mary Alice enjoys at first the same positive image Stingo had of Leslie, but once again, after repeated grapplings, he discovers that she will not have intercourse with him although she has no qualms about masturbating him as much as he desires—but he does not desire it. Worse to Stingo than the "Cock Tease" Leslie, Mary Alice is the "Whack-off artist" (432); and as such she seems to Stingo to be suffering from a "form of sexual eccentricity." She is, however, literate, sensitive, and attractive as well as Southern. In a ferocious lapse in his usual self-declared honesty, he mentions that her masturbating him night after night is "almost the first contact of its kind" he has experienced in his life, forgetting to elaborate upon or even mention his riotously sensual experience with Sophie at Jones Beach. As with Leslie, Stingo's patience is brief with Mary Alice, and he tells in no uncertain terms that she has tormented him beyond his capacity of endurance; this he relates in a drunken storm of incoherent words which, as he did with Leslie, he later records in his faithful if less-than-objective journal.

For Mary Alice's perspective, the reader must turn to the actual words Stingo ascribes to her. She tells him that she likes him, but that they are not in love and for her sex and love are inseparable. She even explains that she was "badly burned" by a young man who talked her into sex with the assurance of an engagement that was but an empty promise. As the reader can surmise from Styron's doggedly if delightfully callow young Stingo, Mary Alice has rightly judged him as a young man of that same sort, but his indignation knows no bounds as he curses her and admits once again to "an overpowering longing to perpetrate a rape" on the "cunt" he says she has "locked up" like gold at Fort Knox (SC 435). The strong language which shocks Mary Alice is no less shocking than the expressed desire to rape that reveals a young man, although self-described as a sensitive writer who desires to produce a work based on a young woman's desperate emotional state, thoroughly wound up in his own onanistic images of women. The *best* that might be said of Stingo is that his courage to reveal his feelings is probably therapeutic, and that he sees himself as repulsive even in his journal entry; further, he appears genuinely concerned that his failures with women betoken a latent homosexuality which terrifies him, especially after that fear manifests itself in his first homosexual dream during the night following his drunken tirade against Mary Alice. Stingo, not unreasonably, argues with Mary Alice that her masturbating him is merely a cynical act of female manipulation, literally and figuratively, in which she maintains her value as a virginal commodity in the marriage market by keeping her valuable genitals locked up until a suitably moneyed suitor comes along. In short, he is frustrated by the restrictions women place on themselves as they collaborate in their domination by the male society that bases their worth on sexual reputation and availability. Still, young Stingo is anything but a male protofeminist in his frustrated and verbally abusive tirades against these young women. Immediately after his final encounter with Mary Alice, Stingo learns that Sophie has been beaten yet again by Nathan, but the elder Stingo does not reflect on his own violent urges with Mary Alice; that reflection is left by Styron to the reader.

Perhaps next to Sophie herself, the most important female character in *Sophie's Choice* is Wanda Muck-Horch von Kretschmann, Sophie's neighbor and lover in Warsaw. Wanda and Sophie are brought together, in fact, as a result of their mutual love for music, but the war blasted Wanda's aspirations as surely as it did Sophie's desire to become a music teacher. Wanda is described as a "tall, athletically built young woman with boyish, graceful arms and legs and flaming red hair"; her eyes are "the most arrestingly clear sapphire-blue that Sophie had ever seen" (SC 369). Like Sophie, Wanda was forced to learn German early by her father whose woolen factory relied upon German commerce; but Wanda was more than the daughter of a bourgeoisie German father with a Polish wife. "Wanda was the reincarnation of the young Rosa Luxembourg, whom she worshipped" (369); and she dreamed of a free Poland. Unlike Leslie whom Stingo apparently sees as trapped in her wealthy neuroses, Wanda breaks from her privileged family to become a committed underground member who is fearless and clever, a real "firebrand." Wanda proclaims her socialism to Sophie and constantly tries to appeal to Sophie's sense of decency so that she will join in the underground's struggle to help Jews and sabotage the German occupation. Still, Wanda does not dismiss Sophie for her lack of patriotic fervor; Sophie later tells Stingo that Wanda was a lesbian and that she and Wanda were lovers briefly (476).

In one of the novel's most riveting scenes, Wanda speaks with Jewish ghetto-dwellers who arm themselves in a desperate attempt to rebel against overwhelming forces. They are suspicious of their Polish underground contacts, and for good reason since many Poles turn Jews in for bounty and favors from the Germans. But Wanda is not one of these Poles; indeed, she is of the group that helps Jews escape or hide and procures arms for them. Wanda berates one ghetto-dweller "brazenly," like a "tough man" but with a "certain female softness" as Sophie describes it, for self-pity. Wanda tells the man, Feldshon, that he should not expect the Poles to be any different than they have been through history: "living in a ghetto, which we Poles originated, how could you expect any help from your compatriots?" (SC 472). She asks him how much concern he would expect from "the terrified rats in the building to have for the rats outside in the barrel—the rats whom they've never felt any kinship with, anyway" (473). For Wanda, "everyone's a victim. The Jews are victims of victims, that's the main difference" (474).

From this no-nonsense woman, Sophie receives affection, physical love, and help in the camp when she yearns to find out about her son's fate. Sophie sees Wanda in her mind as "incredibly brave"; she has limits, however: after Feldshon and the others leave, Wanda sits at their table and weeps openly. Her frank appraisal of the Nazi's omnivorous war machine leads her to tell the Jewish Resistance leaders that they are not the only targets of Nazi hatred, that they will not stop with the Jews. "Because once they finish you off they're going to come and get me" (SC 475), underlining yet again a running theme throughout the novel. In a way, Styron's creation of Wanda balances his creation of the loutish Stingo, who is obviously mocked for his chauvinism and narcissism. Where Stingo is tormented by sexual longings perpetuated by "disturbed" coquettes, Wanda has no time for such foolishness, and the reader is called upon to draw the contrasts sharply between the two. By acting in some sense as a foil to the almost absolute heroism of Wanda, Stingo contributes to her story, emphasizes its true voicing, and redeems his own curlike behavior. Stingo is offered up as a criticism of males and male domination as part of a redemptive process that is one of the novel's purposes, as surely as "Lord Jim" in Conrad's novel, which Wanda discusses with Feldshon, redeems himself for his abandoning of his responsibilities with his own subsequent death and suffering. Like other heroines, then, Wanda must be sacrificed because that is the reality of the world Styron describes. She is found out in Auschwitz and slowly strangles on a hook; but her voice carries on through Sophie's and then Stingo's renditions of her courage. Her succinct conclusion that "everyone's a victim" is validated in the narrative's unyielding exploration of even the most petty forms of degradation we see in Stingo's masturbatory visions. Even Stingo can be seen as a victim of his society and its general callousness toward the marginalized which is the legacy of a culture formed by the notions of elite, primarily if not exclusively male, ruling groups who define the value of human beings according to their own calculus of domination. In the midst of human suffering and degradation, Wanda stands out as a character thoroughly deserving of admiration, and yet as a lesbian and a socialist she could not be further from the patriarchy's ideal of woman. In Wanda, Styron makes a courageous statement which befits the character herself and calls into question authoritarian systems that condemn heroines like Wanda. Dale Marie Bauer explains that women such as Wanda act and speak actively against the patriarchy, of which Nazism is surely one of its most virulent forms, because to do so "engenders" them and therefore empowers them. "For women to speak is an empowering act, but also an engendering act . . . when speaking, women mark and determine themselves simultaneously as objects of their own voices and as subjects" (158).

From Wanda we turn to Sophie the survivor. The discourse of the narrative provides portrayals of Sophie beginning with images of her when she is very young, long before she encounters Stingo in that eventful summer of '47. In chapter 4 we see her first efforts

to explain to Stingo her origins in Poland, but because of the traumata she has suffered she represses much of the "truth" of her
story, a fact which Stingo does not know at first. Indeed, the elder
Stingo directly addresses the reader on a number of occasions to
point out Sophie's mendacity, but the Stingo of June 1947 listens
with innocence to Sophie's drama as it unfolds. Still, Styron presents a narrative that mirrors his own readers' dilemma: we know
that Styron and his elder Stingo narrator are already acquainted
with the "truth" and core of Sophie's "choice," but like young
Stingo, we do not yet know the *context* of the "entire" story. Young
Stingo, like the very readers of his story about Sophie's story, must
follow the development of her narrative, attaching meaning as he
hears it; but unlike young Stingo, readers are privy to the elder
Stingo's own Holocaust research after thirty years of musing on
Sophie's fate. In spite of this knowledge, however, we are still be
subject to Styron's manipulation of his narrative. As Richard Law
explains, the novel alternates intensely detailed passages with sections of abstraction, "drawing the reader into a rhythm of confrontation and evasion"; and this rhythm is further enhanced by the
"complementary but quite different narrative perspectives" of the
two Stingos and Sophie herself (Law 1990, 45–46). But Sophie's
view is always through Stingo's reconstructed imagination; and the
elder Stingo is, of course, a reconstruction of aspects of Styron's
own experience. As Law reiterates, "the book gives expression to
many voices . . . even as it assimilates them to its own ends" (46).
Dale Marie Bauer would argue that the very inclusion of these
voices, in a Bakhtinian sense, insures that the carnival of voices
will both support and subvert the ends, the intentions, Styron may
have had in mind.

In considering the particularities of Styron's presentation of Sophie, the retelling of her story to Stingo is crucial. Stingo first hears
her tale as she unravels it during one of their half-dozen or so
lunches in Prospect Park in central Brooklyn, just across from
Yetta's place. Her other revelations take place in their rooms at
Yetta's as well as at the Maple Court, a "full-fledged bar" in Flat-
bush (SC 181). Suggesting that Sophie's story may be told in
strictly chronological terms, Styron has Stingo report that she tries
to "begin at the beginning" of her life. "In Cracow, when I was a
little girl . . . we lived in a very old house on an old winding street
not far from the university" (79). With this kind of "once upon
a time" opening, we can see Styron constructing a traditional
chronological narrative whose apparent simplicity and seductive
charm will be torn apart as both young Stingo and the reader learn

more. In any case, Sophie informs Stingo that she had been born in her parents' house, spent her childhood there, and lived there after she had been married; in point of fact, she lived in what may more appropriately be referred to as her father's house from her birth until the Germans occupied Cracow and in November of 1939 took both her father and her husband in a roundup of Polish university intellectuals and shot them. Sophie rhapsodizes about her life in prewar Cracow as idyllic: she lived "high up on the fourth floor" of the house when she was little, and she had her own room (79). She loved to read her books of fairy tales and watch the real storks in their nests high above the streets; lying in the dark of her room she listened to the sounds of horses' feet on the streets below. Sometimes she would listen to the clock tower of the church of St. Mary's near the center of Cracow, and she imagined herself inside the great clock. "I would just float around on a spring and watch the levers moving and the various wheels turning and see the rubies, red and bright and as big as my head" (80). As we have seen, another of Styron's female characters who commits suicide has a similar dream of being "inside" a clock: Peyton Loftis. Sophie concludes her initial gush of fond memories with: "They were wonderful times, those years between the wars . . . we lived in a wonderful civilized way, the best kind of life you can imagine, really" (80).

She continues that her goal in those halcyon days was to live the life her parents had lived and "perhaps become married and become a teacher of music like my mother" (SC 81). Her mother played the piano, and Sophie, "warm and comfortable and secure," heard the beautiful notes of Schumann or Chopin as they reached her on the fourth floor. She explains that her father and mother "was [sic] wonderful people"; her father was a "pacifist" (82). After marrying Casimir, nicknamed Kasik, a student of her father's—although she says she was married "very, very young"—she was in a state of "being a little girl," thinking her comfortable life would last forever (83). At this point she tells Stingo that she was "so happy with Casimir" and loved him because he was generous, loving, and, importantly, intelligent—like Nathan, she says (83). But the Germans came; they took away and eventually shot the two men in her life who had, in effect, defined her very existence. She and her mother took her children to Warsaw where she found work.

In this section where Sophie narrates (through Stingo) her early days, she laments that she did not have a chance to bid farewell to her husband Kasik. On the evening before he was caught up in the maw of the German extermination machine, they had had a fight and slept apart; in spite of her conviction that Kasik knew of her love for him, she feels guilt because she had told him to "drop dead" in the heat of their last argument. "I have lived long with this very, very strong guilt which I can't lose," she says, "even though I know it has no reason" (SC 87). This is Sophie's first proclamation of guilt in the narrative, and it appears to be out of proportion with the act, the "silly fight" she had with Kasik. As the reader and Stingo later comprehend, the guilt she feels goes beyond her parting in anger from her husband; her claim that the guilt "has no reason" is likewise an apparently false claim on her part. But she is in a sense correct about her feelings of guilt over Kasik: in psychoanalytic terms, guilt arises from the sublimation of primal desires and *becomes* the unconscious (Eagleton 1983, 165). Guilt itself pours forth from the unconscious, the seat of guilty desires; so the unreasoning unconscious, by definition, "has no reason" as Sophie intuitively suggests.

In another session of Sophie's oral history, this one later at the Maple Court, she tells Stingo that he is very lucky to "still have a father"; she confides, "I miss my father so" (SC 197). Amplifying a bit, she adds that she no longer grieves as she once did, but she misses him. "He was such a good man." Sophie, who a little earlier in the scene says that religion is for "*des analphabetes,* imbecile peoples," is suddenly incensed that a good man like her father "risk [*sic*] his life for Jews and die, and the Jew-killers live, so many of them, right now" (198). This proves to her, she says, that there is no reason to believe in "this God" who turns his back on good people. But this conversation is cut off as Stingo heads off for the toilet and returns to find Nathan in one of his rages. This brief interchange is offered without comment from the elder Stingo on the veracity of Sophie's claims about her father. Styron is here more concerned with moving Nathan's abuse of Sophie into the foreground of the narrative than speculating yet again on the nature of her manipulating the "true" nature of her father's attitudes toward Jews. The reader is thus left to consider at this juncture that Stingo the elder has cast doubts on Sophie's honesty, but the narrative has offered no other discussion about her father.

The next time we hear of her father and her life before the war occurs as Sophie explains that her father's insistence upon her learning shorthand provided her with a measure of "salvation" at Auschwitz, for she uses her language skills and shorthand speed to get closer to Kommandant Höss. In fact, "she breathed a small prayer of thanks" to her father, or "Professor Bieganski" as she often thought of him, for having her learn the skill when she was sixteen, back in Cracow (SC 222). A few pages later, however, the reader finally becomes aware of "Sophie's most flagrant evasion": we are told that her father was not, after all, the benign paterfamilias and brave libertarian she had painted him. Her fabrication is "another fantasy served up to provide a frail barrier, a hopeless and crumbly line of defense between those she cared for . . . and her smothering guilt," reports Stingo (237). In fact, Bieganski was a rabid anti-Semite who wrote vicious tracts promulgating the extermination, the vernichtung, of the Jews in Poland and elsewhere in Europe. The supreme irony of his life story is that his entire family, save Sophie, was itself exterminated by the German Reich he so admired and supported.

Sophie does maintain, however, that she had not been *completely* mendacious with Stingo earlier. Her stories about an idyllic childhood in peaceful Cracow were true; it was a place, she still maintains at this point, "of surpassing warmth and security" where "domestic serenity" was supplied by her mother, a "bosomy, expansive, loving woman" (SC 238). But over this sunny patina of her mother's calm lay "the constant, overwhelming reality of her father"; he exercised over the household a "tyrannical domination" inflexible in the extreme but cunning and subtle enough that Sophie discloses how she was a grown woman before she realized that "she loathed him past all telling." And even when she did realize her true feelings, reports Stingo, "she could find no voice" to express her hatred. In Dale Marie Bauer's terms, the inability of heroines in American fiction to find a voice *of their own* with which to address the patriarchy informs this passage. Like Lily Bart, Sophie has for her entire existence relied upon male definitions for identity, for expression, and when Sophie is confronted with the truth of her feelings, she lapses into an anguished silence.

Sophie's subservience to her father, explains Stingo, "was as complete as in any neopaleolithic pygmy culture of the rain forest, demanding utter fealty from the helpless offspring" (SC 241). This comparison, no doubt, is to offset completely Sophie's earlier fabrication of the "civilized" life Sophie had claimed for the Bieganski household. Sophie's submission was "part of her bloodstream, so much so that as a little girl growing up she rarely even resented it" (241). A major part of this fealty was bound up in her Polish Catholicism where patriarchal veneration was appropriate and "necessary," even something Sophie admits she may have "relished" sharing with her mother; she concedes to Stingo that in even her worst recollections of her father he "was not actually cruel to either of them" (241). So without any conscious resentment, she accepted his domination even after her marriage to Kasik.

In what Stingo refers to as "a sketch, a fragment, among the most odd and unsettling" of those Sophie relates to him is the one that includes images of her married life and her infatuation with Dr. Walter Durrfeld, which informs her later raucous awakening to her sexuality with Nathan. In June of 1937, Durrfeld, a director of I. G. Farben, is being courted by Sophie's sycophantic father, and so she is "dragooned" into entertaining her father's important German guest, but she is genuinely impressed by the man's physique, his cleanliness—especially his fingernails, and his breadth of knowledge. She finds herself "strongly" attracted to him, for the first time in her life physically attracted to a man with such abandon. We learn, meanwhile, that her husband Kasik is impotent and has been for some time before Durrfeld's visit. In fact, Kasik blames her for his impotence, saying her body leaves him with no sensation. "I cannot stand even the smell of your bed," he tells her with contempt (SC 386). Thus is Sophie for the first time in possession of "electrifying desire" for another man. As Durrfeld tells her that she must visit Leipzig to see Bach's grave, she feels "wickedly" excited. "His voice seems to be an amorous melodic murmur, cajoling, politely but outrageously flirtatious, irresistible" (387). But she regards Durrfeld from "a point of view that is singularly female," reports Stingo: "he is attractive, she thinks, then in a dampness of mild shame banishes the thought. (Married, the mother of two little children; how could she!)" (384). This "female" point of view is nothing if not the interiorized *opprobrium* of the patriarchy and the reinforcement of the conjugal rights of men over women in matrimony. Stingo's very insistence on Sophie's view being "singularly female" gives the lie to its "singularity," for its origins are clearly rooted in the value of a young woman as a sexual commodity. Sophie succeeds, says Stingo, in putting Durrfeld out of her mind after his visit; he became "another innocuous flirtation consigned to the dusty unopened scrapbook" (388).

The next revelation of her relationship with the powerful men in her life occurs on the day she types up her father's article that specifies the solution to the Jewish problem as *Vernichtung;* she is humiliated by her father for typing mistakes. "Your intelligence is pulp, like your mother's," he says to her (SC 245). She realizes, finally, that her father has no more feeling for her "than a servant, some peasant or slave," and although she wants to study and teach Bach, she dares not tell her father of her real desires. She has no way of saying "Fuck you, Papa" as she wishes to at that time. She is suddenly overcome with a "sharp stab of hatred"; and she says to herself, "I hate him—with a kind of terrible wonder at the hatred which entered into me" (246). Not only is her father a despot at home, she comes to understand, but he is also willing to suggest the extermination of a whole people. It is Sophie's sudden awareness of her father's involvement in the Final Solution compounded with his contempt for her even as a grown woman and mother that brings about her wrenching emotional change. Even so, she does not tell her father of her resentment; she sits at his table with her husband and simply refuses to take the tea her father offers her. She has, as she said, no voice with which to speak; she is, indeed, afraid she will faint from the violence of her hidden feelings. This lack of voice, the subsequent psychic suicide, or *psychogynicide,* and her silence before the patriarchal gaze recall Elizabeth Ermarth's discussion of female casualties in literature. Sophie tries to explain to Stingo, an essentialy nonthreatening male, but she still has problems expressing her moment of "terrible wonder" at her hatred for her father: "there is a truth I must tell you," she says to Stingo, "that even now I can't understood [*sic*] or truly make clear" (246). She has begun to reveal her true feelings about her father; no longer does she say he was a "good" man who saved Jews.

Hard upon the heels of this shattering revelation, Stingo learns of Sophie's hatred for her husband as well. After her moment of realization, she slips by both husband and father in the house hallway as they go off on errands to secure attention and perhaps a favored position with the German occupation forces. Stingo relates that in her *emended* version of the story, which he is convinced was finally truthful, she says she felt no bereavement over their seizure that fateful day in November of 1939, but her "entire sense of self—of her identity—was unfastened" almost as much as her "sweet, unthinking, submissive" mother. She did not, however, share her mother's grief for the men; she had become too alienated from them by then.

When Sophie first meets Nathan in the summer of 1946, she adds in her guarded narrative to her Jewish lover a bit more to our understanding of her prewar years, and she sketches an abbreviated version of her arrival at Auschwitz. She tells Nathan, according to Stingo, that she has nothing left from her past. "Nothing at all. So that is one of the reasons why, you see, I feel so uncomplete" (SC 142). She speaks of her father as a "talented photographer" who was "very good" and "sensitive"; Sophie chiefly recalls the photo of her mother and herself that was lost, a photo of the two of them "at the piano" and taken by her father. At this stage in the discourse of the narrative, we begin to see that Sophie's glowing portrait of her tyrannical father is a fabrication she builds as she talks with Nathan; that she needs this ersatz father figure precisely because of her loss of identity. In effect, she rebuilds a new psychic fatherland on the ashes of the memory of her father. It is not until she is abused so egregiously by Nathan that she shares with Stingo—perhaps as with a brother or a confessor— her *real* father. In Nathan her father has been resurrected but with manic intensity. Stingo rounds out this brief section by having Sophie report that she had lived with her children and her ailing mother in war-ravaged Warsaw for three years before she was sent to Auschwitz-Birkenau in April of 1943.

Sophie's accounts of the years in Warsaw are scattered throughout the latter parts of the narrative, and it is instructive to piece them back together into a kind of straightforward chronology. We see her presented by Stingo as she recalls various stages of her life with Polish underground members who share her bed and try to convince her to aid the Home Army of resistance fighters with her language skills. Sophie finds a job in a tar-paper factory and passes by the Jewish ghetto every day, so she is a witness to the slow hemorrhaging of the community. She claims that like other Poles she assumed the Jews were at first being transported to labor camps, but because of her ties with her underground roommates, she learns soon that her father's vision of *vernichtung* had become a reality. Feeling shame, but not guilt, as she explains it, she tells Wanda about her father; Wanda surprises her by reacting with calm, even though Wanda is one of the Poles who tries desperately to help Jews. Sophie confesses further to Wanda, as she will to Stingo, that she has lied about her father and her husband's fighting for Poland in the invasion. Sophie's image of herself at this time in Warsaw is that she was a "coward" among courageous Poles (SC 468). She describes Wanda at length, admiring her "hypnotic" intensity: "she was like a tough man . . . but there was enough in her that was young and female, a certain softness, too . . ." (470). As I have noted, she confides in Stingo that Wanda was a lesbian with whom she has slept "once or twice," but "it didn't mean much to either of us, I think" (476); she loved Wanda "because she was better than me, and so incredibly brave." Sophie also has Wanda's half-brother Jozef as a lover, and the nineteen-year-old shares her bed not out of love, as she puts it, as much as for companionship and warmth.

At the close of her last reminiscence about her life in Warsaw,

Sophie reflects that on one particularly freezing night, she opened the windows of her apartment and let in the icy wind. She says, "I can't tell you how close I came to hurling myself with my children out into that darkness just then—or how many times since then I've cursed myself for not doing it" (SC 476). Still, she does have other memories of the Warsaw times that include her children in more positive terms. She describes her daughter Eva and her son Jan returning through the war-ravaged streets after a flute lesson; Sophie had engineered the lessons because "she could not consider raising Eva without giving her knowledge of music. One might as well say no to life itself" (373). Sophie shares this love of music with Wanda as well, but Eva is "mad for the flute" and has a natural gift for the instrument. Eva is described as having her yellow hair in pigtails; she has lost her front teeth. As the children are receiving instructions from their tutor on the flute, a squadron of Luftwaffe bombers drones over, overpowering the fragile notes Eva sends up to the window from below. Sophie is suddenly struck with the "grip of an aching, devouring love" followed by "joy that was inexplicably both delicious and despairing. . . ." (374). Just then she answers Wanda's demands that she help the underground; she refuses to get involved because of her children, and she cuts Wanda off with German: "*Schluss—aus!* That's final!" Ironically, she and her children are later sent to Auschwitz along with Wanda and other freedom fighters in spite of her determination not to get involved.

After her young lover-assassin Jozef is murdered by Ukranian guards and he bleeds to death in front of Sophie, she is taken prisoner herself for the crime of trying to smuggle a ham to her tuberculosis-ridden mother. In the middle of March 1943, she finds herself caught up in a roundup of the Home Army and soon recognizes a badly beaten Wanda at her side. Consoling about the children who are also in custody, Wanda offers soothing whispers "at once sisterly, maternal and like the attentions of a nurse" (SC 368). And so Sophie is in the care of her lover and "sister." It should be mentioned here that Sophie's relationship with Wanda, who often addresses her as "darling," complements Sophie's needs for a strong figure in her life; she has admitted to losing a sense of identity after her father's death, and she fills this void with the powerful presence of Wanda who is both direct, which Sophie admires, as well as "female" and caring, which Sophie so desperately needs after the abuse of her father and husband. Thus Wanda also doubles as a mother figure for Sophie after her mother has been destroyed mentally and physically by her husband's removal. In

Wanda, Sophie sees the strength she never observed in her own "sweet" submissive mother; we can also see in Wanda's "mothering" of Sophie how submissive Sophie has remained throughout her Warsaw experience, a trait she will take with her through Auschwitz to Yetta's in Brooklyn where Stingo will first encounter her "plaintive and childlike" voice in 1947, almost eight years after her separation from her father and her husband.

Apart from this waiflike consistency in Sophie, one of the supreme ironies of the novel that Stingo drives home is that her capture was due to the Resistance and to its efforts to help Jews escape the ghetto. The dozens of members rounded up with Sophie were corralled and sent to the same fate Jews suffered: "and Sophie too—Sophie the stainless, the inaccessible, the uninvolved—was adventitiously ensnared" (376). And although she does admit the shame she feels when she sees the ghetto, Sophie also honestly reveals that she felt "safer" for her children and herself because the Jews were the special target of the Germans' extermination plan. As noted, Wanda rightly proclaims to a group of Jews that all Poles, all people, are eventually the targets of the Nazis. In dialogical terms, that the devout Catholic child and grandchildren of Professor Bieganski should end up in Auschwitz is Styron's compelling history lesson on tyranny: no one is safe from monologism and its attempt to drown out multivocality and dissent.

Clearly, Styron portrays the Nazi state as the patriarchy gone berserk, a state where domination and then submission to the Fatherland are taken to their genocidal limits. But as the elder Stingo reflects from his own research into Richard Rubenstein's *The Cunning of History* (1975), although the Nazis were the first slaveholders to "fully abrogate any lingering humane sentiments regarding the essence of life itself" (SC 236), the horrors of their domination can be seen as "a full flowering and expression of central tendencies" in the entire patriarchal Judeo-Christian tradition (Law 1990, 57). Thus the genocide promulgated by the Nazi's society of total domination is the legacy of a system of rationalization *privileged* by the patriarchy in Western culture. Law continues, "The Nazi's program of industrialized slaughter . . . is therefore an extreme, *but probably repeatable,* expression of that cultural legacy" (57; italics mine).

When Sophie first narrates the story of her arrival at Auschwitz, Styron has Stingo relate how she in fact originally tells Nathan about her ordeal, even though she had refused earlier. In "tearing open a nearly healed sore" she attempts to share at least highlights of her experience with Nathan to whom she feels she "owes" an outline of her recent history. That Stingo describes her as opening a wound is underscored by his report that she is "gratified by the emotionless, truly pedestrian tone she was able to sustain" while she unfolds an abbreviated version of her imprisonment to Nathan She says, matter-of-factly, "In April of 1943 I was sent to the concentration camp in the south of Poland called Auschwitz-Birkenau" (SC 143). From this toneless, studied beginning she graduates to an explanation of the workings of the two camps: Auschwitz housed slave labor and Birkenau was "for just one thing, and that was extermination" (145). She is saved from the gas chambers, she discloses, because she was of the right age and in relatively good health; she was in Auschwitz for twenty months before the camp was liberated. Importantly, she shares very little else with Nathan besides these bare facts; it is with Stingo she allows herself to recall the scene of her first arrival at Auschwitz, but not until the final pages of the narrative when they have fled New York for the trip south and away from Sophie's latest tormentor, Nathan.

A number of chapters before the close of the novel, Stingo manages to report the results of research he has completed concerning the day upon which Sophie arrived at the camp. It was April Fools' Day, a day that he has been unable to enjoy since his keen awareness of the terrible events of Sophie's first day of April in 1943. Stingo claims with vehemence, "I hate April Fools' Day as I hate the Judeo-Christian God" (SC 379). In his detailed report of the actual numbers of Jews and resistance fighters who were gassed, he chronicles the delay that lasted to dusk as the SS men halted and then resumed their grisly work. Those prisoners remaining in the cars were finally ordered out and the doctors took over the selection process which lasted over an hour. Stingo's prose is as terse as Sophie's first account of that day. "Sophie, Jan and Wanda were sent to the camp" (380). The other half of the prisoners are ordered to their deaths in Crematorium number two at Birkenau, and they include "the flutist Eva Maria Zawistowska, who in a little more than a week would have been eight years old."

In Sophie's own account, details about the ancient first-class railroad cars are interspersed with the note that she took courage from Wanda's voice advising the people stuffed in the car to remain calm and quiet. Eva begins to wail loudly, and the child's screams momentarily terrify Sophie more than the word they all receive about the doomed Jews. Jan manages to shush his little sister, but the wait continues long hours, during which time, "Sophie stared straight ahead, composed her hands in her lap and prepared for death, feeling inexpressible terror but for the first time, too, tasting faintly the blessed bitter relief of acceptance" (SC 481). Suddenly they are released into light and onto the ramp where she meets the "Nordic" Dr. Fritz Jemand von Niemand whom Sophie relates looked like a militarized Leslie Howard, a favorite actor of hers.

Instead of remaining quiet under his first questioning, she speaks up in her perfect German and excites his drunken, demented attention. Styron, in fact, has Niemand, whose name translated means "someone from no one" (Colville 1986, 116), arch his eyebrows and look at Sophie with "inebriate, wet, fugitive eyes, unsmiling" (SC 483). The doctor's *patriarchal gaze,* an arresting example of the image discussed at length in the work of Bauer and Ermarth, fixes Sophie: "she was not strong enough to return his gaze" (483). She senses from his manner that something is terribly wrong, that the rationality of her language, her perfect German, would not save her; it was, indeed, "leading somehow to her swift undoing" as she stood there under "his gaze—the new look in his eye of luminous intensity. . . ." (483). The Doctor's response to her faith in Christ the Redeemer, the central male figure in the Judeo-Christian tradition that Rubinstein critiques as irrevocably bound up in Nazi domination, is his challenge to her to choose which of her children should be gassed. The Doctor abandons his role as healer because his duty to the patriarchy, the Fatherland, has demanded it of him, and he becomes the executioner of little Eva, even though his trick with the language has placed Sophie in the role of the one with the choice. In his "oddly abstract voice, like that of a lecturer examining the delicately shaded facet of a proposition in logic," he taunts her, "So you believe in Christ the Redeemer?" (483) His control of her language, of her choice, leaves her in total shocked disbelief. The patriarchy that has supported her, educated her, identified her, languaged her, now forces her to assume responsibility for its cruelty and masks it in sophistry. "You're a Polack, not a Yid. That gives you a privilege—a choice" (483).

By suggesting later in the narrative that Niemand is in a religious crisis at the moment he orders Sophie to choose, Styron underlines Richard Rubenstein's point that the camps themselves were "manifestations of the basic religious traditions of the West, not departures from them" (Law 1990, 58). In discussing this "night side" of the Judeo-Christian tradition, Rubenstein points out that "[w]hat makes the problem so serious is that there is no escape from [this] . . . ethos of exclusivism and intolerance . . . as long as our fundamental culture is derived from a religious tradition that insists upon the dichotomous division of mankind into the elect and the repro-

bate" (Rubenstein 1975, 93). Styron personalizes the experience o.
the dichotomy explained by Rubenstein by involving the reader ir
the wrenching human drama of Sophie's choice, implying that as
a member of the culture each reader is a "potential perpetrator as
well as [a] victim"; and at the root of this dehumanization is the
power to divide human beings (as Niemand does with "Yids" and
"Polacks") "into the elect and the reprobate," into defining categories which are to Rubinstein implicit in "the illness we call Judeo-
Christian civilization" (93). Sophie does not see her daughter's face
as Eva is led away—with great gentleness, the narrative tells us—
by Niemand's aide; Sophie is blinded by her own tears, and Stingc
reports that she was grateful that she had not seen Eva's final
expression, for she was almost driven mad "by her last glimpse of
that vanishing small form" (SC 484). That Sophie "chooses" to
send her daughter to the gas instead of her son is no choice at all.
The Nazi slave-system has determined Eva's value, not Sophie.
The patriarchy, in the person of the Doctor, has no use for the
little girl *or* the little boy, and so they are silenced victims of their
own grandfather's *vernichtung* policy.

Imprisoned in the terrible slave-capitalism of Auschwitz, Sophie
endures the death-in-life of the camp until she is reassigned to work
at Kommandant Höss's house. A few days before she goes to Haus
Höss, she meets Wanda, whom she has not seen since their arrival
some six months before. As usual, Wanda implores the reluctant
Sophie to work for the underground and to spy on Höss, perhaps
to even smuggle out a radio. Sophie has a sudden flash of insight
that she will never see Wanda again, "this brave, resolute, luminous
flame of a girl" (SC 390). In light of their previous relationship,
their sisterhood is even more apparent to the reader as Wanda
urges Sophie to "use" Höss. "For once you've got to forget that
priggish Christer's morality of yours and use your sex for all it's
worth," she says; "give him a good fucking and he'll be eating out
of your hand" (391). So it is that Wanda gives Sophie the idea to
seduce Höss in order to help her get Jan safely enrolled in the
Lebensborn program. Wanda leaves, and again Sophie is racked
with insecurity; she feels "weak and hopeless, with a sense of
inadequacy" in the face of Wanda's dedication and strength of purpose (392).

These two "sisters," the one battling for her own and her child's
survival while the other continues her underground war against the
overwhelming strength of the Nazi patriarchy, meet for a final
moment and then part, both young European women caught up
in the madness of their "rational" civilization as it seeks through

domination to "purify" its destiny *über alles*. Wanda is the last person from her life before Auschwitz that Sophie sees alive; later, after Sophie leaves Höss's "employ," she receives a note from Wanda with news of her son's health, but after that nothing. She learns afterward Wanda is found out, tortured, and hanged on a hook where she slowly strangled. Says Sophie of her, "She was the bravest person I ever knew" (SC 412), even though previously she had identified Wanda as the root of her problems because of the latter's constant reminders that Sophie bore a responsibility to humanity to work for the underground against the Nazis. Wanda's courage and protofeminist consciousness, awakened by socialist ideals, are clearly respected by Styron in the narrative; and her death is depicted as a result of her being such a dangerous threat to the powers-that-be. Although her sister Wanda attempts time and again to give her a new voice as a patriot and as an emancipated socialist woman, Sophie is a woman who endures in silence because *she has no voice*. Indeed, as we have seen, Sophie's father had, literally, taken over her voice by insisting she learn German before all other languages (although in conversation Sophie prefers mellifluous French). Her father also *chooses her voice* in that he has her remain a copier of male language as his stenographer; she becomes a skilled *transposer* of words, but she has not been raised to be a *composer* of words.

Sophie remains, then, a passive woman-child in search of a strong father–possessor who is loving as well as protective, sensitive as well as commanding, the kind of man she was attracted to in Walter Durrfeld. Having been defined by men's desires for her, she is adrift without such men in her life. Looking ahead, we can see why, when Stingo first sees her, she pleads with Nathan that the two of them need each other, to which Nathan makes a series of replies that compare her to various terrible diseases. It is Sophie who desperately needs Nathan's *defining* albeit pathological maleness. Styron again underscores the idea that we all are victims of dehumanizing forces, whether we fight them, join them, or merely suffer in silence; indeed, in the case of Sophie, her passivity brings on the same punishments as the active Wanda endures. Perhaps Sophie's suffering is worse if we consider the terrible guilt feelings she endures long after the others have had their trials ended by death. Another facet of Styron's cautionary tale may very well be that if the "uninvolved" Sophie—as beautiful, educated, passive to male dominance, and Aryan as she is—can suffer, then who is "safe" from the gaze of Dr. Jemand von Niemand, who is himself the son of a domineering father?

Stingo reveals in his narrative that Sophie tells him of two major events that take place during her stay at Auschwitz that she conceals from Nathan because he would not "understand" the delicate balancing act of subterfuge she has built up around herself to endure her massive guilt feelings. The two events were, of course, her arrival at the camp and her "very brief" relationship with Kommandant Rudolf Höss of KL Auschwitz; the scene in Höss's attic office is related to Stingo over beers on a "rainy August afternoon at the Maple Court" in 1947 (SC 220), about four years after the actual events take place. Stingo begins this section of the narrative by relating how clear his own memories of her narrative are for him; they possess a "cinematic" quality because of their intensity, but also because the event centers around October the third. This date's importance for Stingo is manifest; it is the birthday of three of his "heroes": Thomas Wolfe, Nat Turner, and his own father. It is also the anniversary of Sophie's marriage to Casimir Zawistowski in Cracow. We may infer from this and from other textual information that Sophie was married in 1933 at the age of eighteen; thus, she is twenty-eight years old the day she overcomes her fears and begins her plan to seduce the Kommandant and rescue her nine-year-old son Jan. Stingo is also able to supply a letter that he wrote on the day of Sophie's arrival in Höss's house, a note of "birthday felicitations" sent to his father when the young Stingo was at Duke University in the V–12 officer's training program (220). Thus dovetailing his life with the overwhelming suffering of Sophie's, Stingo manages for the reader a path by which to enter Höss's upside-down universe; the innocent Stingo becomes our white, Anglo-Saxon, Protestant Virgil into this hellish landscape.

As Höss's amanuensis, from the Latin for "slave at handwriting," Sophie is able to live a life of bare subsistence that far exceeds the starvation and cruelty beyond the compound walls that separate the Kommandant's house from the camp itself. Styron uses Sophie as a means of penetrating the mystery of the mind of Höss and of the entire scheme of the Nazi Final Solution. But as a witness with a mission for herself and her son, she is more than an observer-victim. In an odd turn of events, Sophie finds herself more appreciated for her stenographic gifts by Höss than by her father. Sophie even suggests a few phrases for Höss and is promptly complimented, for which she feels "a glow of satisfaction, almost pleasure" after long hours of impersonal businesslike interaction that day (SC 224). Sophie has been working in Höss's house for ten days previous to this monumental day and has it seems nothing at all to reveal about those other banal workdays than that Höss has at least grown less strictly formal with her (255). During another dictation, Höss abruptly halts and muses on the sight of his stallion Harlekin in "full poetic flight" (225). In a reverie, Höss speaks aloud of the animal's majesty and its breed. "The greatest horses in the world, these Polish Arabians," a statement which drives home the point that this man is, after all, a Nazi who has more praise for Polish horses than for Polish people; but he soon returns to his official tone. Nonetheless, Sophie has begun to hope for a chance to effect her plan to save Jan; she has returned, in a sense, to a familiar role: handmaiden to a powerful man, in this case a skilled transposer-of-the-language handmaiden. That Sophie begins to feel more and more in her element, or at the very least more sure of herself, is important to note because earlier on this morning of October third, she has had a "feeling of strangeness and loss such as she had never known." Stingo reports that earlier that morning Sophie collapsed in nausea as the stench of burning flesh reached her from the crematoria; so shaken is she that she cannot recall her own name. "'Oh god, help me!' she called aloud. 'I don't know what I am!'" (266). That morning her identity crisis reaches a critical stage, and now with an opening in Höss's mood signaling familiar avenues of possible success with the necessary obeisance, she at least knows what she is: the secretary-hand-maiden again.

As she types his previous dictation concerning the overabundance of Greek Jews to be exterminated, she translates the jargon of *Special Action* into its real-world language. This important translation, especially for the reader, draws attention to the necessary obfuscation and subsequent creation of "professional" languages through bureaucratic circumlocutions. It is a commonplace that a control of law and its language, and therefore the languages of regulation and bureaucracy, has been firmly in the hands of a elite male professional groups who for centuries have defined the very existence of selected groups of people. Slaves were defined as people-as-property, and women, until relatively recent reforms induced by suffrage in largely Western cultures, were likewise defined as little more than chattel goods in a patriarchal system of householders' rights. Sophie, serving as Styron's translator and ours, clearly glosses Höss's intent: to use Greek Jews as members of "death commando units" at his ovens until they, too, will be exterminated. Stingo explains that Sophie, who had been so shocked by her father's endorsement of *vernichtung* years earlier, now reacts hardly at all to the gravity of Höss's real message. Six months before what she was transcribing would have seemed "so monstrous as to have surpassed belief," but now such news is simply part of the commonplace events of "this new universe she inhabited, no more to be remarked upon than (as in the other world she had once known) the fact that one went to the baker's to buy one's bread" (226).

As her workday continues, Höss suddenly asks her a rhetorical question, and she becomes so flustered that she is taken off balance and her pencil flies out of her hand; but she can muster no reply, nor can she even return his smile, such is her dominance by his role as her absolute master, her Kommandant. Still, there is a conversation of sorts building between them as he asks if she is Catholic; she responds with a spontaneous "Are you?" for which she instantly criticizes herself as "idiocy." But he responds impassively that he has lost faith in Christ; her surprise is with his treatment of her question as worthy of a reply; again, it appears she receives more consideration from Höss than from her own father. Then comes a moment of great import for Sophie: she looks up from her work to find Höss gazing straight into her eyes and complimenting her kerchief. Sophie is so taken aback that she stammers a thank-you and continues feverishly to speak of his kindness and Frau Höss's and so on, all the while hoping fervently that she may be able to maneuver this powerful man somehow. But he is abruptly called away from the room. During the intervening few minutes in which she is alone to assess her "progress" with Höss, she decides that she will take Wanda's advice and "appear attractive to him," even to appear "sexy," or as she tells Stingo, "Looking as if I wanted to be asked to fuck" (233).

Finally, some forty pages later in the novel, Styron returns us to Sophie waiting patiently for her Kommandant who returns only to be struck by a migraine, doubtless stress-related. After the attack subsides, Höss asks Sophie how she came to work at his house, a rare and coveted billet for prisoners. She ascribes her fortune to fate, which she tells Höss brought her to him because only he can understand the grave mistake that has been made by her imprisonment. She hastens through an argument in which she pleads that she is indeed *judenfeindlich,* anti-Semitic, like her professor-father. But he wants to hear none of this, and craftily reorganizing her efforts and resources, she recounts the story of how attempted lesbian rapes brought her to the attention of a block leader who recommended her to Höss's staff. Sophie dramatizes the homophobic elements of the story, recognizing Höss's own chronic hatred of homosexuals and using it to her advantage. She speaks further, in careful "obsequious solicitude" (SC 274), establishing her under-standing of the complexities of the Jewish problem that plagues him: he cannot kill them fast enough to satisfy Berlin. Surprised at her vehement hatred of Jews, he remarks that she must have a knowledge of the crimes of which Jews are capable. "So few women have any informed knowledge or understanding about any-thing" (275). And with this he articulates a basic prejudice shared by those in any power structure toward marginalized and disenfran-chised groups. The very patriarchal norms that promulgate the "moral" necessity of female ignorance use the results of such a system of neglect to verify their initial arguments. The vapidness of such assumptions as Höss's were ably discussed and dismissed as early as the eighteenth century by Mary Wollstonecraft in *A Vindication of the Rights of Woman*. And yet in one of the most technically advanced societies in Europe, in the middle of the twen-tieth century, assumptions such as Höss's held the field.

But Sophie, having worked so diligently to get Höss to this mo-ment of "shared" convictions, presses her case further by prof-fering her only copy of her father's tract against the Jews to him. She also regales him with stories of an imaginary younger sister who was sexually assaulted by a Jew, but Höss responds that Jews "are perpetrators of many forms of gross evil but they are not rapists" (SC 278). He reminds her, identifies her, that she is, after all, "a Pole, and therefore an enemy of the Reich." He then launches into a lecture on her true place in the Nazi worldview, validating Wanda's contentions that no one is "safe" from dehu-manization if the Nazis succeed with the Jews.

> Indeed, there are some in highest authority . . . who consider you and
> your kind and nation on a par with the Jews, Menschentiere, equally
> worthless, equally polluted in the racial sense, equally justifying righ-
> teous hatred. Poles living in the Fatherland are beginning to be marked
> with a P—an ominous sign for you people. (278)

Sophie bursts into tears at this, which unsettles Höss who suddenly claims she has been flirting with him, and, in his sexist mind, he blames her. "You have made it very difficult for me . . . distracting me from my proper duties." It is a backhanded sort of tribute that Höss would find a woman who has lived in Auschwitz for six months guilty of flirtation. Styron's persistent description of So-phie's beauty would seem to be dramatically vindicated if we are to believe that Sophie can be considered attractive to the most powerful man in the camp after six months of near-starvation and deprivation, along with severe mental and physical abuse.

Höss, however, does react more supportively as he says her flirtation cannot completely be her fault because she is "an extremely attractive woman" (SC 280). Her identity as a mere Pole has been laid out, but she is a valuable Pole in that she reminds him of an actress, a dream woman, who played Gretchen in *Faust*, a woman he recalls simply as Margarete. "There is something about the pure and radiant beauty of a certain kind of woman—fair of skin and of hair . . . that inspires me to idolize that beauty . . . to the point of worship" (281). Karen Horney has shown that such celebration and adoration of the female has its actual origins in a "dread of woman" on the part of some men (Horney 1967, 136). Dorothy Dinnerstein has discussed at some length this "dread" that a "goddess" produces in a man, feelings apparently deeply rooted in fears and sometimes disgust toward the mysteries of the fertile female body which can in a sense "capture" male genitalia (Dinnerstein 1976, 125). Sophie, says Höss, inspires him in the same way as his Margarete. Enrolled in his "pantheon" of Madonnas, Sophie is briefly assaulted by him as he tries ineffectually to possess this re-presentation of his Aryan Dream Woman. "Trembling like a sick man," he kisses her only to be rudely interrupted by a knock at the door. The obvious contradiction in this man's desire "to worship" Sophie after damning her as racially impure brings to the fore another aspect of patriarchal domination: women are simultaneously praised and damned for their complicity in the false visions men create for them in society: the Madonna is put on a pedestal and celebrated for her ignorance of a "man's" world, whereas the whore is reviled (but secretly desired) for her "knowledge." In patriarchal societies where knowledge is power, the women who gain knowledge are seen as impure, as unnatural; but submissiveness is likewise scorned, finally, precisely because it "confirms" that women are contemptible beings lacking knowledge and thus power.

Interrupted, appropriately, by family business, Höss returns to Sophie, but his ardor has cooled. He admits his desire to have intercourse with her; it would allow him "to lose" himself and find "forgetfulness" (SC 282). He claims they could have met "in a spiritual way" with a common understanding. "But they have got rid of me" (282). By "they" he means Berlin, and he too must be on his way as she must go back to her place in Block Two. She desperately pleads her case in a last gasp, flinging herself at him and tearing at his shirt; he finds the "demonstration" offensive—

that she thought he could be "manipulated" by a show of "affection." But Sophie continues pleading, explaining to Stingo that her mind-set was brought about by the Nazis themselves, and she would have done anything—killed Jews or even other Poles—if Höss had promised her some time with her son Jan. "And this is why . . . I know the Nazis turned me into a sick animal like all the rest, I should feel so much guilt over all the things I done there. And over just being alive" (286).

So long has it been her reflex to consign herself to male authority figures, especially those in positions of great power, that she cannot conceive that Höss would not keep his word. This reflection on Höss's word is important in that it is an example of the sort of message Elizabeth Ermarth draws from the beginning of Plato's *Republic*. Ermarth describes the scene of Socrates' meeting with his friend Polemarchus who "playfully" threatens to detain him and prevent Socrates from entering the city. "How can you possibly persuade such as will not hear?" asks the powerful Polemarchus; "By no means" is the brief and knowing reply (Ermarth 1983, 1). Ermarth sees this as the classic confrontation between the rule of force and the rule of agreement or true consensus. Polemarchus' jest is no joke to the patron saint of dialogue and persuasion: "Violence forecloses on consensus," concludes Ermarth; "You cannot communicate with someone who refuses to listen; also implied here is that those who refuse to listen opt automatically for the rule of force rather than for that of persuasion and agreement" (1).

That the rule of force which refuses to listen is rooted in an androcentric patriarchy is implicit in Ermarth's discussion. As such, this realization of the true nature of authoritarian systems—that of force—allows the reader to see how the strategies of dehumanization employed by the ruthless force of the Nazi turns Sophie from an already submissive daughter into a "sick animal" willing to do anything for Höss in order to save her offspring. Victims become the very worst of the victimizers; the oppressed turn on themselves in desperation to accomplish the bidding of the oppressor and thereby survive; for a brief time, the victim can *identify* with the victimizer and achieve a kind of release from the pain of subjugation. The patriarchy's control of the Word, in this case, Höss's absolute control over the lives of Sophie and her young son Jan by means of his "word of honor," is cynically reinforced by the fact of Höss's refusal to "back up" his own word of honor.

The lesson is that those who have the ultimate power over the word may revoke any or all provisions extended to the oppressed. Sophie laments that Höss did not keep his word, even though she questions herself for trusting a man so: "Why should I think this SS man might have a thing called honor? Maybe it was because of my father, who was always talking about the German army and officers and their high sense of honor and principles and such" (SC 411). As Ermarth suggests in her discussion of the scene from Plato's *Republic*, control of the word and the rule of force go hand in hand; but ultimately force dictates the role the word will play in human interplay. How could Sophie have influenced or argued with Höss to keep his word, his honor? As Glaucon succinctly replied in the scene with Socrates and Polemarchus, "By no means." The patriarchy which proclaims its own vaunted approach to dialogue as an "open exchange" can, as it requires, shut dialogue down if its authority is threatened in any way. Höss's excuse to Sophie echos Ermarth's explanation of the irreconcilable difference between the rule of force and that of dialogue. "To bring [Jan] here would be dangerous—it would compromise my position" (410), that is, his position in the authoritarian hierarchy of an absolutist state, the patriarchy of the Third Reich. Above all else, even above the lives of innocent children, Höss must preserve the status quo of the Reich's power structure; Sophie's dialogue about putting her son in the *Lebensborn* program, as convincing as it may be, is doomed to failure precisely because her words are met by the irresistible force of the Reich. As a "non-person" in the Reich's own linguistic "logic," her voice is not privileged and therefore may not be used as a basis for argument. Although the patriarchy of the Reich allows it to except *itself* in the person of Höss from keeping its own "word of honor," it allows no exceptions for the marginalized because in that exception would lie a *recognition* of the rights due a person. But Sophie is not a person; she is only a female Polack.

In their last exchange, after his "apology" for not producing Jan for Sophie to see, Höss's utter disengagement from dialogue with others not affiliated directly with the Reich's power base is evident in his dismissal of her. "Go now," he says abruptly. Sophie, still forced to play the submissive even at this point, actually thanks Höss for "helping" her (SC 413); but he interrupts her to ask if she recognizes the music playing on the phonograph. Sophie does, but in a limited but clear gesture of resistance plays "dumb," and "finds" herself saying to him, "No, not really," she replies: "Why?" This simple question of hers, one that echoes her earlier evasive response when Höss asks if she is Catholic, is lacking in slavish deference to his immense authority over her and causes Stingo/Styron to note that Höss must have been "disappointed." From his point of view, she has disappointed him in that she is not, after all, the ideal Aryan woman. The irony, of course, is that she is extremely well-versed in music, but she chooses to *appear* ignorant precisely because Höss might discern some modicum of satisfaction from being able to share that moment with *her,* his Polish substitute for the Aryan Dream Girl. The scene reveals that the Nazi experiment in exclusion is doomed to failure because such a practice cannot *continue* unchallenged over time; its will-to-monologism is continually undercut by the voices of the oppressed, as is demonstrated in this slight scene of Sophie's interiorized rebellion against the hegemony of Höss's musical taste. "Each internalization of repression contains the possibility of rebellion" (Bauer 1988, xii).

As Dale Marie Bauer argues from a feminist point of view, inclusion/dialogism is the nature of language in spite of patriarchal attempts by force to rule out other vernaculars, other marginalized voices. In short, multivocality or inclusion will eventually win out in language and literature, and, significantly, in society, because such diversity is at the very heart of the nature of things, as can be seen in the existence of Sophie as a character: her voice, representing as it does the multitudes of the silenced, speaks through a male and becomes part of what Walter Ong appropriately refers to as the *Grapholect* (Ong 1982, 8). Styron's re-creation of Sophie is testimony to the accuracy of the idea of the dialogic novel as Bakhtin envisions it; the voice of a woman is the central character in Styron's attempt to "understand" Auschwitz and by extension the powers that enabled the Nazis to succeed to the extent that they did. Sophie not only enters the Grapholect but in a very real way directs the discourse by driving Stingo to try to understand his obsession for her and thus to study and investigate the Holocaust, not as a unique phenomenon but as a legacy of Judeo-Christian culture. The entire patriarchal system's exclusivity is undermined at its vicious zenith in the Third Reich by the testimony of "a piece of Polish *Dreck*" (SC 412).

After her dismissal by Höss, Sophie returns to the steno pool barracks where she struggled to survive for another fourteen months until she is relocated to a camp for displaced persons in Sweden. In Sweden, Sophie decides to commit a "great sacrilege" by committing suicide in a church outside the camp because she wishes "to show and prove" her hatred of God who she believes has abandoned her. She reaches the church and actually succeeds in cutting into her wrist as she converses with God; in this conversation, Sophie addresses the all-powerful *patriarch of patriarchs* in a contemptuous tone, reminiscent of the tone she took with her father when he offered her tea belatedly in that Cracow café so many years before when she realized how much she hated her father. God asks her why she should want to desecrate his holy place the church by killing herself there. She replies, petulantly, "If You don't know in all Your wisdom, God, then I can't tell You" (SC 409). Sophie explains that her reasons are her secret, and she begins to cut herself only to pause as she reflects that Höss is still alive. "I know it sounds like *folie*, Stingo," she says, "—well I have this understanding which comes in a flash that I cannot die as long as Rudolf Höss is alive. It would be his final triumph" (409). Sophie dismisses God as the patriarch who failed to live up to his implicit bargain with her: she has offered her obeisance and submissive devotion, her entire identity, in return for security and for the care of a protective father. But God, in the figures of her father and then the state in Höss, fails to live up to the contract. But when she moves to New York she discovers Nathan, who opens her up sexually and thereby thrusts her into another, although somewhat more dauntingly physical contract with a man, one that will prove fatal ironically because she is "saved" in the first place from suicide by the continuing existence of a mass-murderer. After Höss's hanging, Nathan's driving death wish pervades her existence until *Thanatos* cannot be rejected any longer.

Sophie arrives in New York City, the "kingdom of the Jews" as Stingo calls it, in the early months of 1946, whence she had "been brought . . . under the auspices of an international relief organization" (SC 88). For Sophie America becomes "the New World in spirit as well as fact," and she indulges herself "greedily" in the pleasures of music, food, and literature (89). Before she meets Nathan and discovers his death wish, she enjoys New York as a place where she can recover a sense of inner solace "along with the awareness that there were things to live for, and that she might actually be able to reclaim the scattered pieces of her life and *compose of them a new self,* given half a chance" (89; italics mine). Sophie's desire to "compose" herself, in both senses of the word, but especially that of seeing herself as a new text, a new identity which she could author herself, are important aspects of her new American self because it is in New York that she takes on the English language through which she communicates her previous selves eventually to the innocent Stingo. Styron reproduces and mimics Sophie's at times comic English syntax to highlight her voice's fresh assaults on the organization of the grammar as well as the sensibilities of her auditor Stingo. Hers is a distinctive voice in American literature which itself has a history of including dialects as a means of accessing cultures and their representative speakers. In an effort every bit as bold as Mark Twain's inclusion of Black English in *Huck Finn* and in his own voicing of Nat Turner, Styron has Sophie sift through German, Polish, and cosmopolitan French, finally arriving at an English which gives her voice its vitality and integrity. Styron's is an American novel heavily invested in the multivocality of the American century even though that multivocality is framed by the likes of a Stingo, Sophie's troubled transliterator.

June 1946 brings into Sophie's reconstructed life-world "a disastrous ending to the precarious equilibrium she had devised for herself" (SC 91). She experiences a digital rape that forces her into a headlong retreat from the life she had been building. Lasting no more than thirty seconds, the invasion of the single loathsome finger during a blackout on a crowded subway car fills her with more horror and revulsion than "a straightforward conventional rape" would have, Sophie later tells Stingo. This act strips her "bare"; she returns to her room, thinking of the "womblike perfection of that clock into which as a child she had crawled in her fancy, afloat on a steel spring, regarding the levers, the rubies, the wheels" (94). As music had been her spiritual balm as a child, Mozart's *Sinfonia Concertante* in E-flat major buoys her as she listens to the radio during her "malignant depression" following the rape, and she once again manages to return to her job at Dr. Blackstock's chiropractic office. The violation of the rape reminds her of the blackness of Auschwitz, and further reinforces the bleak outlook that had almost led to her suicide in Sweden. The rape also establishes in her mind her vulnerability even in the apparently "safe" streets of New York far away from the Nazi camps and Höss; the machine of dehumanization and victimization that legitimizes violence against women resides in any stranger lurking in the shadows of the subway. Later, because she is "Catholic and Polish and a child of her time and place . . . a young woman brought up with puritanical repressions and sexual taboos as adamantine as those of any Alabama Baptist maiden" (98), she is embarrassed to report to the good doctor that she has had bleeding as a result of the rape. Unfortunately, Blackstock's chiropractic aggravates the problem and prevents her from seeking proper medical help, which in turn leads to her collapse in the library—where Nathan finds her and "rescues" her.

Such is the serpentine route Styron uses to reveal the complexities of Sophie's relationship to Nathan. The rape causes the bleeding that Blackstock misdiagnoses which directly leads to Sophie's image of Nathan as a "Doctor" who will cure her of her illness, her chemical deficiency, "anemia." By June of 1946, ironically as a result of her desire to read the "male" American poet Emil Dickens, she falls, literally, into the hands of a savior-Jew who will give her a new identity, a new language as a *shiksa*. In fact, the first thing Sophie apprehends about Nathan is his overpowering voice: "she moved her head listlessly, conscious of something else, a voice, a man's voice, orotund, powerful, raging. . . ." (105). His first words about her, spoken in a blast at the rude librarian, refer to her as "that nice and lovely girl there with a little trouble with the language." As he talks with her, he calls her a "sweetie" and "honey": "Ahh, you're so beautiful, how did you get to be so beautiful?" (105) From the raging Nathan who scorns the librarian, he changes to a *"gentle monologue,* lulling, soothing, murmurously infusing her with a sense of repose" (105; italics mine). Sophie is again in the hands of a powerful voice, another monologue, but another one split, as her father and Höss had both been, between the contradiction of dominating force and gentle dialogue.

When she first meets Nathan, she assumes, as I have noted, that he is a doctor, a physician, who will cure her; this immediate trust of a complete stranger is understandable if we remember the societal trust embedded in the appellation "doctor": "she thought he was a doctor even later as with a kind of commanding encouragement he held her against his arm" (SC 134). And when he leaves, she feels a "terrible panic" that he might not return to her apartment; Sophie admits that it was *"absolument fou"* for her to know a man for only forty-five minutes and feel an "emptiness" when he left, but, she tells Stingo, "I was crazy for him to come back" (135). When he does return, she tells Nathan in an abbreviated way of her trials in Auschwitz; she even defends herself from his first criticism of her and her job with a chiropractor whom Nathan from the start regards as nothing more than a "humbug." Sophie reacts by claiming she could find no other work, and she explains in an apologetic tone that she would like to do "something better" but she has no talents. "I am," she says, "a very uncomplete person. I wished somehow to teach, to teach music, to become a teacher of music—but this was impossible" (141). It is partially impossible, of course, because of her father's early resistance. At this point in her life, although it is fairly early in the narrative itself, Sophie has experienced the erasure of her Polish life along with the trauma of the camp. Her magnificent understatement that "it was impossible" for her to become a music teacher culminates in

 er further remarks that first night with Nathan when she explains
hat she has "nothing left from the past. Nothing at all" (142). And
his, she says, is "one of the reasons she feels so "uncomplete."
And, continuing in her understated way, she concludes: "It would
 ave been wonderful for me to have had the career in music that
 thought I would have. But I was *prevented*" (142; italics mine).

 "Prevented" she certainly was, but she continues in this vein of
 arefully laying down a version of her story that she deems accept-
 ble to the volatile Nathan. She has edited her life around the
 xpectations of men, and her account to Nathan is no exception.
 She sticks to the bare facts of her twenty months in Auschwitz, but
 she does falsely embellish her "loving" father's character. Stingo
 xplains that there was another rationale for her "understated"
 approach to her past: not many in America were in any meaningful
way informed about the camps, and any continued explanation
 causes her "lacerating pain." Another explanation offered by the
 elder Stingo as he reveals bit by bit how Sophie in turn revealed
her story is that guilt figured largely in her major and minor alter-
ations of her narration. The word "guilt," Stingo discovers, "was
often dominant in her vocabulary," and it becomes clear to him
 "that a hideous sense of guilt always chiefly governed the reassess-
ments she was forced to make of her past" (SC 147).

 With that, the elder Stingo launches into a summary of Simone
Weil's point that terrible suffering often stamps the very souls of
victims with a self-scorn or disgust that can become self-hatred
coupled with a corrosive guilt; paradoxically, Weil notes, this guilt
does not necessarily afflict those who commit crimes, as can be
witnessed in Rudolf Höss's own book on his Auschwitz leadership
which Stingo quotes at some length later in the narrative. Höss's
excuse for not reacting with revulsion to the extermination orders'
immorality is perfect bureaucratic logic, the locus of Weil's point
that "real evil is gloomy, monotonous, barren, boring" (SC 149):
 "Whether this mass extermination of the Jews was necessary or
not was something on which I could not allow myself to form an
opinion, for I lacked the *necessary breadth of view*" (152; italics
mine). This chilling abdication of even the most rudimentary moral
awareness points up that Styron answers the question "Where was
God?" at Auschwitz with the question "Where was man?" (513)
In a cruel twist, we find Sophie racked by torturous guilt which
Höss does not feel, guilt about her own survival. In another sense,
her guilt is the result of her failure time and again to take a more
active role in the struggle against the Nazis. Her reluctance to "get
involved," understandable though it may be, results in terrible guilt

feelings, and this aspect of her story emphasizes one of the novel's most salient themes: no one is untouched when others are dehumanized and brutalized.

After Sophie's "reconstruction" by Nathan when he procures for her superb dentures and a regimen of food supplements and health care that all contribute to her physical revival, they become lovers and he embarks upon her sexual rejuvenation after a lifetime of repressed desires under first her father and later her husband. Durrfeld is her only other admitted "desire," but her meeting with him at Auschwitz proved that even he has been radically altered by the Third Reich. For all that, Sophie's description of the dream she has just before she sees Durrfeld at Höss's office deserves attention precisely because it is so sensual, in the "carnal" meaning of the word. Sophie is described by Stingo as being "untroubled or untouched by sexual desire" while in the camp, but this "total absence of amorous feeling" throws into a more pronounced "focus" her dream of the German Man. Having a continuing interest in the psychoanalytic orientations found in much of literary modernism, Styron uses dreams in this narrative, as he does in previous works, to suggest possible explanations for characters' behavior.

Sophie's dream of the German Man is ripe with detail: the man is middle-aged, jovial, fair, attractive; more than merely attractive for Sophie, he "made her melt with desire" (SC 401). The dream scene is a beach, and Sophie wears a "transparent skirt" in which she feels "unashamedly provocative" (401). She enters a chapel, stands nude before the altar where the unnamed Man, also naked, scowls which excites her, "inflaming her lust." The man orders her to fellate him and then directs her to "kneel at the altar beneath the skeletal cruciform emblem of God's suffering, glowing like naked bone" (402). He enters her from the rear in a "cloaklike embrace," as she hears "a clattering of hoofs on the floor, smell[s] smoke, crie[s] out with delight as the hairy belly and groin swarm[s] around her naked buttocks. . . ." Sophie finally recognizes the Man as Walter Durrfeld whose name she had heard spoken many times in Höss's office before the dream occurs; but the Durrfeld she encounters in the dream "metamorphosed into the devil" as will Nathan.

Sophie boasts to Stingo about how Nathan provides nearly everything she possesses, music, entertainment money, her teeth, her clothes, and her diaphragm. She has never used a diaphragm before, but she accepts it with a "rush of liberating satisfaction, feeling that it was the ultimate token of her leave-taking from the church" (SC 314). She also tells Stingo that she has become accusomed to Nathan's sexual appetites and his performance, particularly when he is on a "pill jag" and filled with amphetamines; these essions are "no mere fun" for her. "Sex with Nathan in his amphetamine thrall . . . was unharnessed, oceanic, otherworldly. And t went on forever. . . ." (324). Her multiorgasmic delight in Nathan s escapist, however: "at last liberated (adieu Cracow!), uninhibited, self-absorbed bliss: his extravagant ability to make her ome—to come not once or twice but over and over again until an lmost sinister final losingness of herself has been achieved, a sucking death like descent into caverns during which she cannot tell vhether she is lost herself or in him, a sense of black whirling lownward into an inseparability of flesh" (331). For Sophie, it eems, both Eros and Thanatos are commingled in her sex with Nathan, and her pilgrimage seeking the Man who excites her to elf-abnegating carnal amnesia reaches its own climax in Nathan's nsatiable drug-addled frenzies of lust and sadism. So intense is he when Nathan brings her to orgasm, she cries out in Polish— he only time she thinks or speaks in the language anymore—"*Wez mnie, wez mnie,*" which she translates to mean "Take me, take me" (331) in a sense of abandon, a sense of her losing herself in he "downward" whirl of their sexual union which erases for a vhile her feelings of total alienation from the male gods who previously had defined her existence.

The passage that defines more clearly the death-in-life pact Sophie seems to have made with Nathan includes their ill-fated trip o Connecticut during which Nathan's severe drug abuse results n Sophie's brutal beating and subjection by her self-styled "savor." It begins as they motor up the Merrit Parkway toward a Connecticut hideaway and the promise of blissful lovemaking in the country. But after his drug frenzy plunges him into deep jealous ages and paranoia, they stop at the roadside only to have Nathan age again. He orders her, as does the German Dream Man, down on her knees to accept him, but Nathan's variation is to have Sophie "accept" his urine in her mouth and then curse her for having no ego at all" (SC 340); this blaming of the victim is hideously eminiscent of Höss's impatience with Jews whose sheer numbers confound the capacity of even his extermination camp. In his renzy, Nathan orders her to fellate him, calling her "Irma Griese," after the infamous and inhumanly cruel matron of Auschwitz. But so low is her own self-esteem that, even at the moment of his shouted curses that she is an "Irma Griese Jew-burning cunt," Sophie feels she "cannot live without [Nathan] . . . aware of the riteness of the thought but also of its absolute truth" (335). His death, she explains, would be her final agony. In that coppice near the roadside of the Merrit Parkway, Nathan kicks her three time and succeeds in breaking a rib; but his attempt to urinate in her mouth brings him to an inner crisis, and he begins a "crash" that is abated only by heavy doses of barbiturates which Sophie, even at this cruel juncture in their relationship, helps him find. Leading him back like a "wounded man" to the car, Sophie, for the firs time, feels pity for Nathan: "Poor Devil" (342). Stingo traces her memory of that climactic scene: "it is the very first time she has experienced an emotion having to do with Nathan that resembles anything so degrading as pity. She cannot stand pitying him" (342).

Later, in their motel room as they both drowse in a drugged haze, Nathan plays with tiny capsules of cyanide perched on his lips as he lectures her on the subtle differences between life and death and how intertwined they are in nature. HCN, he says, is spread throughout nature, but sugars form glycosides with cyanide and change its deadly form, "only a molecule's organic distance," into a tasty macaroon crunch (SC 332). Sophie flushes the cyanide down the toilet, a little concerned about polluting Connecticut water, but relieved when the toilet swirl removes this suicide dose. Thus does Sophie's desperately flawed Dream Man combine Eros and Thanatos. Terry Eagleton's portrayal of the psychoanalytic view of the ego's attempt in the modern world to find a blissful inanimate state where it cannot be injured is instructive here in reference to Styron's portrayal of Sophie. "The ego is a pitiable, precarious entity, battered by the external world, scourged by the cruel unbraidings of the superego, plagued by the greedy, insatiable demands of the id" (Eagleton 1983, 161). Eagleton explains that Freud's compassion for the ego is a "compassion for the human race, labouring under the almost intolerable demands placed upon it by a civilization built upon the repression of desire and the deferment of gratification" (161). By claiming that he is trying to understand Auschwitz by exploring Sophie's experience, Stingo and therefore Styron are, like Freud, concerned with the embattled modern ego. And although Nathan frees her from minor guilt feelings over her lust to fellate him (and others, like Stingo, whom she eventually does), he dominates her ruthlessly and dooms her to spasms of life-threatening guilt over her complicity with the Nazis. And because there is in some sense a truth to Nathan's basic claim about her complicity, as the narrative demonstrates when she takes a strategically rabid anti-Semitic stance with Höss, her patched-up psyche unravels further after the Connecticut incident. The victim having identified so long with the victimizer's "truth," she is all too susceptible to being defined by the "orotund" Nathan who provides not only sexual escape but the promise of ultimate oblivion and that black whirling downward spiral into the "inseparability" for which she yearns: nothing less, that is, than a death wish.

Even after and in spite of all her suffering at the hands of the century's most egregiously patriarchal society and its male figureheads in her life, Sophie does not find her own way to define herself; she does not find her voice of legitimacy as a woman undefined by a man. She is destined to be a female casualty, and Styron's use of her in the novel underscores that very point; in Elizabeth Ermarth's terms, the heroine must be sacrificed in order for the prevailing male consensus to survive. Having given her a voice, however, Styron continues the dialogue in a novel that confronts the very patriarchy that has empowered him to speak *for* it. The development of the novel, as Bakhtin theorizes in terms that complement Nathan's HCN lecture,

> is a function of the deepening of dialogic essence, its increased scope and greater precision. Fewer and fewer neutral, hard elements ("rock bottom truths") remain that are not drawn into dialogue. Dialogue moves into the deepest molecular and, ultimately, subatomic levels. (Bakhtin 1981, 300)

The very nature of the novel directs the discourse in which Styron involves himself; in keeping with its development, Styron's creation of Sophie challenges the notion of patriarchy as do Stingo's masturbatory fantasies. Styron's framing of Sophie's story inside Stingo's *Bildungsroman* invites us to examine the limits of fiction as a means of experiencing others' lifeworlds. Stingo's self-conscious narrative also exposes the reader to a critique of previous notions of texts as closed entities. At least on an emotional level, it should be noted that for Sophie there is no closure in the saga of her survival; it reverberates through an entire life which is a process of surviving one man's domination only to succumb to that of another. Finally, Sophie's voice can be said to "survive" even the domination of Stingo's narrative efforts at closure.

It is at this juncture in Sophie's own life-narrative that Stingo enters; in fact, Stingo's first "sense" of her is as a disembodied, overheard voice involved initially in tempestuous lovemaking and later burdened with the sadness of a lover's quarrel. From Stingo's point of view, Sophie is at first a "plaintive" voice, pleading with a sonorous male voice,"a husky and furious baritone" in its tone

(SC 38). As we have seen when he first catches sight of her, he refers to her as "a rosebud quivering in a windstorm," but there remains "something plaintive, childlike in her voice" (47). Stingo tries to comfort her after Nathan's stormy exit, but Sophie argues with Stingo that Nathan is "right about so much"—even right that she should be berated for stealing menus. Stingo opines that taking menus should not be considered grand larceny, but again Sophie defends Nathan's point of view: "No, I know it was wrong. What he said was true, I done so many things that were wrong. *I deserved it,* that he leave me" (51; italics mine). Abandoning his attempts to "restore her self-esteem," Stingo describes her "beautiful body" with "all the right prominences" in little more than cliché terms, except that he notes a certain "odd quality" to her skin signaling some severe emaciation recently overcome. Of course, he is reading the signs after the fact of his awareness of her tattoo from the camp, but he continues in the narrative to catalog her "wonderfully negligent sexuality" because, as he has told us, he is an "exposed nerve" of a virgin at twenty-two. Stingo is especially fascinated by Sophie's "truly sumptuous rear end" which despite "past famine . . . was as perfectly formed as some fantastic prize-winning pear" (51). In her dream of Durrfeld, Sophie's lover also prefers to take her from the rear, emphasizing perhaps a predilection for submission on Sophie's part and a desire for dominance on Stingo's. Even so, Stingo catches himself in midfetish and muses as Sophie ascends the stairs at Yetta's that "there must be some perversity in this dorsal fixation," however dimly he realizes it. In this first meeting we see themes raised that will continue to be examined as both Stingo's and Sophie's stories evolve: his seeking for a context for his own life in which he resolves his feelings of sexual inadequacy and Sophie's own journey to regain a childlike innocence and total trust in a male figure, as she had had in her early days in Cracow in her fourth-floor room where she heard her mother's music and watched the fantastic storks.

Of the several scenes involving Stingo and Sophie, most are taken up with her telling and then retelling differing versions of her experiences before she arrives in New York. The focus in these passages is directed primarily at Sophie's past, although a past sifted through the lust-struck eyes and ears of the priapic Stingo who after but ten minutes with Sophie fantasizes about wooing "this ex-starveling with her taste for fancy restaurants and expensive phonograph records" (SC 53). Indeed, of the sixteen chapters of the novel, Styron has dedicated *half* to what may be called solely Sophie's concerns: her lives and the men who dominated her different incarnations. In the early chapters of the novel, Stingo is introduced to the problematic relationship Sophie shares with Nathan, and notes with fascination that when Nathan returns after the row he witnessed, Sophie is "flushed with high spirits and joy" (57). Stingo describes her as having a "sparkle" in her eyes and a "pink exultant glow that colored her cheeks like rouge," all of which contributes to her "radiant face" which appears to him as "irresistible" (57).

As discussed at the outset of this chapter, the convergence of two other important women in Stingo's life occurs just before he physically meets Sophie: he receives news of Maria Hunt's suicide and later recalls the recurring dream he has of his mother in her coffin and her terrible suffering eyes. Thus is the reader prepared to see Sophie as Stingo views her: as an antidote to his morbid reflections on the deaths of Maria and his mother. Stingo's early descriptions of the Sophie of June 1947 continue to reflect his infatuation; he discloses that when Nathan nuzzles her, she emits "a gay burbling laugh" complemented by "the most faithful imitation of a cat's electric purr" Stingo has ever heard. These flights of descriptive fantasy are offset, however, by Stingo's growing awareness of Nathan's violence toward Sophie as Morris Fink retells Nathan's propensities to be a "golem," a monster. The combination of repulsion-attraction that Stingo feels for both Nathan and Sophie is, of course, a mirroring of Sophie's relationship with Nathan in particular and males in general, especially males with dominant positions in her emotional life.

As noted earlier, Stingo's first mistake in identifying Sophie regards her ethnicity; he automatically assumes she is Jewish, but Nathan informs him that Sophie is a *shiksa* or a "goy girl." In another disclosure, Stingo learns that it is Sophie, not Nathan who insists on their "dressing up" in period costumes on Sundays and holidays; it is also Sophie who teaches Nathan about music, and in this sense she has achieved her fondest desire to become a music teacher, for she not only instructs Nathan, but Stingo as well, who envies them their varied and expensive collection of classical music. Stingo is also made aware of Sophie's ability to at least in some sense discard her "wounded, submissive role and actually stand up to Nathan in a frisky way, beginning to manipulate him out of sheer charm, beauty and brio" (SC 74). This observation takes place well before Stingo understands the advancement of Nathan's mental illness and his drug abuse. At this early stage, the awe-struck Stingo can but exclaim his wonder at Sophie who "was able to work upon Nathan such tricks of alchemy that he was almost instantaneously transformed—the ranting ogre become Prince Charming" (74).

Thus charmed himself, thus seduced, he journeys off with them to Coney Island, and in the process begins a journey into Sophie and Nathan's lives that will take him far beyond "as strange a place as Brooklyn." But his inconsolate lust overtakes him at one point as Sophie says that they are all going to be "great friends" and a "lovely phosphorescence" envelopes her face; Stingo struggles with calming his ardor as she squeezes him. He is planning his domination of her at that moment of good feeling, a further comment in the narrative upon the hidden agendas of all the characters, of even the "innocent" young man from the provinces. Stingo muses that even as he enjoys her squeeze, he sees this attention of hers as a "compromise," and that there is a distinct "inequity" in Nathan's "custodianship of such an exquisite prize" (SC 76). Although Nathan's jealous rages against Stingo at the close of the novel are indeed psychotic, in this scene we see the groundwork for Stingo's own complicity in the tragedy that follows; like Sophie's own complicity with anti-Semitism by association, Stingo's involvement in their breakup is mostly inadvertent but suggestive of the same kind of tainted motivation: selfishness. Indeed, Stingo reveals his innermost thoughts at the very moment when the three of them are embarking upon being "the best of friends" as Sophie would have it. "I returned Sophie's squeeze with the clumsy pressure of unrequited love, and realized as I did so that I was so horny my balls had begun to ache" (76). Even with the "sensitive" and "enlightened" fledgling author from the South, Sophie remains a "prize" to be won or wrestled from her previous captor, Nathan. Her beauty and her charm, even after her loss of flesh and teeth, reduce men to their primal roles.

Here Styron is once again laying before the reader the social situation of the late 1940s which inheres today and informs the reader's experience of Sophie's world then. Styron so completely envelopes the reader in Stingo's mind-set that the passage ends with Stingo's purple-prose rendition of his "premonition" darkening his own sunny erotic glow with a deep sense of foreboding about the summer ahead with Nathan and Sophie: he longs, suddenly, to rush from the train and escape. But he stays, he says, and that is why there is a story to tell. Like Stingo, the reader will stay on the "train" of Sophie's story and "plunge" on toward Coney Island with him; but the reader is also forced to consider at this juncture what exactly is to be found at the conclusion of this journey into Sophie's life-world as told through Stingo's apprehension.

The elder Stingo frames an answer pages later as he explains that his attempt to understand Auschwitz through re-creating Sophie's experience as closely as he can is his way of dealing with the images that have "haunted" him since he first met Sophie. The reader, too, has a desire to "textualize" Sophie to some extent, in order to scrutinize her world; above all, Styron presents readers with an opportunity to listen to her voice, her testimony, in its multiple contexts.

A few other key scenes reveal the way in which Sophie and Stingo become "best of friends" in the course of the summer of 1947. Just before his reunion with his father, they both meet in the Maple Court, and he describes her from his "stunned" perspective as one "still moronically in love with her" (SC 191). He lavishes on her a word-devotion that refers to her features: "the lovely swerve of her cheekbone below the oval eyes with their sleepy-sullen hint of Asia . . . the fine, elongated, slightly uptilted 'Polish *schnoz* . . . which terminated in a nice little button'" (191). So taken is Stingo, who is off on his own fantasy date with Leslie, that he rhapsodizes Sophie "created a continuum of beauty that was positively breath-taking" in the drab confines of the Maple Court Bar. He admits that he is as taken as he had been that first visit to Coney Island (192). Her perfume and her revealing dress, unusual for her, put him into a state of "erogenous dreamery" as he glances at her "liberated" breasts, which he refers to as "slightly freckled, pretty demi-globes." Still, he notices other details with his "novelist's eye"; she has dentures that at times come loose, her "neck still had unbecoming little wrinkles, slack flesh pulled at the back of her arms" (192). As they wait for Nathan, they are accosted by two nuns who are asking for charitable donations and who cause in Sophie a violent reaction, from which the nuns withdraw gasping. Sophie explains that two nuns are "bad luck" and the two were especially "awful-looking." But she continues her tirade. "I would hate nuns even if I cared about religion. Silly, stupid virgins!" Stingo describes the nuns in an apparent effort to corroborate Sophie's contention. "They looked Italian and were extremely ugly." One has a "wen" that Stingo determinedly describes in detail, as if to intensify the contrasting beauty of his own vision of Sophie.

Nathan arrives in his manic state, and Stingo presents Sophie's changed appearance. "Like a terrified child clutching at Daddy in the vortex of a mob, Sophie squeezed down on my fingers" (SC 202). Her hand quivers as she holds her wine glass, and in "dumb reflexive obedience" shares a toast with Nathan. The evening disintegrates from there and ends with Nathan calling Sophie "the Coony Chiropractic Cunt of Kings County" and screaming about her canny ability to survive at Auschwitz; she responds by calling him a liar as she groans in torment. Stingo's courage fails him and he goes to the toilet rather than chastise Nathan for his behavior; when he returns they have gone, but later Morris Fink tells him that Sophie returned "bawling like a baby" and "cryin' her eyes out the whole time" as she and Nathan packed up to leave Yetta's (212). The reader in this passage is faced with the manic behavior of Nathan as well as Stingo's apparent cowardice in the face of the other man's rages. Stingo is unable to defend the "honor" of Sophie, and as the young inexperienced "warrior" that he is, he retreats and gives the ground to Nathan. Stingo's failure to "face down" Nathan complements Sophie's failed attempts to stand up to her father, her husband, Höss, and Nathan.

Styron adroitly maneuvers the scene into a revealing critique of the power of force, especially male force which often holds behind it the threat of physical violence, as Elizabeth Ermarth explains, the rule of force here successfully challenges the rule of dialogue. Even young Stingo is cowed by the rages of Nathan, as is the streetwise Morris Fink who likewise refuses to intercede on Sophie's behalf. Stingo's failure to challenge Nathan in this scene is recreated later in the narrative when he fails to pursue Sophie back to New York after their Washington, D.C., tryst, and his guilt will assail him as Sophie's guilt on a larger scale assaults her. Stingo's guilt eventually leads him to give voice to Sophie's horrible "choice"; Sophie's guilt plunges her into suicide and silence. In either case, facing the patriarchal, authoritative, powerful male "gaze" paralyzes them both. Thus is it possible to see Stingo's efforts to uncover Sophie's voice as a manifest *tribute* to Sophie as well as an attempt by Styron to expiate his own sense of guilt as a member of the male patriarchy; his narrative can be seen as documenting *his own complicity,* for all his enlightenment, in the exploitation/domination of women.

It is instructive to note that the chapter which unfolds the story of Nathan and Sophie's tempestuous and even sadistic Connecticut trip is also the chapter in which we can find Stingo's most troubling erotic fantasy. He is staying with his father in a hotel room, after the crushing events of Nathan's blowup at the Maple Court. Stingo lies awake as he experiences seizures of guilt punctuated by spasms "of erotic mania" (SC 295). Stingo recalls that he had been severely punished for abandoning his invalid mother to a cold freezing afternoon because he had neglected to return to light her fire. He reflects that he resented her cancerous affliction, and the guilt of his complicity in her eventual death through his neglect shoots through him. But as an antidote to this insomnia-fed guilt, he turns his mind actively to sex, and he conjures up a stormy masturbatory fantasy that includes Leslie, Maria, and Sophie, all of whom he describes as "dead" to him: "in effect extinguished, defunct, kaput, so far as each of them concerned my life" (SC 299). And at that juncture of the narrative he is right, but as he is transforming Leslie into Maria, and thus "possessing the heroine" of his own novel, his father interrupts his reverie by going to the toilet.

When Stingo resumes his fantasy, he finds he is "making ravenous love to Sophie. And of course it was she I had wanted all along" (SC 299). So caught up in his fantasy is he that he calls her name aloud as he climaxes and he awakens his father who hears Stingo's cry as "soapy" (300). Besides the humor in such a pun, the reader can reflect upon the transcendent truth that Stingo the younger will achieve his goal of having Sophie later in the book, and thus the elder Stingo will *succeed* in making love to *his* own heroine, Sophie. On another level Styron achieves a union with Peyton Loftis in her interior mind-set by *becoming* Peyton, or Maria as young Stingo names her. Styron also manages, through both Stingos, to possess Sophie, a character who is based on the refugee he himself met on Caton Avenue in Brooklyn in the forties. But as Stingo the younger realizes in the McAlpin room, he is having an orgasm with a "phantom Sophie" and he understands "for the first time how hopeless" was his love for her (300).

In this troubling scene we have Stingo present four women who haunt him then and trouble him for the rest of his life, or, at least until he deals with them in some meaningful way by virtually creating a context, a meaning for them by relating the events of that summer. Like the patriarchal system that has controlled society, Styron/Stingo must finally come to terms with the silenced voices of the marginalized women in his life. And the way Stingo/Styron manages to alleviate/expiate and thus perhaps explain himself is to re-create the voices and let them speak—even if it means that he opens himself and the very foundation of his society to scrutiny.

By August of 1947, after his several adventures in New York and his cathartic Dantesque journey into the Nazi nightmare, Stingo records that his writing desk calls him and he refuses to let Sophie obsess him "as a love object," especially after Nathan's return to her life following the tumultuous Maple Court incident. Reflecting the "proper" view of those times, the elder Stingo says that his younger incarnation "returned happily" to his writing, "yielding [Sophie] up willingly again *to the older man* to whom *she so naturally and rightfully belonged,* and acquiescing once more in the realization that my claims to her heart had all along been modest and amateurish at best" (417; italics mine). Because of this "gentlemanly" withdrawal from the field of battle over Sophie, Stingo is able once again to concentrate on the other "phantom" woman in his life, Maria Hunt, about whom he is penning his first literary masterpiece.

Another male presence enters the story in the person of Nathan's brother Larry, who is a respected member of that most vaunted profession, physician and surgeon. Larry's authoritarian role is clear in his passage as he sets Stingo straight about the true nature of Nathan's *non compos mentis* rages and their bases in paranoid schizophrenia and massive drug abuse. This objective point of view and the information proffered "validates" conclusively for Stingo the misgivings he has about Nathan, but successfully repressed (SC 425). Larry Landau refers to Sophie as "that sweet girl," "this sweet, sad, beautiful, fouled-up Polish girl of [Nathan's]," and "that nice girl" (426–27). But even the admirable and "scientific" mind of Larry has trouble with imagining the outcome of a marriage between his troubled brother and Sophie. If they have a child, muses Larry, and Nathan "goes off his rocker" again, what will happen? "How unfair that would be to—well, to everyone!" Larry emotes. He continues his desperate seeking of a meaningful solution by asking, incredibly, Stingo, the twenty-two-year-old neophyte: "Do you have the answer?" Sighing in frustration, the famous surgeon concludes, "Sometimes I think life is a hideous trap." The impasse that has "unmanned" both Larry and Stingo recalls Law's point about Styron's challenging of privileged, primarily *androcentric,* discursive reasoning and its ability to decode "mysteries" such as what to do about Nathan's insanity. This interchange between Larry and Stingo emphasizes the limits of "rational" discourse when confronted with human behavior in extremis, and it does this by intensifying Stingo's encounter "with the nature of things beyond our language. . . ." (Law 1990, 64). The exchange also gives the reader yet another example of men deciding *for* Sophie what her future shall be; but in this case, Styron portrays the limits of male interdiction and its pronounced impotence when confronted with its limitations.

After a brief hiatus in the area around Nyack, Stingo returns to Brooklyn to find that Nathan has once again exploded and beaten Sophie. His advice to Morris this time is not to call the police, even though Stingo senses impending doom and is "assaulted by Kierkegaardian dread" as he contemplates further dangers from Nathan, now that he is beginning to comprehend some of the implications of Nathan's illness (SC 438). As he is ruminating on these dour feelings, Sophie comes through the door of Yetta's and his description of her is telling. "Oh, my poor Sophie. She was hollow-eyed and disheveled, exhausted-looking, and the skin of her face had the washed-out sickly blue of skim milk—but mainly she looked aged, an old lady of forty" (439). Nathan, he learns, has kicked her arm this time, and she is severely bruised. Sophie explains that Nathan has threatened to kill her and "this man" whom he alleges had sex with her. Sophie does not say who the man is, but the younger Stingo infers it to be one of the chiropractors Nathan obsessed about before. The reader, however, is fully aware that Sophie's hesitation to name "this man" projects the role directly onto Stingo himself, who has literally become the "other man," which in fact has been his goal from the very outset of the novel. But Stingo's ignorance of Sophie's gentle mendacity is short-lived; Nathan's subsequent phone call curses him squarely for desiring "Polack nooky" while acting the part of the "best friend" who is in reality a "sneaky Southern shitass" (444). The effect that Styron achieves in this dramatic scene is heightened by the reader and Stingo's awareness of how prescient Nathan's judgment remains even in his paranoid, drugged condition; the irony is that in this case Nathan's paranoia is more or less on track about Stingo's longings for Sophie.

Nathan's suspicions of Sophie's faithfulness, although the younger and elder Stingo alike seem predisposed to dismiss them as overwrought mania, are based upon some intuitive mental leap made. More to the point, the reader is made aware of one particular event in which the "betrayal" that Nathan suspects of Stingo's friendship with him is exposed and haunts the narrative itself. During the Jones Beach scene where Stingo actually saves Sophie from a suicide attempt, both get drunk and unleash repressed sexual longings. Sophie probably does so because of her recent breakup with Nathan, and Stingo ascribes his participation to his never-ending horniness. Indeed, Stingo himself curses Sophie before they leave for the beach. In his shower he longs for her and curses her, "Bitch, Sophie!" and "God damn you, Sophie!" (SC 349). He proudly proclaims that Nathan, a "death-force" (349) is gone "kaput!" and that she should love him. "Love me. Love me! Love life!" In this mental frenzy, Stingo sets off with Sophie for a secluded spot on the beach, but along the way a surprisingly defiant

Sophie, fed by bourbon, tells Stingo that after reflecting on the Connecticut experience she is glad Nathan has left her; she says, "it was sick of me to be just this little kitten for him to fondle" (351). Curiously, Stingo feels a need to defend Nathan's behavior as drug-inspired, but Sophie quickly quashes that notion: "people . . . always says that we must pity a man, he is under the influence of drugs and so that excuses his behavior. Fuck that noise, Stingo" (352).

In this exchange we see that Sophie *has* taken on a voice, *Nathan's,* much like Poppy Kinsolving takes on Cass's obscenities in *Set This House on Fire.* And she is reacting the way Nathan would if the situation were reversed; the scene suggests clearly that Sophie is capable of learning a new voice, but, sadly, it is a mimicry of her orotund lover's voice and not her own. She goes on in this vein, cursing Nathan as a man who merely "bought" her with gifts of food and clothes and even health; "he done such a thing only so he could use me, have me fuck me, beat me, have some object to possess . . . he was buying me with it, like all Jews" (SC 353). That her diatribe against Nathan's sexism degenerates into anti-Semitism is revealing. "All my childhood, all my life I really hated Jews," she says to the distraught and shocked Stingo, who dismisses her tirade and is convinced that she is "still daft in love" with Nathan (353). The greater challenge is to the reader who is made aware of her hidden feelings for Jews and Nathan; what is to be made of her anti-Semitism in light of her obsequious, fetishistic submissiveness to Nathan in Connecticut? Again, Styron leads the reader into the heart of the conundrum of the novel: How can Sophie indeed be anti-Semitic and desperately in love with Nathan simultaneously?

On the beach, as Sophie gets drunker and tells Stingo of her involvement with Wanda's brother Jozef, Stingo muses about what he had been doing in 1943 when the Polish underground was battling for its life. Suddenly, Sophie reaches "up into" Stingo's bathing trunks and "lightly" strokes "that spectacularly sensitive epidermal zone down deep where thigh and buttock intersect" (357). She immediately implores him to take his clothes off along with her: "Let's be naked," she says. Stingo rhapsodizes for a paragraph about dreams come true, comparing winning a lottery to this suggestion of Sophie's. Finally, Stingo is in the presence of that which he has so long wished for: "a young female body all creamy bare, with plump breasts that had perky brown nipples, a smooth slightly rounded belly with a frank eyewink of a bellybutton, and . . . a nicely symmetrical triangle of honey-hued pubic hair" (358).

Sophie clambers into the ocean for a swim, but Stingo remains bound to the beach, embarrassed about his erection. Sophie returns to tease him about his "hard-on" and they fall upon each other: "we rolled like dolphins into each other's arms." Sophie grasps Stingo's "schlong" and strokes him to a quick orgasm for which he is heartily ashamed although she laughs and tries to reassure him that such a reaction is normal. Her way of reassuring him about the commonality of such ejaculation only serves to agitate him more; she talks of her sex with Jozef who was as young as he and a virgin too. And to Stingo's amazement, as Sophie talks of Jozef, her dead lover, and of Stingo's virginity, she "massages" her face with Stingo's semen. He refers to her reminiscences of Jozef as "running off at the mouth like a tobacco auctioneer" (SC 361); he simply cannot believe that "his" Sophie can switch from masturbating him to a casual recollection of Jozef: "Could women, then, so instantaneously turn off their lust like a light switch?" he asks of himself. But he also asks if he is "merely an instant surrogate Jozef, flesh to occupy space in an ephemeral fantasy" (361). Revealingly, Stingo seems not to connect this thought to his own ability to substitute women, even dead women, for one another in his own fantasies. Styron presents Stingo caught up in the throes of agonizing lust suddenly released, and we see him finally confronted with Sophie as a mature, sexual being, with real experiences that he cannot control as easily as he can control his image of her in his fantasies. He is shocked to learn that women can indeed lust for men and then, like men, discuss other loves quite casually. His Madonna-image of Sophie, reminiscent of Kommandant Höss's, is replaced and confounded by the reality of her appetites and her body inches away, which again parallels Höss's reaction to her. Stingo wants her to concentrate on his needs and to keep her lovers to herself. It is a point in the novel where the reader, the two Stingos, and Styron can all confront the enigma who is Sophie and can be confronted by her, literally, naked before the world.

After Sophie's reverie about Jozef and their lovemaking in Warsaw, and her sudden and vehement attack on Wanda, she plunges into despair, and Stingo relates that he has finally come to understand "Slavic melancholy" as he witnesses her sobs. She implores him to hold her. "Oh Christ, I feel so lost . . . I'm so alone!" she cries (SC 362). Stingo nods off only to find she has jumped into the ocean, "slicing her way . . . bound for Venezuela" and suicide.

He swims to her, saves her, but she berates him for his efforts, "Why didn't you let me drown? I've been so bad—I've been so awful bad!" (364). She reiterates that "no one has such badness"; he gets her dressed, back to Brooklyn, and into a bed for a nap from which she awakens seemingly little affected by her near-drowning. Stingo muses in a passage following that Sophie needed to delve into her past with him because "perhaps she felt that there was really *no returning to the present* unless she could come clean, as they say, and shed light on what she had concealed from me as well as (who knows?) from herself" (365; italics mine).

Stingo the elder in his presentation of this scene seems to underplay its importance in the narrative. From the first chapter the reader has been reminded of the younger Stingo's propensity for viewing his world in terms of his sexual fantasies, yet when he has his "goddess" in his arms, naked, both before and after her attempt to swim into oblivion, he does not lapse into his usual starved monologue of unending priapism. In fact, he merely relates that "Eros had fled." After her rescue, instead of the usual sententious journal entry or soliloquy over her breasts or "perfect rear," Stingo abruptly ends the scene and spends one single paragraph thinking of Sophie's motivation for telling him of her "nethermost reaches" of the past. Although it *appears* that Stingo has matured to a point where he can actually be more than a walking libido, in the remaining one hundred and fifty pages of the book, this is not the case.

As we have noted, Stingo's chief criticism of Mary Alice Grimball is her indefatigable ability to masturbate him, something he claims never to have experienced before; but he has—with Sophie at Jones Beach where he achieved an intimacy he had not thought possible. He seems, however, to have minimized the importance of the incident at Jones Beach out of all proportion. It remains an important scene in which Stingo is exposed, literally, to Sophie as a mature and lusty woman with a sexual past that Stingo appears incapable of dealing with. He reflects not once on his manual sex with Sophie when they are both nude and "rolling like dolphins" in each other's arms, but he spends pages on his memories and journal entries on Leslie and Mary Alice, although he contends that it is Sophie he has wanted "all along." This curious lapse in character in both the younger Stingo's behavior and the elder Stingo's penchant for relating in minute detail his youthful sexual peccadillols may have a specific function. The absence of Stingo's further musing on this scene may be a means of emphasizing

Stingo's inability to grasp the true nature of Sophie's profound despair, even after he has "matured" into the elder Stingo.

The lack of commentary from Stingo may also emphasize his guilty complicity in Nathan's subsequent manic rage at the close of the novel; Stingo may be blocking from his consciousness the Jones Beach scene specifically because it points to his physical involvement with Sophie, as Nathan suspects. Even though Stingo has finally conceded to Nathan the latter's "rights" to the "prize" Sophie, he has not been the "innocent" or "uninvolved" friend that he protests to Nathan that he is: Stingo must share some responsibility. Perhaps the narrative is suggesting that Stingo is as guilty of complicity in the case of Sophie and Nathan as Sophie is in her efforts to remain "uninvolved" in the Nazi's War against the Jews. Both are engaged in some denial, because both may love Nathan, but they also fear and loath him as well. In short, even the lad Stingo *is* guilty of victimizing his own "best friends" on some level.

The final tryst scene in Washington, D.C., is noteworthy in that it is the final time that Stingo sees Sophie, and it is the section of the narrative revealing Sophie's "choice." After reaching a run-down hotel, Stingo, without reflecting on his last "close encounter" with Sophie, reverts to the reveries on Sophie's body that populate earlier sections: he describes the "blue-veined" skin of her exposed breast and begins to fondle that breast as Sophie sleeps. He catches himself, and admits that "there was something sneaky, almost necrophiliac in the act. . . ." (SC 458). After she awakens, they take a drunken walking tour of the city and return to rest some more after their exhausting flight from the mad threats of Nathan; eventually they make love in their room. Although Giorgiana Colville contends that Stingo is merely *dreaming* his lust-scene with Sophie, the narrative discloses that "the dream melted instantly away at the sound of her whisper. 'Oh . . . now, Stingo darling, I want to fuck'" (496). Stingo claims that their lovemaking was "mutually inexhaustible" and that for him this was the result of his virginity and the fact of his holding in his arms—although he had done it before—"the goddess" of his unending fantasies (496). As for Sophie, Stingo opines that she was reacting to her own "good raw natural animal passion" but she was also taking a "plunge into carnal oblivion and a flight from memory and grief." And like all the other men in the narrative who express their desire to get her into bed, from Von Neimand to Durrfeld to Nathan, Stingo achieves another of his sexual fantasies: he ejaculates in Sophie's mouth, after which he falls into an oblivion of fatigue and sexual contentment.

When he awakens, of course, Sophie has fled back to Nathan's arms, leaving Stingo her last words in a note. In the note Sophie obligingly tells Stingo twice what a "great" lover he is (as he has always suspected, even in the beginning of the novel as he fantasizes about Mavis Honnicut) but she closes with a feeling of severe anguish. "I love Nathan but now I feel this Hate of Life and God FUCK God and all his Hande Werk. And Life too. And even what remain [sic] of Love" (SC 500). Sophie does not achieve the escape from grief in her "carnal oblivion" with Stingo. In her case the battle between Eros and Thanatos is over.

The last description of Sophie alive is rendered through the reported recollections of Morris Fink who sees her last and who runs an errand for her. She returns to Yetta's while Stingo sleeps and later fumes in Washington, D.C., and she puts on the costume from the thirties in which Stingo had first seen her "dress up" with Nathan. She asks Morris to buy whiskey, which he leaves by her room door, only to find it there hours later. Morris reports that when he last sees her she has a "curious glint of mild amusement" on her face; he also sees her "tongue run across her upper lip, interrupting the words she had been poised to say" (SC 502). Morris sees no "negative" emotions or signs of distress. Stingo himself never does see her face again because when he finally returns in a frenzy of guilt-ridden worry, he finds what he has feared: Nathan and Sophie "entwined in each other's arms" as suicides from cyanide poisoning; and Larry Landau advises Stingo not to look at their faces. Sophie is buried next to Nathan because she has "no closer relative" than her savior-tormentor. Young Stingo grieves and eventually leaves Brooklyn to finish his first critically acclaimed book about Maria Hunt's suicide; later he will write of Sophie, the one he "had wanted all along" (299).

That Stingo is clearly one of the men who seek to possess and dominate Sophie has been discussed earlier in this study. That Sophie is finally unable to run from Nathan and follow Stingo to the peanut farm existence he offers her in Washington, D.C., is yet another comment upon the various kinds of domination she must "choose" among in her life. Sophie could not choose the peanut farm in the South because it is another camp, another enclosed space in which she would have to kowtow to yet another man's whims of propriety and conduct. Stingo attempts to become Sophie's father by engineering her "escape" from Nathan. The irony is that Stingo's escape is to Sophie another form of entrapment and

nother camp. Imprisoned in her father's home, in her marriage to
er husband—a father surrogate, in Höss's camp and dreamworld,
n Nathan's world of Jewish rage and guilt, and finally in Stingo's
mages of her as a Southern *hausfrau,* Sophie is finally driven to
he oblivion she has sought but not found in sex. When she rejects
jod in her final note, she turns finally from the identities thrust
pon her by men and enters into her own final "role" as she dresses
ike a "Clara Bow, Fay Wray, Gloria Swanson" figure (SC 502).

Even in the frieze of death with Nathan, she is seen by Stingo
s part of a couple, peaceful and "frozen" in "a grave and tender
mbrace forever" (SC 507). But his romantic point of view here is
elied by his refusal to see the tragic death-grip that Nathan has
ad on Sophie since the beginning of the narrative; Stingo's own
verblown foreboding points out Nathan's repeated cries to her
hat they were dying as they lived their apparently enjoyable if
nanic lives. Nathan's is not a "tender" embrace; it is the death-
rip of Thanatos, a detail young Stingo does not realize fully in
ime and the elder Stingo will not comment upon, perhaps because
e is still smitten more by his romantic image of Sophie than the
eality of her real voice. But Styron presents her through his narra-
ors as a multi–voiced character full of human contradictions and
earning both for life and death, domination and submission. If the
ovel is Styron's most fully realized text in terms of structural
omplexity and thematic concerns, as John Kenny Crane suggests,
hen Sophie is surely his most accomplished character, framed
hough she is by males.

Styron's major concern in the fictive world of *Sophie's Choice*
nay finally be not what fiction can reveal about a woman's experi-
nce through the eyes of a male narrator–author, but what a reader
an learn from such a fiction about the underlying assumptions of
he male point of view, the patriarchal consensus, that strive to
lefine Sophie. The focus of the novel in this sense is not Sophie,
ut the two Stingos and their complicity in the horrors of dehuman-
zation and domination. Styron lays bare the midtwentieth-century
nale point of view in all its sexist and racist ambiguity and explores
ts dark sides, even in those with the best of intentions. The results
re all the same for Sophie, no matter what the intentions of those
nales who define her. She is sacrificed because she has not been
ible to identify herself *as* herself *by* herself, as a person outside of
he context of male sexism. From Daddy's little amanuensis to
Nathan's Nazi-sucking whore, she has had her life defined by men's
lesires and not her own. As the Jones Beach scene with Stingo
:learly shows, even well-read and educated if inexperienced male

lovers selfishly desire her to fulfill only *their* onanistic dream images and reject her real-life incarnation. As the Nazis strove to reduce the world to their Master Plan, so too each male charac ter at midcentury desires to dominate the women in his life and to fashion his own plan for realizing the overarching demand: of a patriarchal society which supports and encourages such domination.

If Dale Marie Bauer is correct in her interpretation of Bakhtin's premise that "all literature is ideological and hence social," then she is correct again in reasoning that novels such as *Sophie's Choice* that incorporate opposing modes of thinking, even naive modes like young Stingo's, undermine patriarchal norms of reading as well as "dominant, centralizing conventions" (Bauer 1988, 161) Further, in reading, we are all engaged in a dialogue with the text as such; as Bauer explains, in the novel we are not mere observers or witnesses of dialogue (as Wanda reminds Sophie in several scenes) but are participants in it. Bakhtin claims that "every liter-ary work faces outward away from itself, toward the listener-reader, and to a certain extent anticipates possible reaction to it-self" (Bakhtin 1981, 257). Thus readers face in some sense a ver-sion of the struggles of Wanda and Sophie, and even Stingo; just as these characters face the external authority of their cultures and the complexity of their own inner dialogic responses to those social hierarchies, readers struggle with their responses to the discourse in the novel and to their own resisting interplay with that discourse. As a result of this process, both characters and readers are *engen-dered*. Styron's novel allows readers a means of experiencing "the dialogue between authoritative discourse and inner speech" (Bauer 168). And in our active participation we form ourselves as readers; indeed, we form the very texts we read as much as we form our-selves. Reading in this sense involves the development of the self between what Caryl Emerson refers to as "two modes of discourse, the authoritative and the internally persuasive" (Emerson 1983, 225). An awareness of the gap between the inner and the outer worlds of discourse functions, claims Emerson, as an important aspect of self-definition through discourse and "as an index of indi-vidual consciousness, as a measure of our escape from fixed plots and roles, as a *prerequisite for discourse itself*" (259; italics mine).

Styron's novel, then, presents readers with interpretations *of acts of interpretation* and readers in the act of reading not only their own, dated texts—as Stingo presents his journals from long ago to shore up the reality of the world he creates for Sophie—but also evaluating their own ways of seeing/reading their former textual *selves*. In this way, Styron's "backward glance" frames the narrators' subjectivity such that readers are drawn into not only interpretation but a reflection of the act of reading itself, in addition to the critique of society inherent in the novel. As Bauer comments, "Reading is not 'free,' but an activity determined by the text and by the ideological discourses one brings to bear on the text" (Bauer 1988, 15).

As a kind of epilogue to this discussion of *Sophie's Choice,* we may explore the idea that, although the life of Sophie Zawistowska directs most of the movement of the discourse of the novel, Styron directs noteworthy narrative attention to the roles of mothers in the discourse. At one point Stingo suggests that mothers (and fathers) are at the core of existence "somehow" (SC 462). Stingo's own mother haunts him in his recurring dream of her accusatory gaze reaching out from her coffin, holding him partly responsible for her early death. He speaks of the cancer which has been devouring his mother's bones and eventually leads to her invalidism. One of his chores is to keep her fire stoked in cold winter months, but one afternoon he "abandoned her" (296), and guilt about this act is with him throughout the narrative and arises at particular moments of crisis: when he first meets Sophie, when he discovers Maria Hunt's death, when Nathan ends their friendship, and when he and Sophie are fleeing from Nathan. Stingo recalls with anguish his "deserted mother" and how as a young boy he "became sick with alarm" at his deserting her. "Jesus Christ, guilt.. . ." is his groping attempt to explain his feeling ten years later in the McAlpin Hotel. The event of his deserting his mother for a joyride in a Packard has been marked on his mind by his father's punishment: he is himself locked in a cold shed for hours, so he would feel the desolate cold his mother had felt. The punishment serves its purpose on the young Stingo's conscience, but in another sense his punishment does not erase his resentment of her illness and death; he wanted and still wants, even as the elder Stingo, a healthy vibrant mother figure in his life.

My point here is in contradistinction to the view expressed by Georgiana Colville's that Styron/Stingo seeks to "kill" his dead mother over and over in his characters. Rather, Stingo attempts in his life to find and realize a communion with a vibrant older woman with whom he can lose the visions of death that he clearly associates with his dying mother. In fact, Stingo recalls his punishment in the freezing shed as part of his memory of his mother and his "crime," as he puts it, against her: "in my mind it would inescapably and always be entangled in the sordid animal fact of my mother's death," a "disgusting" death in its horrible "transport of pain"; his mother dies on a stifling July day, "faded away in a stupor of morphine" (Colville 1986, 297). Stingo's thoughts as he describes her horrible death continue to emphasize his perceived complicity in her death: that his abandonment "sent her into the long decline from which she never recovered" (298). His dream of her piercing eyes riveting him from her coffin restages the actual moment when he finally arrived home to find her half-frozen, her hazel eyes wide in their terror and damning him for his selfishness.

Styron's use of Stingo's guilt complex is primarily that of a bridge by which both Stingo and the reader might in some way access the depth of Sophie's guilty feelings for surviving the extermination of her entire family and, in reality, her entire way of life. Sophie's vision of her mother contrasts sharply with Stingo's and doubtless adds "sting" to his own guilt feelings. Sophie is sent to Auschwitz ostensibly because she was caring for her ailing mother's tuberculosis by smuggling ham during her illness. Yet Sophie too feels a sense of guilt that she never does find out what happened to her mother; she assumes her mother died a starveling's death in Warsaw. In Sophie's case, however, she was not joyriding in a Packard but being shipped by train to a concentration camp, a point not lost on the sensitive Stingo as he time and again points out what inane adolescent activities he participated in as Sophie and her family endured unimaginable hardships. As to her memories of her mother, Sophie refers with wistful appreciation to her mother's piano-playing and her mother's gentle if submissive soul. After her father and husband are taken by the Nazis, Sophie in effect becomes a parent to her devoted and devout mother whose nerves collapse. In this sense, Sophie has a more fully realized relationship with her mother than does Stingo, one in which she had actively cared for both her mother's emotional and physical needs as best she could. And as a mother herself, Sophie does not fail in trying to provide for her children in the most trying of circumstances, although her deep guilt over her own abandonment of Eva strikes to her very core. That Sophie's own maternal nature predominates in many of her relationships, especially those with Nathan and Stingo, is ample evidence of her socialization; she is reared to be a mother, and perhaps it is the violent wrenching of her children from her, above all the other horrors she endures, that causes her to see her God as turning his back on her, as abandoning her at her moment of crisis, at her moment of choice. But we must remember that Sophie is *forced* to abandon her little girl Eva to the gas chamber by a society that has decided it has no use for this girl in its corporate slave labor camp for I. G. Farben. The rule of the Fatherland snuffed out Eva's brief life because it can see no *place* for her in its business ethic; in Eva's case the patriarchy defined her as having even less value than a slave.

In his portrayal of women in *Sophie's Choice*, William Styron ironically focuses on the males who define women's lives. As Richard G. Law has written, the mature Stingo's "saving knowledge" after his encounter with, and final rendition of, Sophie's harrowing experiences is his awareness of his own capacity for evil, "including his monumental self-centeredness and his capacity to use others as instruments" (Law 1990, 64). Thus in the novel, Styron's lesson to his readers is that the locus of human evil in the form of dehumanization and domination is not some monstrous "other," but rather in each person's capacity to victimize another, whether the reduction of people to slave labor in a brutal camp like Auschwitz or the degrading of a woman into a sexual object reduced to her body parts for onanistic gratification. Styron also adds another dimension to his exploration of the human capacity for evil by presenting the complex and problematic nature of collaboration and complicity with regards to human cruelty. Sophie may not have actively endorsed her father's anti-Semitic tracts, except in the extreme stress of Auschwitz, but her silence and later determination to remain uninvolved in Warsaw are in reality "choices" themselves. Perhaps it is no exaggeration to conclude with Styron that no choice is apolitical, no decision without political consequences.

However, the important point that reaches out time and again to the reader from the voices assembled in this novel is chiefly that, no matter how assiduously women submit themselves to the strictures of the Western Judeo-Christian system, they are left disenfranchised and marginalized in the end. In fact, it is precisely because of the Judeo-Christian ethic, argues Mimi Gladstein, that women are pushed into the space of the "other" and thereby subjected to opppression. Gladstein writes:

In brief, the concept of other, which sees man as subject and woman as object, has strong roots in the story of Genesis and the Judeo-Christian ethic, the dominant theology in our culture. In the mythology of the Christian West and therefore of the American mind, woman was created, not as a separate, unique entity, but from the body of man and for the purpose of complementing man. She is therefore not an end in herself, but a functionary of man's fulfillment. Man is the subject; woman is the object, the other. (Gladstein 1986, 2)

In terms of feminist dialogics, Sophie is sacrificed no less than her sister Wanda. In Sophie's case, she "forgets" that "discourse/dialogue is an ongoing activity" and she loses her powers of resistance (Bauer 1988, 167). Wanda, on the other hand, is strangled and has her voice of dissent literally choked out of her. Wanda realizes the power of engagement, and even as a marginalized lesbian character whose courage Höss would dismiss as the result of her "unnatural" sexual preference, she struggles to subvert the dominance of the Nazi patriarchy to undermine that hierarchy's definition of her as a "perversion" of the submissive Aryan woman-ideal. Sophie fails, in dialogic terms, to attain a full awareness of how her suffering is the result of androcentric ideology; and her "failure of engagement" further marginalizes her into silence. Bauer sees this kind of failure as a "failure in tandem with the failure of community," a community which finally fails to sustain Sophie even though she is "valued" as a maternal and sexual commodity. Bauer explains, "The individual's struggles against the social conventions which define and inscribe subjectivity into society reveal the structure by which the body (and especially women's bodies) is controlled" (167). But Bauer is quick to point out that "[n]o monologic voice, no individual representation of truth, however, can encompass reality." Nor can authoritarian monologism "resist the other voices which influence it; no voice can be purely monologic" (166). Put another way, "multiple voicing fractures the monolithic and monologic discourse of power" (Hitchcock xvi), as it certainly does in *Sophie's Choice*. Bauer clearly presents a conviction that there is a discernible and insidious "will-to-monologism" in patriarchal discourse that must be offset by a feminist reevaluation of women's marginalized voices which shows how these "silences" have "a material presence in novelistic discourse" and in *HIS*tory itself (Hitchcock 1993, 20). Styron can be said to have achieved a rendering of such a presence in the character of Sophie.

6

Postscript: Feminist Dialogics, the Language of Authority, and the Novels of William Styron

USING Bakhtin's notion that the self is "authored" as it interplays with language, which is itself an ongoing multivoiced process of dialogue and discovery, it is appropriate here, finally, to bring in William Styron's own extranovelistic voice, as he comments upon his capability of portraying "female psychology." Still, we must remember that Bakhtin stressed that "language is the otherness in self" while the "subject is authored in communication" (Hitchcock 1993, 10). That is, "[n]o utterance in general can be attributed to the speaker *exclusively;* it is the product of the interaction of the interlocuters . . . the product of the whole *complex social situation*" (Hitchcock 1993, 10; italics mine). With this awareness of Bakhtin's architectonics of social relations and language, we may be, however, tempted to eliminate "answerability" for the speaking subject. That is, Styron's comments perhaps contribute little insight since he himself is "conceived in polyphony" and therefore incapable of an awareness of his complicity in patriarchal norms. In reality, the emphasis returns to a examination of the meaning systems *behind* an individual's utterance and in so doing allows a reader–listener to evaluate more than the individual answering (10).

Styron has revealed in his own answers to interviewers that his novels are "attempts to understand" and bring new light on old subjects (Morris 1981, 61); in this sense, he says, his books are voyages of "self-exploration" as well, in which he engages the reader "on the most basic level" and then by "hook or crook" carries the reader to various levels of that growing understanding (63). An integral part of these explorations are Styron's portrayals of women's sensibilities; and some critics compare Styron's ability to present female characters with those of Tolstoy and Hardy, praising Sophie as another Anna Karenina or Sue Bridehead and suggesting that she is "a symbol of a society and an era" (65). I have pointed out in this study that Peyton Loftis can also be seen as an important American heroine and representative of her generation because Styron articulates through her the significant problems of self-definition encountered by a generation of Americans in midcentury. Styron argues that his is an intuitive insight into female psychology, that his ability is a reflection of Jung's idea "that we all have this component of femininity or this dual sexual nature" (66). Styron elaborates:

> The femaleness in the male and the maleness in the female is part of the mechanics which allow each of us to relate to, without being sexually involved with, both sexes. The femaleness in me allows me to truly understand the femaleness in the female, the maleness (if not carried too far) in the male. As a consequence . . . [a writer] should be able to feel certain female emotions with the same intensity that he feels the male. . . . *I've never had any trouble at all in works I've written in relating or describing women or feeling their emotions.* I simply don't know what causes it, except that I seem to have a sort of *balance* that way. (66; italics mine)

Judith Ruderman disputes Styron's reputed "balance" and asserts that his "female characters seem to be *unreal,* more like ideas than people" (Ruderman 1987, 124; italics mine). Ruderman explains that Styron's "phantom women" are a result of his view of sex "as expressed throughout his career" (125). Styron's growing up in the thirties and forties in the American South enmeshed him "in a sexually repressive culture," and, as a consequence, "he views sex in most instances as a destructive rather than a constructive force; pushed down by society, the sexual urge rises to express itself in perverse ways" (125). Ruderman further argues that Styron's portrayal of women, is, after all, presented through male narrators and reflects their "postpubescent wish-fulfillments" (124). *Sophie's Choice* is more about Stingo and the patriarchal culture that produces him than the inner workings of Sophie's mind. Indeed, with the exception of Peyton's "monologue" and various sections of Helen Loftis in *Lie Down in Darkness,* Styron's novels avoid interior "monologues" for female characters. Styron's novels after *Lie Down in Darkness* are first-person narratives from male perspectives, chiefly that of the WASP-ish Peter Leverett/Stingo/Styron ensemble who view women through a complex of male projections. Nat Turner's perspective reflects a modern male sensibility riddled with the oppression and repression slavery would produce in an early nineteenth-century African-American *male* and therefore further removes the narrative discourse from realistic portrayals of women.

By problematizing in this way Styron's ability to *inscribe* women, especially at the close of this study, I deliberately return my reader to a basic premise of feminist dialogics articulated by Dale Marie Bauer:

> authoritative language constricts *all voices* other than the privileged ones. Bakhtin posits a linguistic community in which the *norms are always in flux,* always open to renegotiation as those conventions are called into dialogic conflict. (Bauer 1988, xii; italics mine)

In reapproaching the points made by Ruderman concerning Styron's portrayal of women, then, it is important to argue that Styron presents the privileged patriarchal consensus—the language of authority—as the determining factor in the dehumanizing of women and other marginalized peoples and in so doing offers up a devastating critique of that authority's ability to reduce people to mere "signs" upon which it may inscribe meaning for its own ends. Women may participate as consenting or otherwise supporting servants of patriarchal structures, as do Helen Loftis and Mrs. Whitehead, but this complicity does not mitigate the importance of the will-to-monologism inherent in patriarchy, nor does it deny the dissenting activity of dialogism within language and therefore within society as a whole. "Each internalization of repression contains the possibility of rebellion," writes Bauer (xii). We might employ here Michael Holquist and Katerina Clark's view of Bakhtin's own sensibility: "This extraordinary sensitivity to the immense *plurality of experience* more than anything else distinguishes Bakhtin from other moderns who have obsessed with language" (Bakhtin 1981, xx; italics mine). Like Bakhtin, Styron has cultivated an appreciation for, and an understanding of, the plurality of experience as well as an instinctively Manichean understanding of the struggles, the "battles" for Bakhtin, between forces that keep things apart (Bakhtin's *centrifugal* forces) and forces that pull things together (the *centripetal*). John Kenny Crane locates Styron's concerns with the "roots of evil" as inhering in a person's abandonment of a feeling of responsibility and interconnectedness with others, a situation that inevitably leads to human suffering. Styron's novels, in which he articulates human suffering and *ventriloquates* it through female characters, suggest that his sensibility identifies concerns also expressed in Bakhtin's theory of the power of novelization. Holquist reports that Bakhtin was convinced of the duel between opposing forces and thus concluded that language (and therefore human existence) was perpetually imbued with a "fragile and ineluctably historical nature" (Bakhtin 1981, xviii). This fragile and yet enduring nature of language as it is employed in the novel—its irrevocable, ongoing "coming and dying of meaning"—is shared by humankind which is itself but another phenomenon, *ventriloquated by language itself* (xviii). The interconnecting forces of language, the centripetal and the centrifugal, interanimate each other and thus is heteroglossia produced. For Bakhtin, then, heteroglossia defines language (and therefore humankind) in an interanimated complex of social and linguistic forces. In this sense, "Language is not a prison house; it is an ecosystem" (Holquist and Clark 1984, 227).

As Bakhtin sees it, "Authorial speech, the speeches of narrators, inserted genres, the speech of characters are merely those fundamental compositional unities with whose help heteroglossia . . . can enter the novel; each of them permits a multiplicity of social voices and a wide variety of their links and interrelationships" (Bakhtin 1981, 262). One might add: *whether the artist wills it or not,* although clearly Styron has meant to present the language of authority as oppressive. Bauer sees characters as representing social, ideological, and stratified voices "which are not univocally the author's" but which compete with the prevailing codes of the society that the author injects, willingly or not, as a topic in the discourse of the novel (Bauer 1988, 6). Thus Styron's sensibility represents itelf and his thematized views of the prevailing consensus, as he critiques it, in a dynamic novelistic discourse containing especially *female* dissenting voices alongside those of priveleged authority. Bauer argues—in terms used by Luce Irigaray—for a perception of the "feminine" in novels as a "disruptive excess" that is a language, a "voice of gender," which moves "beyond the atomic self or body into the larger discursive corpus and which cannot entirely be accounted for in Bakhtin's dialogic model" (6–7). This "voice of gender" is clearly at work in Styron's depiction of women.

In *Nat Turner,* for example, we can witness the dynamics of Styron's voicing of gender as Margaret Whitehead challenges patriarchy by complaining that her brother's "darky sermon" is "folderol" meant to placate the slaves and to insure their passivity, a necessary feature in a rigid slave economy. In doing this, Margaret (Miss Peg) is simultaneously in and "out" of touch with her society; she is the naive character who brings into discussion assumptions that power figures would just as soon leave out of public discourse:

family codes and conventions as well as other communal and class norms. As such, Margaret is what Bakhtin refers to as one of "life's maskers" or "fools" who have the "right to be 'other'" in novelistic discourse (Bakhtin 159). Dale Marie Bauer's work examines such characters in American literature and explores how such as Miss Peg innocently call into question predominantly patriarchal norms because they "see the underside and the falseness of every situation" (Bakhtin 1981, 159).

Through the eyes of Miss Peg, Styron exposes the reader to the hypocrisy and false unity in a culture, the "truth" that masks ideology. Bauer contends that Bakhtin "celebrates" this "fool" and her "healthy failures" to understand and in those failures expose "all that is vulgar and falsely stereotyped in human relationships" (Bakhtin 1981, 162). Margaret Whitehead's efforts to explain her disillusionment with the "special institution" of slavery and Christian apologists, like her brother, who defend the institution meet with her mother's severe disapproval and a claim that Miss Peg must be suffering from the "hysteria" brought on by her menstrual cycle. Thus does the patriarchy silence its female critic, "kill" her in effect with yet another *gynicide* or at least *psychogynicide;* even the innocent "fool" is reduced to her reproductive organs and thus effectively marginalized. "The dominant class in any one society will attempt . . . to represent its interests as the interests of society as a whole," writes Peter Hitchcock, and as its representative, this is precisely how the system employs Richard Whitehead (Hitchcock 1993, 5).

Styron presents other characters in his carnival of voices who also come forward to unmask power structures that enforce conformity; they too, like Nat Turner himself, appear to fail to understand the prevailing consensus, but through their "misreadings" the reader is sensitized to the dialogic interplay of authority and the inner voices of characters. In this category we can place even Stingo as well as Sophie and certainly Peyton Loftis. As Bauer explains, reading in this fashion—reading novels whose characters "misread" their societies' real intentions—allows us to "develop an ability to respond dialogically" to the text (Bauer 1988, 160). Still, reading dialogically does not necessarily mean "taking sides" with characters, "but listening to the refracted speech of the author and *entering the dialogue which constitutes the novel*" (Bauer 1988, 160–61; italics mine). Reading dialogically means observing how a novel, indeed all literature, is ideological and as a result, social; a dialogical reading is therefore attuned to the patriarchal norms of reading and is sensitized to appreciate the significance of opposing models like those of the naive "fool" that undermine "dominant, centralizing conventions" (161).

Dialogic interpretation also allows a reader to identify characters like Richard Whitehead—in some sense a "fool" for the privileged patriarchy—who have internalized the codes and conventions of the patriarchal social fabric so completely that they speak as if their codes were "natural" rather than arbitrarily applied, as was the case with the Christian rationalization of African slavery in the American South. In terms of female voices, the same is true when Mrs. Whitehead scolds Miss Peg for questioning her brother's sermon by invoking the name of Margaret's "sainted father": the older woman defends the patriarchy and rebukes Margaret by sanctifying the "rule of the fathers" which is monologic. As such, the heteroglossia presented in Styron's novels exposes the monologic utterances "which try to pass as 'universal' and 'natural,' but are actually *constructed* and inherently mutable" (Bauer 1988, 162; italics mine).

As I have indicated earlier, Dale Bauer has studied American heroines and concludes that, on the whole, these women are "forced observers, coerced into passive roles because they are excluded by the conventions through which their voices might be heard" (163). Female voices, then, have difficulty in expressing their needs and their own understandings of the overarching patriarchal systems that circumscribe them precisely because of those systems. Styron's heroines certainly exhibit these traits: Peyton and Sophie are driven to suicide; Francesca and Margaret are killed; and other women characters are marginalized and forced to find meaning in a life-in-death experience, a kind of psychogynicide. Suicide or even psychic suicide, however, does not offer any Utopian shelter from the strictures of the patriarchy, for "there is no realm in which coerced silence is power" (165). What feminist dialogics attempts is a *reevaluation* of women's oppression and silence; it is an effort to make intelligible the voices silenced and marginalized. Thus rereadings that examine how marginal voices do in some ways challenge or support the ideologies of various communities are crucial to literary criticism because, as Annette Kolodny suggests, they contribute "an acute and impassioned attentiveness to the ways in which primarily male structures of power are inscribed (or encoded) within our literary inheritance" (Kolodny 1980, 20).

Another important aspect of dialogism that complements a feminist perspective with respect to society and the literature is its "active contestation of meaning" as well as its insistence upon the "right to mean" (Hitchcock 1993, xx). That is, dialogism confronts social and political implications rather than merely absorbing them into commentary. Further, rather than "killing," in the Felmanian sense (i.e., "explaining" and therefore further reducing or marginalizing characters), dialogism insists on a character's material meaning in a given narrative discourse. A dialogics of the oppressed, for example, can identify the inherently prescriptive aspects of patriarchal monologism in the prefatory pages of *Nat Turner* in which Styron has republished the actual text of Thomas Gray's own preface to his *Confessions of Nat Turner* which is also endorsed by the court that tried Turner in 1831. Gray refers to the slaves as "diabolical actors" who enacted "the first instance in our history of an open rebellion of the slaves" (NT xiii). Gray and the rest of the patriarchy in the persons of the white judges cannot bring themselves to identify a "motive" for the uprising, and Gray reports that all the "insurgent slaves" have been dealt with but "without revealing any thing at all satisfactory as to the motives which governed them" (xiii). That the whites cannot identify for themselves the motive of these enslaved men is comment enough on monologism's ability to stifle voices or dissent. Further, the report claims that the slaves were a "band of savages" and yet cowards in the face of "whites in arms," all in the effort to promote and reinforce white supremacy. Nat is seen as having a mind trying to "grapple with things beyond its reach," a mind that "first became bewildered and confounded, and finally corrupted" into the killing of whites. Yet, though he dismisses Nat's mental acumen, Gray sees the insurrection as "not instigated by motives of revenge or sudden anger, but the results of *long deliberation,* and *a settled purpose of mind*" (xiv; italics mine). After contradicting the inferiority theory he has built up, Gray invokes the "diabolic" as an explanation for Nat's ability to plan and succeed in killing white people. The monologism exhibited here by dialogic analysis excludes by dehumanizing and marginalization; feminist dialogics adds a feminist sensibility which empowers readers to appreciate the structures inherent in patriarchy's reduction of women to a *gender-based* slavery.

I have endeavored to show in this study, along theoretical lines suggested in part by the work of Carolyn Durham, Elizabeth Ermarth, and Dale Marie Bauer, how fictive gynicide as a ritual sacrifice of women occurs in the novels of William Styron as a means of revealing the motivation and nature of oppression and dehumanization. Women are victimized, and Styron unflinchingly records their suffering to bring their voices out of the silences that marginalize them. Sophie Zawistowska is Styron's heroine and chief representative of all the "beaten and butchered and betrayed and martyred children of the earth" (SC 515) who fell victim to the patriarchal genocide of World War II, a woman whose survival is complicated by her guilt feelings about her own complicity in the events that doom her; she is yet another victim blamed by the system that brutalized her for being a victim. Her struggles and the struggles of other women characters in Styron's novels reveal "the structure by which the body (and especially women's bodies) is controlled, seduced, and manipulated" by patriarchal norms (Bauer 1988, 167). But the struggles are themselves an ongoing challenge not only to society at large but also to the "interpretive conventions" we inherit largely from patriarchal systems; the struggles of the characters in Styron's novels are ours as well. As characters challenge external authorities or their own inner impulses and desires, during the reading process we readers also challenge interpretive conventions which are represented in the texts as inviolable social codes—"in favor of an internally persuasive 'inner speech'" (168). This development of an inner speech, a sensitivity to the demands of the patriarchy, is a basic element in discourse. Styron's fictions present interpretations focused on the act of interpreting, and therefore readers are encouraged to question interpretive norms as well as consider the dynamics of reading as an interpretive process itself.

"In the act of reading," writes Bauer, "we divest ourselves of the illusion of *monologic selfhood*" (Bauer 1988; italics mine). Reading therefore forces a dialogue with texts and as such exposes the reader to the dialogue between authoritative discourse and inner speech. This study has documented the details of this polemic in the novels of William Styron and has observed the efficacy of Bakhtin's theory of dialogism as its reveals how American heroines "force the polemic to be a communal property" even in the face of powerful and debilitating authoritative norms.

> Thus, the conflicting voices produce the event which draws the reader (as one who identifies) in as one of the many wills called into question by the novel. Identity, then, is always tested and altered. (5).

For Bakhtin, heroines are within the system in spite of the system's ability to silence them at times; thus, female heroines can undermine the patriarchy by continuing to exist as witnesses who see through dominant, prevailing values and articulate alternative, empowering models for the inclusion of voices. Even if one holds the extreme view of Georgiana Colville who sees Styron as a white racist sexist, the voices of the female characters in his novels challenge the prevailing values of the society that enslaves them. My study has presented in some detail examples of Styron's implacable "will to polyphony" which he achieves by building his narratives upon resisting voices that violate the codes of authority with linguistic "impulses" revealing the unconscious wills of those resisting readers in the text (Bauer 1988, 4). As Bauer explains, "The very language which restricts human intercourse produces occasions for its own disruption and critique" (xiii).

As can be discerned from this discussion, in implementing such a discourse-based theory as feminist dialogics, we must realize that texts exist in their own specific contexts with particular historical, cultural, and social implications. In short, one does not read in a vacuum. Feminist dialogics emphasizes the importance of *engendered and engendering* heteroglossia and in so doing also directs attention toward the specific situations in any particular dialogic exchange; that is, it examines the cultural texts involved in narrative discourse and makes conscious the "political unconscious in history," and, importantly, "the words and the silences between and behind them" (Hitchcock 1993, 9). Reading dialogically is an activity which is determined not only by a text, which itself has been determined by a protracted series of cultural interplay, but also by the conscious and unconscious ideological discourses a reader employs in the reading process—as well as a construct of polemic and resistance to the multifarious voices, authoritative and dissenting, represented in the text.

Dialogism allows readers to locate their own voices. "We acquire 'ourselves' by engaging in our own dialogue with others, and especially with texts that challenge our beliefs" (Bauer 1988, 8). Styron's works challenge our beliefs by suggesting that female heroines who become victims of gynicide are sacrificed to patriarchal norms precisely because they have been marginalized by the very defining systems against which they struggle. His insistence upon characterizing human suffering in terms of the experiences of female heroines also articulates his chief concern, a concern clearly congruant with that of feminist criticism which "addresses and redresses the exclusion, the silence, of the female voice" (9).

List of Abbreviations

DV   *Darkness Visible*
LDD   *Lie Down in Darkness*
NT   *The Confessions of Nat Turner*
SC   *Sophie's Choice*
STH   *Set This House on Fire*

Works Cited

Allen, Mary. 1976. *The Necessary Blankness: Women in Major American Fiction of the Sixties.* Chicago: University of Illinois Press.

Alter, Robert. 1979. "Styron's Stingo." *Saturday Review* 6, no. 14 (July 1979): 42–43. Also of interest in this vein: John Gardner, "A Novel of Evil," *The New York Times Book Review,* 27 May 1979: 1, 16–17; refers to *Sophie Choice* as "a Southern Gothic" novel. Benjamin De Mott, "Styron's Survivor: An Honest Witness," *The Atlantic* 244, no. 1 (July 1979): 77–79; Stingo's portrait has "its embarrassments." Alvin H. Rosenfeld, "The Holocaust According to William Styron," *Midstream* 25, no. 10 (Dec. 1979): 43–49; Styron reduces "Hitler's war against the Jews to a literary war." Arnold Wesker, "Art Between Truth and Fiction," *Encounter,* 54, no. 1 (Jan. 1980): 48–57; Wesker sees Styron's treatment of sex as "uniting despair with defiance."

Bakhtin, M. M. 1981. *The Dialogic Imagination.* Edited and translated by Michael Holquist. Austin: University of Texas Press.

Bammer, Angelika. 1992. "The Woman Question—And Some Answers." In *The Philosophy of Discourse: The Rhetorical Turn in Twentieth-Century Thought.* vol. 2, edited by Chip Sills and George H. Jensen, 235–64. Portsmouth, N.H.: Heinemann.

Bauer, Dale Marie. 1988. *Feminist Dialogics: A Theory of Failed Community.* Albany: State University of New York Press.

Beauvoir, Simone de. 1953. *The Second Sex.* New York: Knopf.

Booth, Wayne C. 1982. "Freedom and Interpretation: Bakhtin and the Challenge of Feminist Criticism." *Critical Inquiry* 9 (1982): 45–76.

Clarke, John Henrik, ed. 1968. *William Styron's Nat Turner: Ten Black Writers Respond.* Boston: Beacon Press. [See also "The Uses of History in Fiction," which is an excerpted presentation of a panel discussion at the 34th annual meeting of the Southern Historical Association in New Orleans on 6 November 1968; the panel included Ralph Ellison, Styron, Robert Penn Warren, and C. Vann Woodward; they engage questioners who ask pointedly about Styron's removal of Nat's wife from the story and its implications for the historical novel. The transcription is in *Conversations with William Styron,* edited by James L. West, 114–44. Jackson: University of Mississippi Press, 1985; see especially 135–43.]

Coale, Samuel. 1991. *William Styron Revisited.* Boston: Twayne Publishers.

Cologne-Brooks, Gavin. 1989. "From History to History: The Shifting Patterns of Discourse in the Novels of William Styron." Ph.D. diss., University of Nottingham, 1989. Cologne-Brooks also discusses Styron's use of narrators in "Discord Toward Harmony: *Set This House on Fire* and Peter's Part in the Matter," in *Papers on Language and Literature* 23, no. 4 (Fall 1987): 449–65.

Colville, Georgiana. 1986. "Killing the Dead Mother: Women in *Sophie's Choice.*" *Delta ES* 23 (1986): 111–33.

Crane, John Kenny. 1984. *The Root of All Evil.* Columbia: University of South Carolina Press.

Culler, Jonathan D. 1982. *On Deconstruction: Theory and Criticism after Structuralism.* Ithaca: Cornell University Press.

De Man, Paul. 1983. "Dialogue and Dialogism." *Poetics Today* 4, no. 1 (1983): 99–107.

Dinnerstein, Dorothy. 1976. *The Mermaid and the Minotaur.* New York: Harper & Row.

Durham, Carolyn A. 1984. "William Styron's *Sophie's Choice*: The Structure of Oppression." *Twentieth Century Literature* 30, no. 4 (Winter 1984): 448–64.

Eagleton, Terry. 1983. *Literary Theory.* Minneapolis: University of Minnesota Press.

Emerson, Caryl. 1983. "The Outer Word and Inner Speech: Bakhtin, Vygotsky, and the Internalization of Language." *Critical Inquiry* 10, no. 2 (December 1983): 248–61.

Ermarth, Elizabeth. 1983. "Fictional Consensus and Female Casualties." In *The Representation of Women in Fiction,* edited by Carolyn Heilbrun and Margaret Higonnet, 1–18. Baltimore: Johns Hopkins University Press.

Felman, Shoshana. 1975. "Women and Madness: The Critical Phallacy." In *Diacritics* 5, no. 4 (1975): 2–10.

Fetterley, Judith. 1986. "Reading about Reading." In *Gender and Reading: The Essays on Readers, Texts, and Contexts,* edited by Elizabeth A. Flynn and Patrocinio P. Schweickart, 147–64. Baltimore: Johns Hopkins University Press.

———. 1979. *The Resisting Reader: A Feminist Approach to American Fiction.* Bloomington: Indiana University Press. [For a refutation of Fetterley's approach and other feminist criticisms, see Peter Shaw, "Feminist Literary Criticism: A Report from the Academy," in *American Scholar* 57, no. 4 (1988): 495–513.]

Fiedler, Leslie A. 1966. *Love and Death in the American Novel.* New York: Delta Revised Edition.

Furman, Nelly. 1985. "The Politics of Language: Beyond the Gender Principle?" In *Making a Difference: Feminist Literary Criticism,* edited by Gayle Greene and Coppelia Kahn, 59–79. London: Methuen.

Gladstein, Mimi Reisel. 1986. *The Indestructible Woman in Faulkner, Hemingway, and Steinbeck.* Ann Arbor, Mich.: UMI Research Press.

Greene, Gayle, and Coppelia Kahn. 1985. "Feminist Scholarship and the Social Construction of Women." In *Making a Difference: Feminist Literary Criticism,* 1–36. London: Methuen.

Higonnet, Margaret. 1985. "Suicide: Representations of the Feminine in the Nineteenth Century." In *Poetics Today* 6, no. 1–2 (1985): 103–18.

Hitchcock, Peter. 1993. *Dialogics of the Oppressed.* Minneapolis: University of Minnesota Press.

Holquist, Michael, and Katerina Clark. 1984. *Mikhail Bakhtin.* Cambridge, Mass.: Belknap Press.

Horney, Karen. 1967. *Feminine Psychology.* New York: W.W. Norton & Company.

Huffman, James R. 1986. "A Psychological Redefinition of William Styron's *Nat Turner*." In *Third Force Psychology and the Study of Literature*, edited by Bernard J. Paris, 240–61. Rutherford, N.J.: Fairleigh Dickinson University Press.

Kolodny, Annette. 1880. "Dancing Through the Minefield: Some Observations on the Theory, Practice, and Politics of a Feminist Literary Criticism." *Feminist Studies* 6, no. 1 (Spring 1980): 1–25.

Law, Richard G. 1990. "The Reach of Fiction: Narrative Technique in Styron's *Sophie's Choice*." *The Southern Literary Journal* 23, no. 1 (Fall 1990): 45–64.

Markos, Donald W. 1974. "Margaret Whitehead in Nat Turner." *Studies in the Novel* 4 (Spring 1974): 52–59.

Meese, Elizabeth. 1986. *Crossing the Double Cross: The Practice of Feminist Criticism*. Chapel Hill: University of North Carolina Press.

Millet, Kate. 1970. *Sexual Politics*. New York: Avon Books.

Moi, Toril. 1988. "Feminism, Postmodernism, and Style." In *Cultural Critique* 9 (Spring 1988): 3–22.

Morris, Robert K. 1981. "Interviews with William Styron." In *The Achievement of William Styron*, edited by Robert K. Morris and Irving Malin, 29–69. Athens: University of Georgia Press.

Ong, Walter J. 1982. *Orality and Literacy*. New York: Methuen.

Ratner, Marc L. 1972. *William Styron*. New York: Twayne.

Rich, Adrienne. 1979. "Disloyal to Civilization." In *On Lies, Secrets, and Silence*. New York: W.W. Norton & Company.

Reitz, Bernard. 1987. "'Fearful ambiguities of time and history': *Nat Turner* and the Delineation of the Past in Postmodern Historical Narrative." *Papers on Language and Literature* 23, no. 4 (fall 1987): 465–79.

Rowbotham, Sheila. 1973. *Woman's Consciousness, Man's World*. Harmondsworth, England: Penguin.

Rubin, Louis D. Jr. 1981. "Notes on a Southern Writer in Our Time." In *The Achievement of William Styron*, edited by Robert K. Morris and Irving Malin, 70–105. Athens: University of Georgia Press.

Rubinstein, Richard. 1975. *The Cunning of History: The Holocaust and the American Future*. New York: Harper & Row.

Ruderman, Judith. 1987. *William Styron*. New York: Frederick Ungar Publishing Co.

Schuster, Charles I. 1992. "Mikhail Bakhtin: Philosopher of Language." In *The Philosophy of Discourse: The Rhetorical Turn in Twentieth Century Thought*, vol. 1, edited by Chip Sills and George H. Jensen, 164–98. Portsmouth, N.H.: Heinemann.

Scott, Bonnie Kime. 1987. *James Joyce*. New York: Humanities Press International.

Shinn, Thelma J. 1986. *Radiant Daughters: Fictionald American Women*. New York: Greenwood Press.

Shore, Laurence. 1982. "William Styron's *Nat Turner:* The Monster and the Critics." *The Journal of Ethnic Studies* 2, no. 1 (Fall 1982): 89–101.

Singer, Alan. 1988. "The Voice of History/The Subject of the Novel." *Novel: A Forum on Fiction* 21, no. 2–3 (Winter/Spring 1988): 173–79.

Smith, Joan. 1992. *Misogynies: Reflections on Myths and Malice.* New York: Fawcett Columbine.

Smith-Rosenberg, Carroll. 1986. "Writing History: Language, Class, and Gender." In *Feminist Studies/Critical Studies.* Teresa de Lauretis, 31–54. Bloomington: Indiana University Press.

Spender, Dale, 1980. *Man Made Language.* London: Routledge and Kegan Paul.

Styron, William. 1981. *The Confessions of Nat Turner.* New York: Bantam.

———. 1990. *Darkness Visible.* New York: Random House.

———. 1978. *Lie Down in Darkness.* New York: New American Library-Plume.

———. 1960. *Set This House on Fire.* New York: Random House.

———. 1979. *Sophie's Choice.* New York: Random House.

Wollstonecraft, Mary. 1985. *A Vindication of the Rights of Women.* Excerpted in *The Norton Anthology of Literature by Women,* edited by Sandra M. Gilbert and Susan Gubar, 138–60. New York: W.W. Norton & Company.

Index